DEMOCRACY IN MEXICO

Peasant Rebellion and

Political Reform

DAN LA BOTZ

SOUTH END PRESS, BOSTON, MA

Cover design by Birgitta McAlevey
Original cover art by Steven Johnson Leyba
All inside photos by Dennis Dunleavy
Text design and production by South End Press collective
Printed in the U.S.A.

Library of Congress Cataloging-in-Publication Data

La Botz, Dan, 1945-
Democracy in Mexico: peasant rebellion and political reform/by
Dan La Botz
p. cm.
Includes bibliographical references and index
ISBN 0-89608-507-4: $16.00 (hardcover)
ISBN 0-89608-508-2: $35.00 (pbk.)
1. Mexico—Politics and government—1988 2. Democracy—Mexico—History—20th century. 3. Social movements—Mexico—History—20th century 4. Mexico—Economic conditions I. Title.
F1236.L32   1995
320.972—dc20   95-23162
CIP

South End Press, 116 Saint Botolph Street, Boston, MA 02115

01 00 99 98 97 96   ® GCIU 745-C   2 3 4 5 6 7 8 9

DEMOCRACY IN MEXICO

To my partner Sherry

CONTENTS

ACKNOWLEDGMENTS

I owe thanks to a number of people who helped make it possible for me to write this book.

Cecilia Rodríguez of the National Commission for Democracy in Mexico made it possible for me to attend the National Democratic Convention, in Chiapas in August 1994, as one of the U.S. observers chosen by the Zapatista Army of National Liberation (EZLN).

I stayed at the Casa de Los Amigos in Mexico City while interviewing Mexican candidates, voters, and election observers later in August 1994 and appreciated the special hospitality of the Casa. Fellow guests at the Casa, Paul Haber and Philips Russell, and *Z Magazine* writer "John Reed" shared their views with me. A number of Global Exchange and Humanitarian Law Project guests at the Casa permitted me to interview them about their experience as election observers.

I thank the many delegates to the National Democratic Convention, Luz Rosales and the members of Alianza Cívica, as well as individual voters and election observers who gave me interviews and shared their opinions with me.

Rosario Ibarra de Piedra shared her insights with me at a conference organized by Solidarity and *Against the Current* in Los Angeles.

Mary McGinn at Labor Notes in Detroit helped to keep me informed and shared her ideas about Mexican developments. Labor Notes made it possible for me to attend the Cross-Border Organizing Conference in Juárez where I interviewed many of the labor organizers cited here. Over the years, the Labor Notes conferences have provided me a regular opportunity for discussions with Mexican labor activists.

Several friends and colleagues read the entire manuscript, and made corrections and criticisms, as well as sometimes differing with interpretation of events, among them: Ken Blum, Sam Farber, Peter Gellert, Danny Laird, Ricardo Pascoe, and Ann Twinam.

A number of other people read a chapter or two of the book and made suggestions, among them: Stan Corkin, Wayne Durrill, Jerry Faust, Milton

Fisk, Sarah Heath, Todd Larson, Bruce Levine, Joanne Meyerowitz, Zane Miller, and Thomas Winter. Russel Durst offered helpful ideas. Frances Goldin, untiring literary agent and movement activist, read and edited several chapters.

My father, Herb La Botz, religiously clipped and mailed San Diego newspapers to me, which was extremely helpful.

Lynn Stephen who read my manuscript for South End Press made many helpful suggestions. Project Editor Dionne Brooks and the South End Press collective have been supportive throughout.

As usual, I found it very useful to argue with Rusty Gilbert about all the issues involved.

As always, my greatest debt is to my partner Sherry Baron who makes everything possible. Thanks to my beautiful rambunctious boys, Traven and Reed, for their patience with this project.

My apologies to anyone I may have forgotten.

While I received much help, I alone am responsible for the ideas expressed in this book.

INTRODUCTION

The Chiapas Rebellion of January 1994 appears to be the beginning of the end for Mexico's Institutional Revolutionary Party (PRI). The events of 1994, beginning with the Chiapas uprising in January and ending with the devaluation of the peso in December, have undermined the PRI's support both at home and abroad, creating an unprecedented crisis. The combination of a regional rebellion, several political assassinations, and an economic disaster have brought Mexico to the brink. At this point we can not be sure exactly how or when the end will come. But if Mexico proves unable to carry out a democratic transformation, then it is altogether possible that we will see social disintegration, or perhaps even a military coup.

While this book was prompted by the Chiapas Rebellion, it is not primarily a book about the rebellion. It is rather an attempt to put the Chiapas Rebellion in the larger context of Mexican history and society. The focus of this book is Mexico's struggle for democracy. By democracy, I mean not only free and fair elections, but also human rights and civil rights, as well as the rights of workers.

At the center of the democratic struggle in Mexico today are four forces: the Zapatista Army of National Liberation (EZLN) which leads the rebellion in Chiapas, the National Democratic Convention originally convened by the EZLN, the new movement of "civil society" now embodied in the Civic Alliance, and the opposition Party of the Democratic Revolution. These four forces are the subject of my book. However, I think it is impossible to appreciate and understand the contemporary movements without some historical understanding of the Mexican Revolution, the nature of Mexico's one-party state, the character of the Mexican capitalist class, and the politics of the conservative opposition National Action Party.

In addition to the historical account of the rise of the state and the ruling party, I also include brief biographical sketches of some of the major figures in contemporary Mexican politics—Carlos Salinas, Ernesto Zedillo, Diego Fernández, Cuauhtémoc Cárdenas, Porfirio Muñoz Ledo, and Rosario Ibarra—believing that it is impossible to understand politics without knowing the personalities and characters of the people involved. I also address the ideas of some of Mexico's leading intellectuals and political commentators, such as Carlos Monsiváis, Adolfo Gilly and Jorge Castañeda. Finally, I intend this book to be a kind of survey of Mexico's contemporary social and political movements, so I discuss not only the peasant rebellion in Chiapas, but also the workers' movement in the *maquiladoras* of the northern border, the women's movement in Mexico City, and the citizens' movement for civil rights and political reform. I do not pretend that this survey is either completely comprehensive or precisely representative. But I do believe that it introduces the reader to many of the principal issues and controversies in Mexican society today.

While the Chiapas Rebellion and the December 1994 peso devaluation may have precipitated the current crisis, the roots of the PRI's problems are to be found in the last 25 years of Mexican history. The 1968 massacre at Tlatelolco and the 1982 financial disaster laid the basis for the present situation. For 25 years, peasants, workers, the urban poor, students, feminists, and environmentalists built important social movements that fought for democracy and social justice. Together these forces converge and culminate in the contemporary democratic movement.

In my view, the working class constitutes the all-important absent factor in present Mexican politics. Controlled by the PRI and its "official" unions, faced with economic crisis and severe repression, workers have so far failed to create either independent unions or their own political party. The absent workers' movement is, to my mind, the key feature of the political situation in Mexico.

Since the early 1980s, Mexico has been caught between two powerful forces: on the one hand, a conservative (in Mexico called a "neo-liberal") economic revolution from above, and on the other hand, a radical, democratic movement surging up from below. At the root of the recent violence in Mexico is the conflict between these two revolutions. President Carlos Salinas de Gortari used the state's power to force on Mexico a conservative, free-market capitalism, while the people fought for democracy and economic justice. The state pushed down as the people tried to raise themselves up.

Ernesto Zedillo and the technocrats of the PRI won the 1994 election, but only to find themselves on the verge of economic disaster. The challenge from below—the struggle for democracy—continues to be driven by poverty and injustice. In the long run, the PRI's inability to overcome its continuing economic crisis will provide the motor that drives democratic opposition forces in Mexico to struggle again and again to free themselves from the PRI and perhaps, too, from the domination of capital. The combination of a one-party state and an economic crisis will drive peasants to rebel, civil society to fight for reforms, and eventually force workers to fight back as well. When the working class enters the struggles of civil society, and allies itself with the demands of Indian peasant rebels, the challenge from below may yet bring democracy to Mexico.

1

THE REBELLION OF
FACELESS

Early in the morning on New Year's Day, January 1, 1994, several hundred Indian peasants marched out of the foggy, wooded hills and valleys of Mexico's southernmost state of Chiapas. The soldiers of the Zapatista Army of National Liberation wore ski masks or red bandannas over their faces. But their communiqués would later say that the masks hid nothing, because they were the *sin rostro*, the "faceless" mass of Indians and peasants who had been neglected and ignored by the Mexican government.

The rebel soldiers were the sons and daughters of poor farmers and plantation laborers, mostly Mayan Indian peasants, who lived in nearby villages and towns. The young revolutionaries, a third of them women, wore military uniforms with red and black patches, the colors of labor union strikes throughout Mexico and Latin America. Some of the soldiers were armed with modern automatic weapons, but many more carried rifles of World War II vintage or even old single-shot 22 calibre hunting rifles. Some rebel troops had only wooden rifle stocks, clubs or knives.

The insurgents took the name Zapatista Army of National Liberation (EZLN) from Emiliano Zapata, a leader during the Mexican Revolution. Zapata was assassinated in 1919 by the founders of the modern Mexican state because he demanded an equitable distribution of land to the peasants. According to a legend among the peasants of his native state of Morelos, Zapata

1

can still be seen sometimes, riding his white horse along the crest of the hills. Now, it seemed, Zapata had ridden south, into Chiapas.

On that first day of the new year, the Zapatista Army occupied the city of San Cristóbal de Las Casas and the towns Ocosingo, Altamirano, and Las Margaritas, and attacked the Rancho Nuevo regional military base, all located in Chiapas. The taking of San Cristóbal, the colonial capital of Chiapas, a major center of foreign tourism, and a bohemian artists' colony, was a cunning move. The presence of hundreds of foreign tourists made government repression much more difficult.

In some of the towns, the Zapatistas met little resistance and quickly occupied strategic points. But in Ocosingo, where 600 Zapatistas attacked, 200 of them were pinned down in the market and as many as 15 rebels were killed by enemy fire. The rebels proved unable to take the Rancho Nuevo military base where they had hoped to capture the arsenal and its better weapons.

But as the EZLN spokesman Subcomandante Marcos was fond of saying, "The problem of war is not a problem of who has more guns, more men or more bullets; it's a problem of who is right." As the EZLN marched, Marcos distributed a series of remarkable communiqués and letters explaining the rebels objective, political program, and social ideals. These documents, printed in Mexican newspapers and circulated worldwide on the electronic computer networks would, over the next several months, prove to be the Zapatistas' most powerful weapon, winning them sympathy and support throughout Mexico and soon from around the world.

The opening lines of the Zapatistas' "Declaration of War" proclaimed:

> We are a product of 500 years of struggle....But today we say ENOUGH! We are the heirs of the true founders of our nationality. We are the dispossessed millions, and we summon all our brothers and sisters to join us in this call, as the only way to avoid starving because of the endless greed of a dictatorship that has prevailed for over 70 years now, headed by a group of traitors who stand for the most conservative groups that have sold out the nation.[1]

The Zapatistas based their right to rebel on the Mexican Constitution, and in their first communiqués they cited Article 39: "The people have the right, the inalienable right, at any time to alter or modify their form of government."[2] The insurgents demanded that Salinas resign his office, that the Mexican Senate and House of Deputies cease to recognize Salinas's authority, and called for the creation of a transitional government. The EZLN declared it would march to Mexico City and overthrow Salinas and the PRI.

The Zapatistas timed the uprising to coincide with the first day that the new North American Free Trade Agreement (NAFTA) took effect. NAFTA, the continental treaty negotiated in 1992 by U.S. President George Bush, Canadian Prime Minister Brian Mulroney, and Mexican President Carlos Salinas, had been opposed by many peasants of Chiapas who feared that the treaty would destroy their local economy, and drive them even deeper into poverty.

"People of Mexico," said a rebel manifesto, "The dictators are waging an undeclared genocidal war against our people and have been for many years. We ask your participation in supporting our fight for work, land, housing, food, health, education, independence, freedom, democracy, justice and peace."[3] Those last eleven words were the Zapatistas' minimum program for Mexico.

The surprise and swiftness of the EZLN offensive allowed the Zapatistas to take control of several little hamlets in Chiapas, in addition to the four major towns they had occupied. In the initial attacks the EZLN troops wounded or killed a number of policemen and soldiers. But wherever they went, the rebels scrupulously avoided altercations with non-combatants and treated the civilian population respectfully.

In the course of the EZLN advance, groups of civilians, including many Italian tourists, were inadvertently "captured." But neither foreigners nor Mexicans were killed, kidnapped, or harmed, and all but one of them were released and soon sent on their way. When one or two captives were robbed, EZLN commanders personally apologized for the incidents. In their dealings with civilians, the Zapatistas were courteous to a fault. At one point, the EZLN blocked a road to the ruins at Palenque, but a group of tourists insisted on going through. Finally, in exasperation, one of the young soldiers told the tourists, "We're sorry for the inconvenience, but this is a revolution."

The EZLN took only one prisoner. Absalón Castellanos Domínguez, a rancher and former governor of Chiapas known for his brutality against the Indian peasants, was detained by the EZLN at his ranch near Las Margaritas on the first day of the rebellion. (Castellanos was tried and found guilty of murder and torture and sentenced to life of hard labor by an EZLN court. The EZLN later commuted his sentence and, after a month of captivity, he was released as a gesture of good will intended to promote the peace process.)

In the towns it briefly controled, the EZLN promulgated a number of laws—small tokens of a revolutionary regime which the Zapatistas never had a chance to establish. The one revolutionary law the EZLN could and did carry out was the "Justice Law": "All prisoners in jail will be freed, except those guilty of murder, rape, or those who are narcotics dealers."[4] As the Zapatistas took over the towns, the prisoners were liberated. Four jails were opened, two in San Cristóbal, one in Ocosingo, and one in Margaritas, and some 230 prisoners were released.[5] A few of them reportedly joined the rebel army.

As the EZLN advanced, one soldier stopped to spray paint a short essay on the social conditions in Chiapas:

> "We want land, we want good food, we want decent housing, we want bread, a roof, land: long live our fallen groups, death to the army of the bourgeoisie. We want food."

While the army marched, officers and soldiers talked to reporters, explaining their movement. EZLN Captain Arturo responded to the government's suggestion that outside agitators were responsible for the uprising. "No one is behind us," Captain Arturo said. "The people gave us all that we have. They gave us the money to buy arms and uniforms because we want what they want—land, a roof over their heads and work." Another EZLN officer, Lieutenant Jesús, head of the unit occupying the town of Altamirano, told of the secret preparations for the revolt. "We explained to the people that the struggle was clandestine and that no one could know. The majority supported us because they knew this was an army that was going to liberate all of the country."

Some EZLN leaders projected a long struggle not only for reforms, but for socialism. "There is no longer any way to survive the situation in Mexico," said Lieutenant Jesús. "There is no work, there is no land, no education. There is no way to change that in elections. This is not going to be a war of two or three years. This could be a war of 25 or 30 years. Our thinking is that we have to build socialism." Another rebel soldier said simply, "We are for socialism like the Cubans have, only better."[6]

Attempting to deflect criticism of the PRI and Salinas, government spokesmen claimed that the EZLN leaders were either Catholic priests, Guatemalan revolutionaries or other foreign agitators. At times the government insinuated that Samuel Ruíz, the Bishop of Chiapas, known for his support for the Indians and criticism of the government's human rights record, was responsible for the uprising.[7]

4

The Clandestine Revolutionary Indigenous Committee (CCRI) of the EZLN categorically denied the government's claims. "The leadership and ranks of the EZLN troops are mainly indigenous people of Chiapas, and that is because these indigenous people represent the most oppressed and dispossessed people in Mexico, but also, as you see, the worthiest...There are also in our ranks, Mexicans from other social backgrounds and from different states in our country. The members of the Clandestine Revolutionary Indigenous Committee...belong to the Tzotzil, Tzeltal, Chol, Tojolabal and other groups." The CCRI asserted "our struggle is national and does not limit itself to the state of Chiapas."[8]

The Zapatista uprising and photos of Subcomandante Marcos in his ski mask dominated the newspaper headlines. National television carried reports of the Chiapas Rebellion throughout Mexico. In those first few days of January many ordinary people identified with and sympathized with the Chiapas rebels. Though many were critical of the Zapatistas' use of violence, ordinary Mexicans empathized with the plight of the indigenous peasants.

Factory workers in the *maquiladora* plants along the U.S.-Mexico border, poor people in the slums of Mexico City, peasants in poverty-stricken villages throughout the countryside, even many middle-class and upper-class Mexicans felt that the poor people of Chiapas had been driven to rebellion. Since Mexico had only become urbanized in the last two generations, many of those in the cities had come from other similar little villages and could empathize with those who tried unsuccessfully to eke out a miserable living from the soil.

The Chiapas rebels' complaints about poverty, low wages, lack of decent housing, poor diet, disease and lack of health care were problems not only of other peasants, but also of the urban poor. Even the middle class had suffered through the lost decade of the 1980s as its economic security and social status were undermined by currency devaluations and economic reorganization. Many Mexicans saw the rebels as people much like themselves who had been pushed to the wall.

Certainly no one who had seen the poorly armed and badly equipped EZLN soldiers considered them a serious military threat. The real danger to the government was political. The audacity and courage of the young Indian men and women, and the selflessness and idealism they expressed in such patriotic and nationalist terms gave hope to the hopeless. People began to think that change might be possible. Perhaps this is why after the hesitation of the first day or two, President Salinas moved quickly to crush the rebels.

At the orders of President Salinas, the Commander-and-Chief, the Mexican Army and the Air Force counter-attacked. Salinas and his general staff mobilized 10,000 troops, several tanks and a number of armored personnel carriers. Apparently in an attempt to strike at the social bases of support for the Zapatista uprising, government troops not only fought the EZLN, but also terrorized the communities. Throughout the conflicted parts of Chiapas, residents later told reporters and human rights organizations that, as the Mexican Federal Army moved into the towns, soldiers broke down doors and dragged men and women from their homes.

Soldiers beat, tortured, and killed a number of townspeople. In the most publicized incident, in Ocosingo five men were found dead, face-down with their hands behind their backs as if they had been tied. Human rights activists believed they had been summarily executed by the Mexican Army.[9] Many such violations of human rights were reported, and many more must have gone unreported in the isolated smaller villages.

The Mexican Air Force also contributed to the indiscriminate repression. Mexican Air Force planes had been flying overhead since January 1, but on January 4, both government airplanes and helicopter gunships began to strafe, fire rockets, and bomb not only Zapatista targets, but also local communities. Two aircraft zoomed in and strafed San Antonio de los Baños, a little village in the mountains above San Cristóbal de las Casas.[10] In that town and several others, aircraft fire or rockets damaged buildings and killed animals while the residents hid or fled.

Mexican Air Force planes also fired on unarmed reporters and other civilians. Bruno López, a correspondent for Univisión television network, told newspaper reporters that he and his crew had been shot at by government planes.[11] EZLN soldiers fired back, and a few Air Force planes were hit and damaged and a couple were reportedly put out of commission.[12]

Through the combination of air power, massive numerical superiority and more sophisticated weapons, by January 5, the government had retaken control of the four major towns held by the EZLN and drove the insurgents back into the jungle. In the first week of fighting, the Mexican military claimed there were 93 deaths. The government's official death toll would eventually reach 145 for the 12 days of fighting, although the Catholic Church estimated more than 400.

Thousands of peasants began to flee the fighting and the repression of the Mexican Army, leading legions of refugees to tramp out of the conflicted area. Eventually, the numbers would reach 35,000 people seeking refuge from the violence in Chiapas.

The Mexican Army brought in more troops, and soon 15,000 soldiers blocked roads and highways, and stopped cars and buses. The soldiers detained and held many young men for questioning, some of whom were threatened and beaten. Surrounded or occupied by the Mexican Army, many villages were cut off from the outside world. Some towns were without adequate food, medical care or other social services.

On January 6, Salinas appeared on television and spoke to the nation, demanding that the rebels surrender before any dialogue could begin. Salinas distinguished between "the action of a violent armed group," and peasants who might have joined the rebellion because of "trickery, pressure or desperation." He promised "benign treatment" to those who had been duped. Meanwhile, the Mexican Army and Air Force pressed their attack.

While the rebellion in Chiapas appeared to be in retreat, new outbreaks appeared in other parts of Mexico. On January 6, a group calling itself the "Urban Front of Mexico City of the Zapatista National Liberation Army" issued a statement apparently rejecting calls for dialogue with the words, "this struggle will take many years." Early in the morning of January 8, a bomb exploded in an underground parking lot of a Mexico City shopping center—damaging the structure, but injuring no one. At the same time, two 90-foot electrical towers were blown up, one in Puebla and the other in Michoacán. The EZLN issued a communiqué declaring that it was "fighting the police and Federal Army and not the parking facilities in shopping centers." The EZLN denied responsibility for those attacks, or for any other attacks, on civilian targets.[13]

Political opposition to the government and support for the rebels also began to appear. On January 7, the several thousand supporters of the leftist Independent Proletarian Movement (MPI), made up mostly of bus drivers and factory workers, demonstrated in Mexico City. They demanded that the Salinas administration stop its military actions, officially recognize the rebels, and begin negotiations with them. Five days later, on January 12, nearly 100,000 people gathered in the Zócalo, Mexico's national plaza, in a massive demonstration calling upon the government to stop its military attacks on the rebels and negotiate. Cuauhtémoc Cárdenas, presidential candidate of the center left opposition Party of the Democratic Revolution, had initially supported the EZLN's demands but condemned their violent methods. Now, however, he appeared in the Zócalo as a defender of the indigenous uprising. The indigenous rebellion in Chiapas was reviving the Mexican left.

The uprising had become a full-scale political crisis for Salinas. Mexican and international human rights organizations and newspapers around the world criticized the Mexican government for the Air Force strafing and bombing of villages and for the Army's summary execution of unidentified civilians. The Mexican stock exchange dropped 6.32 percent on January 10, the biggest loss since the crash of 1987. Brokerage houses in the United States began to suggest that their clients withhold investment from Mexico until the problems in Chiapas were settled. The Chiapas Rebellion threatened to spill over into electoral politics, and perhaps even lead to a defeat for the PRI on August 21.

Faced with these developments, Salinas had little choice but to negotiate a political settlement with the rebels. On January 6, the EZLN had made known its conditions for peace talks: recognition of the EZLN, a cease fire, withdrawal of federal troops, an end to the bombing, and the formation of a national mediation commission.[14]

Without precisely agreeing to accept the rebels' demands, Salinas carried out a series of shrewd measures which would, between Janaury 10 and 12, lead to a truce. First on January 10, President Salinas removed from his cabinet the Minister of the Interior and former Governor of Chiapas, Patrocinio González Garrrido. As governor of Chiapas, González had been denounced by international human rights organizations because of his repeated use of state violence, including murder and torture, against indigenous activists. González's presence in the cabinet was an embarrassment to the Salinas' administration and an impediment to a political resolution of the Chiapas situation. Salinas replaced González with Attorney General Jorge Carpizo McGregor, a former Supreme Court Justice, former rector of the National University, and a former head of the Mexican government's National Human Rights Commission. Many Mexicans perceived Carpizo, who was not officially a PRI member, as the cleanest man in the government.

That same day, President Salinas appointed Foreign Minister Manuel Camacho Solís as special commissioner to negotiate with the Chiapas rebels. Unlike Salinas, Camacho was a populist-style politician who had made his political reputation as a reformer while mayor of Mexico City. Camacho had been one of Salinas's closest associates over the years, and was furious when, just a few months before, Salinas had passed over him as his presidential successor, and appointed instead Luis Donaldo Colosio, head of the National Solidarity Program. Camacho accepted the difficult assignment of negotiating with the rebels, seeing it as an opportunity perhaps to put himself back in the presidential race. Like Carpizo, Camacho was seen as a relative liberal within Mexico's authoritarian political system.

Finally, on January 12, Salinas declared a cease fire and offered amnesty to rebels who laid down their arms. In a presidential address to the nation, Salinas said he was sending a "message of conciliation, peace and respect for human rights." He also promised to "redouble attention to the social demands of the indigenous community in the highlands and the jungle of Chiapas." The Mexican Army lifted its roadblocks on highways and roads and allowed human rights organizations and medical workers to enter the area.

With Salinas's cease fire order and the offer of amnesty, the initial 12 days of fighting ended, but the political crisis only continued and deepened. The Zapatista Army of National Liberation failed to conquer Chiapas and could not continue its threatened march on Mexico City. During the 12 days of fighting, the EZLN succeeded in challenging the economic policies of President Salinas, in undermining the legitimacy of the Institutional Revolutionary Party, which has controled the Mexican government for 65 years, in questioning the morality of the multinational corporations, banks, and the new world order advocated by the United States. Though checked militarily, the Chiapas Rebellion of 1994 remained the most important political challenge to the Mexican government in 25 years.

□□□

Surrounded by 15,000 troops, and trapped in their jungle hideouts, Marcos and the Zapatistas lost the military initiative, but they still held the political advantage. After Salinas's Air Force strafed the villages, much of Mexico and the world was on their side, and with the national presidential race only eight months away, Salinas could not crush their movement with iron and fire or he might jeopardize the PRI's election victory.

The Zapatistas' most important weapon was now the word. Day after day, puffing on his pipe, Marcos talked over the heads of negotiators and government troops to the people of Mexico and the world. Marcos, alternating between military leader, political propagandist and poet, captivated Mexico with his style. Marcos' combination of wit, irony, humor, and sophistication delighted Mexicans of all classes.

9

Marcos sent almost daily communiqués to Mexico's left-wing newspapers and magazines—*La Jornada, El Financiero,* and *Proceso*—held press conferences, gave interviews, sent letters to school children, and wrote poems to the people. The EZLN's little newspaper, *El Despertador* or *The Alarm Clock,* was a wake-up call to the people. A newspaper the size of a hand and small enough to put in a pocket, began to appear as if by magic in cities throughout Mexico. The miniature newspaper, contained the EZLN's revolutionary laws and proclamations.

Though the pro-government Televisa and Azteca networks limited and distorted their coverage, the rebellion was televised to cities and towns throughout Mexico. Every word the Zapatistas uttered was recorded, entered into the computer, translated by volunteers into English and other languages, and, through services like *Peacenet,* made available throughout the world. The "direct communiqués from the guerrilla leadership served as a block against disinformation."[15]

The early months of 1994 were the time of hope. In Mexico, the EZLN had transformed politics. The rebels had uncovered the dirty underside of Salinas's vaunted economic reforms, revealing the poverty of the nation's Indians. Salinas's violent reaction to the uprising of the underdogs left him standing before the world with blood on his hands. The EZLN's cry for democracy strengthened the hand of civil society and the opposition political parties with their demands for electoral reform. The rebels' very existence, as an organization independent of the state-party, encouraged democratic currents in labor unions, peasant organizations, and particularly other indigenous movements to organize and struggle in their own ways for democracy and social justice. Perhaps most importantly, the Zapatista rebellion immediately shifted the Mexican political spectrum to the left by recreating a radical pole that had disappeared when the old left dissolved itself into the Cuauhtémoc Cárdenas campaign in 1988. Throughout Mexico, things began to stir.

On January 27, with the world's attention focussed on Mexico, Salinas was forced to sign a formal pact with the opposition parties conceding a series of electoral reforms for the coming August 21 elections. The agreement called for impartial election authorities, media equity, no use of public money for private campaigning, and limits on campaign spending. The pact was flawed since control of the electoral process ultimately remained in the hands of the PRI's Minister of the Interior, but the PRI-government had made concessions that encouraged hope.

Peace talks between the Zapatista Rebels and the Mexican government opened in San Cristóbal de Las Casas on February 21, mediated, at the request of the EZLN, by Samuel Ruíz, the Bishop of San Cristóbal. The talks between the PRI-government and the EZLN, carried on in Spanish and several Indian languages, involved 19 members of the Zapatista leadership, two of whom were women. The leader of the PRI's delegation at the peace talks was Peace Commissioner Manuel Camacho Solís, the former mayor of Mexico City who had been chosen for this difficult job because of his reputation as a populist. Marcos was most prominent in the EZLN delegation, though the press and the public were also captivated by Commander Ramona.

The EZLN's principal demands were for immediate economic and social reforms in Chiapas and for democratic reforms in the nation. The negotiations went on for over a week, ending on March 2, in a tentative 32-point agreement in which the government promised housing and hospitals, roads and electrification, semi-autonomy and respect for Indian culture. The Zapatistas' demands for electoral reform and democracy were referred to the national legislature.[16] Marcos and the other EZLN negotiators promised to submit the agreement to the Indians in the communities for their approval. But in the meantime, the rebels, fearing treachery, would keep their arms.

The Chiapas Rebellion and the apparently successful negotiations had a tremendously liberating impact upon the Mexican people. After years of defeat at the hands of the PRI, after decades of repression and coaptation, finally some sectors of Mexican society stood up to the one-party state, and had apparently won. A group of Mexico's most humble people, the poorest Indians from the poorest state, had succeeded in stymieing the Harvard-educated president. In some circumstances there is nothing more radical than a victory of the underdogs.

The combination of the Zapatistas' daring uprising, their democratic and egalitarian ideology, and their masterful propaganda made the EZLN the rallying point for Mexico's democratic forces and social movements. The Mayan rebels took moral leadership of the Mexican nation. Though the Zapatista Army of National Liberation still remained isolated militarily, the rebellion and its news coverage sparked a series of democratic movements that spread like a brush fire throughout Mexico. In one of the early communiqués, the Zapatistas called upon Mexicans throughout the country not to rise in armed rebellion, but rather to do what was appropriate under their circumstances in the struggle for social justice. Many Mexicans, it appeared, were ready to respond to the rebels' call.

The first indigenous group to offer solidarity to the EZLN was the "Council of Guerrero 500 Years of Indigenous Resistance," made up of Tlapanecos, Mixtecos, Nahuas and Amuzgos. The Council sent a delegation to Bishop Ruíz with a message of solidarity for the EZLN: "We recognize your great courage in taking up arms, exposing yourselves to death and fighting to give birth to a just life for the Indians and the non-Indians of Mexico."[17]

From one end of Mexico to the other, many of the nation's appoximately 10 million indigenous people, over 10 percent of Mexico's total population of 86 million, began to organize and protest. In Chiapas itself, the PRI helped establish the State Council of Indigenous and Peasant Organizations (CEOIC) on January 12, 1994, hoping to counter the influence of the EZLN. But the new peasant confederation immediately became radicalized, and at a meeting with President Salinas in Tuxtla-Gutiérrez on January 25, CEOIC leaders publicly derided Salinas, announcing that they supported the EZLN and raised their own demands.

In Juchitán, Oaxaca, not far from Chiapas, the Zápotec Indians who work on the coffee and sugar plantations expressed support for the rebellion in Chiapas. At the other end of Mexico, in Tijuana, Baja California, the Pai-Pai and other local tribes inspired by the Zapatistas formed a "Pro-Ethnic Committee." In the San Quintín Valley of Baja California, the Independent Center for Farm Workers and Peasants (CIOAC) which represents thousands of migrant workers, many Zapotec, Mixtec and Triqui Indians from Southern Mexico, organized a march "Against Exploitation, Poverty and for Peace in Chiapas."[18]

The Chiapas State Council of Indigenous and Farmers Organizations (CEOIC), called the First National Conference of Indigenous People and Peasants in San Cristóbal de las Casas on March 13 and 14. The conference, attended by representatives of 500 indigenous organizations from nearly all the states of Mexico, asserted the right to rebellion and, as a gesture of solidarity, flew the flag of the EZLN. The conference members organized a national demonstration for April 10 in Mexico City in which tens of thousands marched to commemorate the 75th anniversary of the assassination of Emiliano Zapata.[19] In their many different demonstrations and meetings, Mexico's indigenous people demanded the right to their historic lands, a living wage, an end to repression, genuine political liberty, regional autonomy, and a life of dignity.

Small farmers, whether Indian or *mestizo*, inspired by the Mayan peasants, also organized to demand their rights from the Mexican government.

The upsurge began in Chiapas as farmers seized town halls in market towns like Teopisca. Then the movement spread to other states as small farmers organized new groups like the militant El Barzón, which seized government buildings or circled agricultural banks with their tractors to demand debt relief.

But it was not only Indians and farmers who protested. The sparks of the democratic movement blew throughout Mexico and some landed at the Metropolitan Autonomous University (UAM) in Mexico City, touching off a strike there in the first week of January 31. The strike, involving everyone from professors to janitors, stopped classes for some 45,000 students. The University Workers Union (SITUAM) leaders explained that they had struck for their own demands and in support of the Indians in Chiapas.[20]

Mexican civil society, the new democratic movement which had begun with the earthquake in 1985, was also inspired by the Mayan peasants. In Mexico City, the Citizens Movement for Democracy, and dozens of other groups from civil society, took to the streets to demonstrate for human rights and electoral reform. Other citizens' groups committed to democratic change began to appear in cities throughout Mexico.

The protests continued throughout January, February and March, as Indians, farmers, middle-class professionals, industrial workers, socialists, environmentalists, feminists and others joined the democratic parades that trooped through Mexico City's boulevards, usually ending up in the Zócalo, the national plaza. By conservative estimates, in the six months between September 1, 1993 and March 1, 1994, there were 750 protests in Mexico City—that is about four protests per day. Some of the protests involved a few hundred, but some rose to the tens of thousands. Protestors did not simply march down the streets, but took to blocking intersections and tieing up traffic.[21]

At the same time that it inspired mass democratic movements, the Chiapas Rebellion also flummoxed the PRI's election strategy. Manuel Camacho, leading the PRI's negotiations with Marcos and the Zapatistas, dominated the headlines and, by proposing new economic and social programs for the Indians of Chiapas, Camacho rose to new heights of popularity. Camacho's growing appeal threatened to eclipse the election campaign of the PRI's official candidate Luis Donaldo Colosio. The PRI faced the possibility of a succession crisis, disrupting the one-party state's smooth transition from president to president.

Between January and March, the Zapatista rebellion in Chiapas had merged with the already existing reform movements of Mexican civil society to produce the greatest democratic upheaval in two decades. Throughout the first quarter of 1994 there was hardly a sector of Mexican society that was not stirred by the rebellion. In January, the EZLN had led an army of perhaps 2,000 soldiers. By March the Zapatistas stood at the head of an amorphous mass movement of hundreds of thousands throughout Mexico. The Chiapas Rebellion threatened to become a democratic revolution.

But in mid-March, the winds began to shift. A cold breeze began to blow over Mexico. In Mexico, it was the time of the assassins. On March 14, unknown assailants kidnapped billionaire Alfredo Harp Helu, chairman of the National Bank of Mexico, one of the world's richest men and an associate of Mexican President Carlos Salinas de Gortari. Harp Helu was part of the inner circle of businessmen associated with President Salinas de Gortari, and his kidnapping seemed at first like another blow at the regime.

Harp Helu was later freed, but at the time, it was not clear whether Harp Helu had been seized by criminals or politicos, and if by politicos whether they were leftists or rightists. The Mexican government suggested that ETA, an organization of Basque revolutionary nationalists in Spain and France, was responsible for the kidnapping. Thus the government raised the spector of political violence, not by a mass uprising confined to Chiapas, but by armed bands of foreign terrorists operating in the cities.[22]

While the Chiapas Rebellion and Manuel Camacho's negotiations with the Zapatistas captured the national attention, the PRI's election campaign went on in a lackluster fashion. Luis Donaldo Colosio held rather pathetic campaign rallies in destitute little villages and poverty-stricken barrios, surrounded by PRI loyalists who came more out of interest in the free tacos and beer than in his declamations.

While Colosio tramped the dusty streets of the villages, Manuel Camacho Solís grabbed the spotlight as the man who seemed to have brought negotiations with the Zapatistas to a successful conclusion. Camacho continued to encourage speculation that he would be a candidate for the presidency. Groups like Democracy 2000, a reformist faction within the PRI, came out for Camacho. Yet it was never quite clear whether Camacho was a genuine alternative, or merely the smiling liberal face of the one-party dictatorship, a stalking horse for Colosio and not his opponent.

Then, suddenly and inexplicably, on March 22, Camacho announced that he would not be a candidate for the presidency. "I am putting the higher causes of the nation above my aspirations," he said. The stock of TELMEX, the recently privatized telephone company, rose 7 percent within an hour, and over 10 percent for the day. Foreign investors breathed a sigh of relief, as Mexican stability seemed assured. There was no explanation of why the ambitious Camacho had suddenly and surprisingly removed himself from the presidential arena.

The very next day, March 23, at a campaign rally on a dusty street in a poor neighborhood in the hills of Tijuana, near the U.S. border, a gunman or gunmen assassinated the PRI's presidential candidate Luis Donaldo Colosio. Once again, as after the kidnapping of Harp Helu, a chill passed over Mexico. Was this a single assassin or part of a conspiracy? Was it the first move by rightists planning a coup d'etat? Or was it another blow by leftist revolutionaries? Again people feared that Mexico was being drawn into a maelstrom of political violence. The hope and optimism created by the Chiapas Rebellion, were overcome by the fear and pessimism of the time of the assassins.

Security forces at the scene arrested a casual laborer named Mario Aburto Martínez, and reporters got hold of a videotape showing Aburto putting a gun to Colosio's head. Upon his arrest Aburto was reported to have said, "We have saved Mexico." Investigators learned that Aburto lived in a poor neighborhood in Tijuana and worked, off and on, in one of the city's many small factories. He was a loner. In Aburto's wallet was found a card identifying him as a member of the Association of Committees of the People, an unknown organization. [23]

Not since the 1928 murder of president Alvaro Obregón by a Catholic religious fanatic had a member of the Mexican ruling elite been touched by the political violence. The Mexican rulers were part of a political aristocracy who lived in a world apart, and these things were not supposed to happen to them. The fact that after 65 years the violence finally touched the political nobility was an indication of the perilous political situation that the country faced.

Why had Colosio been assassinated? Many Mexicans suspected that the ruling Institutional Revolutionary Party (PRI) might be reponsible for the assassination. Their suspicions were understandable, for the PRI-government in Mexico had for decades overseen a system of political repression—not like the dirty-wars in Argentina or Guatemala, to be sure—but terrible enough. The Mexican police constantly violated Mexican law by torturing both common criminals and political dissidents. Cases documented by both Mexican and international Human Rights activists show that Mexican police tortured men, women, and even childen.[24]

The police engaged in extra-judicial execution or assassination, particularly of political opponents. During the 1970s, about 500 Mexicans simply disappeared, presumably tortured and murdered by right-wing death squads run by Mexican police and army officers. In 1989, a former Mexican soldier, Zacarias Osorio Cruz, fled to Canada where he told the Canadian Immigration Board that in Mexico he had participated in the murder of scores of political dissidents.[25]

The greatest number of recent incidents of repression involved the opposition Party of the Democratic Revolution (PRD). The PRD claimed that between 1988 and 1994 it had had 286 of its members either killed or disappeared, and found that many of those murdered had been killed by the police, the army or PRI officials.

At the time Colosio was killed, many Mexicans still remained disturbed about the May 24, 1993 assassination of Cardinal Juan Jesús Posadas Ocampo who was gunned down in the Guadalajara International Airport. The government initially arrested over 50 people involved in the killing in one way or another, but somehow allowed three of the key witnesses to be murdered. The government prosecutor, Jorge Carpizo McGregor, ultimately decided that the Cardinal had been the accidental victim of a shoot-out between two rival gangs of drug smugglers. But in the course of investigating the case, government authorities, church officials and reporters discovered that a number of high ranking police were involved in the drug trade and in the murder. Most Mexicans did not believe the government's account of an accidental killing, and many suspected some sort of conspiracy to assassinate the Cardinal.[26]

Salinas appointed a close associate, Miguel Montes, as a special investigator in the Colosio case. Montes suggested that there had been a conspiracy involving three ex-state police officers of the former PRI government of Baja California. A fourth suspect was an agent of *Gobernación*, the Ministry of the Interior, which is responsible for doing much of the PRI's political dirty work.

As more information became available, many speculated that Colosio had been assassinated by the PRI party leaders of Baja California because four years before he had forced them from power. In 1989 Colosio, then head of the PRI, had compeled the PRI's Baja California leaders to turn over control of the state to the National Action Party (PAN) after businessman Ernesto Ruffo of the PAN won the gubernatorial election.

The patronage plum of Baja California is Tijuana, a city of over a million inhabitants across the border from San Diego, California. Tijuana has become a major center of the *maquiladora* or border industries program with hundreds of factories and warehouses. The city is also a center of the tourist industry with *jai-lai*, horse racing, night clubs and prostitution. Finally, Tijuana is the busiest Mexico-U.S. border crossing, and consequently a strategic center of drug smuggling and illegal immigration to the United States. All of this opened up infinite opportunities for shady business dealings, graft and extorsion of all kinds, much of which enriched the PRI's local police officials and political leaders. When Colosio forced the PRI's local leaders to yield to the PAN, he took from them the goose that laid the golden eggs of patronage and payoffs. The Baja PRI never forgave Colosio and could conceivably have killed him.

Others suggested that under the pressure of the Chiapas Rebellion and Camacho's rising popularity, Colosio had begun to make too many concessions to the new democratic rhetoric. Colosio began to talk like a populist and a democrat, and PRI leaders feared he might act like one. Some speculated that Salinas and other PRI leaders had Colosio eliminated. The most cynical interpretation, was that Salinas, or some conservative police or military figure, had Colosio assassinated in order to raise the spector of a right-wing military coup, and frighten the country back into the embrace of the PRI.

Montes proposed a conspiracy theory which pointed in the direction of the state or perhaps in that of the national PRI leaders. Later, however, unable or unwilling to come up with the evidence, the government prosecutor decided that Aburto alone had killed Colosio. Aburto, was tried by a judge in a federal prison without jury, and on October 31, 1994 sentenced to 42 years in prison for murder.

With the national elections only five months away, Colosio's assassination left Salinas with the task of choosing someone to replace Colosio as the PRI's presidential nominee. In Mexico, the president is limited to one six-year term, and the out-going president, after consulting with party leaders, handpicks his own successor. There is no party convention or primary process; the president simply decides. In the 65 years of the PRI's rule, the president's choice has always become both the party's candidate and the next president. The Mexican Constitution, however, forbids the nomination of a sitting member of the presidential cabinet, so several of the likely contenders, such as Commerce Minister Jaime Serra Puche and Treasury Minister Pedro Aspe, were thus eliminated from consideration. Both Manuel Camacho, the peace negotiator in Chiapas, and Ernest Zedillo, the former campaign manager for Colosio, however, were available.

There was some speculation that Salinas might choose Manuel Camacho, made famous by his negotiations with the Zapatistas. However, many members of the PRI leadership strenuously objected to Camacho. There was also a certain popular reaction against Camacho since he had been an opponent of the now martyred Colosio. In any case, Camacho immediately announced that he would not be the replacement candidate.

Salinas chose as his nominee a man with his own free-market views. Ernesto Zedillo was born and grew up in Mexicali, Baja California, and graduated in 1972 from Mexico's National Polytechnic Institute. Like Harvard-educated Salinas, Zedillo studied abroad, earning his doctorate in economics at Yale University in 1978. Zedillo began his career as a banker in the Banco de México, Mexico's central bank. He rose quickly, and in the early 1980s headed a trust fund created to restructure Mexico's foreign debt. Still quite young, Zedillo served as Minister of the Budget (SPP) from 1987 to 1988, and then as Minister of Education (SEP) from 1992 to 1993. As Minister of Education, Zedillo undertook the revision of the nation's elementary school history books, a process that involved him in a national brouhaha.

While Mexican history books had previously traced Mexico's greatness to the Mexican Revolution of 1910 to 1920, Zedillo's textbooks named former dictator Porfirio Díaz as the father of modern Mexico. Zedillo's new texts did not call Díaz a dictator, and instead praised him for bringing peace and economic growth to Mexico. The new history books also ended in 1964 to avoid having to discuss the 1968 Tlatelolco massacre. Zedillo's new texts caused a tremendous national controversy, and in the end, were never used.[27] In 1993, Zedillo resigned from the cabinet to become the campaign manager for Colosio, his first real fling in electoral politics.

With Salinas's choice of Zedillo as the PRI's new presidential candidate, the stock market steadied. The *Wall Street Journal* was delighted with Salinas's choice of a free-market neo-liberal. But among the PRI party workers there was less elation at the choice of a candidate who was variously described as cold, wooden, and distant. Many in the PRI believed that Zedillo—who had never run in any election—could not hope to win the presidential race. Ramiro de la Rosa, head of the reformist Democracy 2000 faction in the PRI, warned that the PRI would not unite behind Zedillo and that

"A divided party will oblige us to commit massive fraud on August 21 [election day] to stay in power."[28]

In the August 1994 election then, Zedillo would face Cuauhtémoc Cárdenas of the left-center Party of the Democratic Revolution (PRD), who had been cheated out of the 1988 election by Salinas, and Diego Fernández de Cevallos of the conservative National Action Party (PAN), as well as the candidates of six other small parties. The presidential race, however, was not the only or even the most important contest taking place in Mexico during the five months leading to the election. There still remained the struggle between the PRI and the Mayan rebels in Chiapas.

The kidnapping of Harp Helu and the assassination of Luis Donaldo Colosio succeeded in chilling the political atmosphere, and creating fear and apprehension. Television, radio and press commentary linked the insurrection, the kidnapping and the assassination, and suggested a new period of political violence. In the minds of the public there appeared the spector of Mexico becoming another Central America, sucked into a syndrome of violence and counter-violence. Playing to the popular anxieties, the PRI's Zedillo declared himself the candidate of peace and stability.

The Zapatista Army of National Liberation remained besieged in the Lacandón jungle in Chiapas, and as a result of the assassination and the new political climate, seemed increasingly isolated. To overcome their military and political isolation, in June Marcos and the Indigenous Revolutionary Clandestine Committee of the EZLN in Chiapas, conceived the ingenious idea of calling for a National Democratic Convention (CND) to be held in San Cristóbal and in the rebels stronghold in the Lacandón rainforest. A masterpiece of political strategy, the CND would allow the EZLN to establish a broad national movement, even while apparently trapped. Despite the chilling effect of the assassination of Colosio, the events of January to April 1994 had revitalized Mexico's democratic movement.

In just four short months, the Zapatistas' Chiapas Rebellion had had a tremendous impact on Mexican politics. The Zapatista rebellion had strengthened the social movements of Indians, peasants and farmers, and it had given new life to the Mexican civil society's struggle for democracy. The EZLN had also helped to recreate a left pole in Mexican politics. The EZLN uprising strengthened the left wing of the Party of the Democratic Revolution and the many small socialist groups to the PRD's left.

To fully appreciate the importance of these developments one must understand the social conditions in Chiapas, the history of the Mayan Indian and peasant movements in the region, and the ideology of the new Zapatistas. We turn to those matters in the next chapter.

2

PEASANT REBELS:
THE ZAPATISTA ARMY OF
NATIONAL LIBERATION

What had led the Indian peasants to rebel? Before the uprising, in 1993, Subcomandante Marcos wrote a document with the title: "Chiapas: The Southeast in Two Winds, a Storm and a Prophecy." The powerful pamphlet is a guidebook to the forgotten Chiapas, to its rich and powerful, its poor and faceless. As if flying over the state, Marcos points out the enormous industrial and agricultural wealth of Chiapas: huge hydroelectric plants, oil wells, highways, railroads and airports. We see the many large cattle ranches, the coffee, tobacco and sugar plantations, and the farms with their corn fields, soy, and sorghum. All of those products, explains Marcos, are bound for the United States, Canada, Germany, Japan. All of it, he says, has "the same destination—the empire."[1]

Throughout the pamphlet, Marcos contrasts the enormous wealth of the state to the abysmal poverty of the majority of its inhabitants. Perhaps the most striking example is electricity. "Chiapas produces 55 percent of Mexico's hydroelectric energy, and 20 percent of all the nation's electricity," writes Marcos. "However only one-third of the Chiapaneco homes have electricity. Where do the 12,907 gigawatts produced annually by Chiapas's hydroelectric plants go?"[2]

"The wealth of Chiapas," says Marcos, "has done little for the 3.5 million citizens of Chiapas, two-third of whom live in the countryside. "Communication is a grotesque caricature," for such a rich state. The highways serve the industries and tourists, while paved roads never reach many indigenous communities.

"Education?" asks Marcos, "The worst in the country. In primary school, 72 of every 100 children do not finish the first grade. More than half the schools offer only up to the third grade, and half the schools have only one teacher...." Many children get no education because their parents need them to work in the fields or to work at home so another adult in the family can work in the fields. "The health of the Chiapanecos," says Marcos, "shows the marks of capitalism: one and a half million people have no medical service whatsoever."[3]

Marcos continues the tour, showing us the marvelous architectural monuments of Chiapas: the ancient Mayan ruins at Palenque and the colonial Churches in San Cristóbal de las Casas. We see thousands of tourist hotels, and hundreds of restaurants and tourist agencies. But, as we look more closely, the prisons and military barracks stand out as a landscape of repression. Marcos's pamphlet suggests that *Chiapanecos*, especially indigenous people and peasants, face two overwhelming realities: poverty and violence.

Marcos' pamphlet presents a more literary version of the findings of government investigators, academic researchers, and social service organizations. Various studies of Chiapas in the early 1990s found that housing conditions in general were deplorable. Eight out of ten homes had dirt floors, lacked sewer systems, and typically housed nine or more people. For the majority of Chiapas' inhabitants wages were entirely inadequate. Eighty percent of the workforce earned less than US$6.66 and over half the workforce earned less than US$3.32 per day.

Conditions were even worse in eastern Chiapas where the Zapatista uprising took place, particularly in villages like Altamirano, Las Margaritas, Chanal, Huixtan and Oxchuc. Seven out of ten homes in that area had no electricity, eight out of ten homes were overcrowded, and nine out of ten people were illiterate. Yet despite these conditions the Mexican government which spent on the average about US$180 per person in all of Mexico, spent only US$84 per person in Chiapas.[4]

With such low wages, it is not surprising that 80 percent of the children suffered from malnutrition. Because of dirt floors, lack of sewers, poor food, and the absence of medical care, *Chiapanecos* suffered 14,500 deaths each year from curable diseases, with children and infants being the principal victims, mostly dying from diarrhea. After the insurrection, Marcos told reporters, "It's better to die fighting than to die of dysentery."

Depressingly, it seemed Chiapas had always been the same. In the 1950s, Paul Lamartine Yates found Chiapas "possessed the lowest level of well-being in Mexico." In the mid-1980s Thomas Benjamin wrote that "Chiapas is one of the most impoverished regions in Mexico."[5]

In addition to poverty, hunger, and disease, the Mayan Indians of Chiapas also faced the Mexican society's endemic racism. While Mexico's government claims to be a racial democracy, both the government and the society are profoundly racist against the Indian. Since the Revolution of 1910, the Mexican state's vision of social progress has been based upon the idea of a *mestizo*, that is a mixed-race culture. Historically the Mexican state's goal has been the assimilation of the Indian to that dominant *mestizo* society.

"*Indigenismo*," until recently the official anthropological theory in Mexico, called for the integration of the Indians into the Mexican nation. While this has often been put in terms of the "uplift" of the Indian, many Indians would argue that assimilation represents a process of ethnocide—the destruction of the indigenous community.

The unassimilated Indians, who represent a minority within the Mexican population, feel genuinely threatened by the state's policies. Mexico's Indian population is estimated to be between 8 and 12 million, or between 10 and 14 percent of the total population of 86 million. Those 10 million or so people living throughout Mexico, speak 56 different languages. Twenty of those groups have less than 10,000 members and half of them have less than 1,000 members, which means that they are groups in real danger of extinction.[6] For them, assimilation means the death of their people and their culture.

Indian cultures, particularly the Aztec civilization, are glorified by the state. Dead Indians are celebrated in the state museums, depicted in the murals on public buildings, and represented in the statues that line Mexican boulevards. Living Indians, however, more often suffer state neglect and public humiliation.

In Mexican society, racist behavior toward the Indians is an entrenched everyday experience. The word "*indio*" (Indian) is a derogatory term and an insult. Mexicans refer to their Indian maids as "*la muchacha*," the girl, though the woman may be an aging grandmother. Until the 1950s, Indians were not permitted to walk the streets of San Cristóbal de las Casas. Racism, both by the state and by society, has dehumanized the Indian, making it possible for many Mexicans to overlook the indigenous peoples' poverty and even starvation, and to accept the torture and murder of Indian people.

A more immediate cause of the Chiapas Rebellion was the amendment to Constitutional Article 27 that President Salinas had pushed through the Mexican legislature. As a result of the changes, Mexican law was altered to permit the privatization of communal land holdings. The changes in Article 27 were intended to bring Mexico's property laws into line with those of the other partners to NAFTA, the United States and Canada.

It would be difficult to exaggerate the importance of Article 27 in Mexican life. In 1917, in the midst of the Mexican Revolution, the delegates to President Carranza's Constitutional Convention, under enormous pressure from rebellious peasants like those led by Emiliano Zapata in Morelos, adopted Article 27 unanimously. Article 27 proclaimed the Mexican nation the owner of the lands and waters of the nation, established an agrarian reform to redistribute land to the peasants, and provided for communal ownership of that land.[7]

Article 27 provided the constitutional basis for President Lázaro Cárdenas' great agrarian reform of 1934-1940 in which 20 million hectares of land were distributed to over 776,000 peasants.[8] Much of the land was distributed to Indian communities or *ejidos*. The *ejido* is a unique Mexican form of corporate land holding, sometimes in collective form, and sometimes in individual plots. By 1994, *ejidatarios* and their families made up 15 million Mexicans, that is, a number greater than Mexico's entire population at the time of the Mexican Revolution. As a result of agrarian reform, out of Mexico's five million farm laborers, four million work their own land, while one million are agricultural wage laborers.[9]

During the 1930s, Lázaro Cárdenas's distribution of land to the *ejido* laid the basis for a revival of agriculture and a renaissance of the Mexican peasant villages. But since the 1940s, the exhaustion of the soil, the enormous growth in population, and inadequate support from the government, meant that the *ejidal* and communal lands declined and the peasantry sank into poverty. By the 1980s, most *ejidatarios* could no longer support themselves by farming, and many worked as wage laborers. Nevertheless, for millions of Mexicans, Article 27 still held out the hope of land ownership and economic improvement.

When Salinas amended Article 27, peasants who had no land lost all hope of ever acquiring any. With the end of land reform, many poor people in the countryside lost confidence in the government. The state-party's historic connection with the peasants, dating back to Lázaro Cárdenas, was severed. Under the new amendments, peasants were free to rent or sell their interest in the *ejido*, and agricultural corporations were permitted to buy the land. Those changes made it possible to break up indigenous village and *ejidal* lands, threatening the continued existence of the Indian community.

The *ejidal* and communal land played a particularly large and important role among the people of Chiapas. Of Chiapas's total population of 3.5 million, one million *Chiapanecos* lived on *ejidal* or communal land. The people of the state of Chiapas therefore felt more threatened by these reforms than any other group in any state in Mexico.[10] Other peasants worried that NAFTA, by eliminating tariff barriers and quotas, would eventually flood the Mexican market with U.S. and Canadian corn, and lead to the economic ruin of their farms and villages. That is why Marcos called NAFTA, "a death sentence for the Indians."

In Meso-America, for two thousand years the Indian communities had been organized around the farming of corn, often on communal land. As Rigoberta Menchú, a Nobel prize-winner and a leader of the Mayan Indians just over the border in Guatemala, wrote in her moving autobiography, "Maize is the center of everything for us. It is our culture."[11] If the Indians lost their land and the ability to farm, they would no longer exist as a culture and a people. NAFTA and the changes in Article 27 did not represent a new economic order for the Indians but rather threatened to destroy a two thousand year old civilization.

□□□

The Chiapas rebellion of January 1994 was not the first. As the EZLN manifesto asserted, such rebellions had been taking place for five hundred years. The economic motor which for centuries drove the Indian or peasant community to rebel was the expansion of the capitalist market.[12] Each expansion of the market or capitalist crisis led to a new wave of resistance: 1524-1530, 1693-1727, 1865, 1911, 1929-1940, 1975, 1982, and 1994.[13] Whenever the Liberals attempted to dismantle the self-sufficient community and introduce capitalist relations, a Virgin appeared to the Indians, talking revolution.[14]

The Spaniards conquered Chiapas in the 1520s, subjugating the Mayans. With the labor of the Mayan villagers, the Spanish colonists established vast *haciendas* and ranches that produced staples—sugar, cacao, vanilla, corn, wheat, cotton, indigo, cochineal, and hides—for sale in the European metropolis. By the eighteenth century the *haciendas* absorbed many of the Indians who lived and worked in peonage. While Chiapas traded on the world market, the internal world of Chiapas remained seigneurial or quasi-feudal.

The Mayans divided their time between the *hacienda* and their economically self-sufficient communities, where they grew corn, preserved their language, and much of their religion. Periodically the Mayan Indians rose in revolt against their Spanish or, later, Mexican overlords. In the largest revolts in 1712 and 1865, Indian women had religious revelations calling upon the Maya to expel the *Ladinos* (Spaniards) from Chiapas. In both uprisings, the Indians organized an Army of the Virgin which drove out Spanish landlords and distributed land to the peasants. Both revolts were crushed in blood.

The greatest expansion of Mexican capitalism in the nineteenth century took place during the regime of the dictator Porfirio Díaz from 1876 to 1910. That economic expansion produced the Mexican Revolution, but strangely enough the revolution hardly touched Chiapas. An isolated Indian uprising in 1911 was put down by the new revolutionary president, Madero. Later Carranza's Constitutionalist Army came to Chiapas, but proved unable to defeat the local landlords. Consequently the Mexican Revolution came and went, leaving Chiapas virtually unchanged.

The revolution's impact was mostly felt in the post-revolutionary period as the Indians of Chiapas turned from armed uprising to labor organizing as their chosen form of resistance. In 1917 and 1918, socialist organizers from Tapachula began to recruit into unions the Indian laborers working on the coffee plantations in the Soconusco region of Chiapas. In 1918 and 1922, the unions struck and thousands of coffee workers brought the harvest to a halt. In Chiapas, the socialist workers succeeded in forcing the Obregón government to expropriate some coffee *fincas* (plantations) in the Soconusco and turn them into *ejidos*. In 1925 the socialists of Chiapas even succeeded in electing a socialist governor. But the governor was murdered, the ranchers took back political control, and the Chiapas socialist movement was driven underground.

During the 1930s, many of the anarchists and socialists joined the Communist Party and continued their organizing efforts among the Indian coffee workers. Some of the coffee workers were Tzotziles from San Juan Chamula and other Mayan communities of the Chiapas highlands. These workers created clandestine organizations, engaged in armed self-defense, and despite severe repression, continued to operate in the shadows.[15]

The election of President Lázaro Cárdenas in 1934 transformed the movement. Cárdenas intervened in Chiapas in 1936 supporting reformer Efraín A. Gutiérrez for governor against the local landlords' candidate. Gutiérrez won, and his election opened the way for Cárdenas's agrarian reform in Chiapas.

Cárdenas then appointed Erasto Urbina, a talented organizer, to head the Union of Indigenous Workers (STI) in Chiapas. Urbina and the STI organized 30,000 Tzeltal and Tzotzil Indians who worked on the coffee plantations. Taking control of the planters' laborers, Cárdenas's party became a force in the region for the first time. Cárdenas also made Urbina the director of the Department of Indian Protection. Working through Indian and *mestizo* rural school teachers, Urbina extended his influence among the Indian laborers on the German-owned plantations and the Mexican *haciendas* of San Cristóbal, Ocosingo, Chilón and Simojovel. With President Cárdenas's backing, Urbina provided the Indians with guns and organized the seizure of plantations in the towns of San Juan Chamula, Oxchuc, Zinacantán, and Chenalho.

Through actions like these, the victorious Indian leaders displaced the *Ladino* merchants and office holders and took power in the towns. The Indians also won permanent and legal control of some farmland. On March 19, 1939, the first anniversary of the nationalization of the oil industry, Cárdenas carried out the largest land distribution in the history of Chiapas, distributing 7,988 hectares of land to six *ejidos*.

These measures would appear to be an overwhelming victory for the Indian communities and workers. But few Indian *ejidatarios* could make a living from the *ejidos* alone; many still needed to work on the plantations to survive.[16] And the indigenous labor union, which should have been protecting the workers, gradually evolved into a contracting agency providing laborers to the plantations.

Precisely because of Cárdenas's agrarian reform, the once powerful plantation workers' unions declined in influence. Many labor unions gradually converted themselves into coalitions of committees petitioning for land. By 1939, when the agrarian reform was carried out, many wage earners and union members had been converted into peasants working their *ejidos*. The socialist workers settled down to become the peasant base of Cárdenas's nationalist party-state.[17]

While begun under communist leadership, the fight for workers' rights and agrarian reform in Chiapas was completely taken over by the

Cardenists.[18] The labor unions and peasant leagues followed their communist leaders into the newly created labor (CTM), while peasant organizations (CNC) affiliated to the Mexican ruling party, the future PRI. The Communist Party's work, and the decades of organizing by anarchists and socialists that had gone before, ultimately served not the peasants, but the new Mexican one-party state.

The Indian leadership in the villages also changed at about this time. The state laws of the 1930s required each community in Chiapas to have a village government with elected civil authorities. Among these officials were *escribanos* or scribes: literate, bilingual Indians who served as middlemen between the Mayan community and the state and national government. The *escribanos,* or scribes gradually evolved into a new generation of *caciques* or political bosses allied with the PRI. These political bosses also exercised economic power through their control of beer and soft drink monopolies, trucking businesses, and local loan-sharking.

In the late 1940s, the state turned to the right. In 1948 in Chiapas and throughout Mexico, the government used the police, the military, and gangsters to attack major Mexican labor unions, deposing the elected leaders and replacing them with PRI loyalists.[19] By the 1960s, the Chiapas CTM "had lost its ability to influence or control in any meaningful way the working class of the state."[20] By the 1970s, the peasants of Chiapas found that the governments' peasant union, the CNC, "not only would not help them but often participated in attacks against them."[21]

Still, from the 1930s to the 1970s, the distribution of land to the *ejidos* served as the "socioeconomic safety valve" for Chiapas. During the 1950s and '60s there was another great land distribution in Chiapas, raising the number of families on *ejidos* from about 71,000 in 1950 to more than 148,000 by 1970. By 1988, one million Chiapanecos lived on *ejidal* land.

But since the 1960s, the *ejidos* had fallen far behind private agriculture. Land distributed to the peasants was often on the poorest soil and the government failed to give adequate financial support to the *ejido* farmers. Compared to large private farms, the *ejidos* had fewer tractors and less modern equipment. The *ejidos* became quite overpopulated, and many *ejidal* parcels were not adequate to support a family. "The high density of population in *ejidos* led to soil degradation, severe deforestation, and the near-disappearance of wild game."[22] The tens of thousands of families living on the *ejidos* found themselves sinking deeper and deeper into poverty.

Unable to make a living on the *ejidos*, Indian peasants often sought work as laborers on the coffee plantations. In many cases they were still involved in either *ejidal* or private farming and constituted a quasi-proletariat. By 1970 "80,000 day-laborers worked on *fincas* and plantations, often living in huts and receiving less than the minimum wage."[23]

The government's economic development programs only worsened the crisis in Chiapas. The Grijalva-Usumacinta hydroelectric complex, built in the Central Valley in the 1970s, provided jobs and electric power. On the other hand, hydroelectric dams at Malpaso, La Angostura, and Chicoasén created artificial lakes and flooded 200,000 hectares of land, exacerbating the peasant land crisis. Oil was discovered in the La Reforma fields of northern Chiapas, near Tabasco. The oil industry jobs often went to migrant workers from other states, however, and the oil workers' higher wages brought inflation to Chiapas, driving up prices for poor peasants. But perhaps the Indian peasants' biggest problem was cattle.

By the 1950s, the Indians of Chiapas found themselves in an intensifying struggle with ranchers. When Lázaro Cárdenas distributed land to the peasants in the 1930s, he issued "certificates of non-affectability" to cattle ranchers so that their lands were exempt.[24] As a result, cattle ranches and herds grew. In 1950 there were 480,00 head of cattle in Chiapas, in 1960 the cattle numbered 790,000, by 1970 the herds had reached 1.25 million.[25] The growth of the cattle ranches and plantations concentrated economic power in the hands of the big landowners and helped to push peasants on to the worst land or off the land altogether. Cattle grazing displaced the Indians' *milpas* or cornfield, and, according to Thomas Benjamin, "production of corn and other basic grains stagnated, and the people became desperate."[26]

The cattle ranchers and landlords of Chiapas entirely dominated local government, and worked in close cooperation with the PRI's police and the Mexican Army to repress the peasantry. Total estimates of peasants murdered by gangsters, police and army units working for the landlords reached into the thousands. In 1980, for example, in the Cholón district, the Mexican Army attacked the village of Golonchán, where they killed 15 people and wounded 22 others. That, of course, was a massacre, but the murder of four or five peasants at a time has been common since the mid-1970s. Many other Mayans suffered beatings, torture, and unjust imprisonment.[27] Governor Absalón Castellanos, the man taken prisoner by the EZLN, became infamous for using police and the armed forces to murder peasants.

By the 1980s, Chiapas had changed fundamentally. Oil, hydroelectric plants, ranches and coffee plantations all contributed to a larger social phenomenon: the final penetration of the capitalist economy into the Mayan village. "During the oil boom of the 1970s," writes anthropologist George Collier, "a new player began to take center stage in the indigenous hamlets of Chiapas. Money."[28] The cash economy led to growing economic differentiation in the countryside, which changed everything about village life: kinship declined in significance, elders lost their hold over the young, and that, in turn, undermined the basis of the PRI's political machine.

Some indigenous peasants became entrepreneurs: truckers, contractors, and wealthy farmers. Other peasants lost their land: men became wage laborers and women piece workers.[29] Indian villages themselves became torn by a class struggle between the propertied and the propertyless. Whether the peasants became richer or poorer, the PRI tended to lose its grip over them. Chiapas's peasants became open to other forms of social and political organization.

Some poorer Indian peasants began to move into the Lacandón rainforest to get farmland. The Spanish conquerors and Mexican landowners had exterminated most of the original inhabitants, so that few people lived in the rainforest until the 1950s when highland Indians and other Mexicans in search of land began to migrate there. During the 1960s, thousands of highland Mayan Indians migrated into the Lacandón carrying on slash and burn agriculture.

President Echeverría's government attempted to regularize the situation in the Lacandón rainforest in 1971, deeding land to various Indian groups. The PRI also carried out another agrarian reform in the area, distributing land in the form of *ejidos* to the Lacandón community.[30] But these measures may only have succeeded in encouraging more squatters, for the migration into the forest continued and gained momentum. By the 1980s, about 70,000 Tzeltal, Chol and Tzotzil Maya had moved into the Lacandón. The eastern lowlands and the Lacandón rainforest became a magnet for immigrants not only from the highlands, but from other parts of Mexico.[31]

The new villages in Las Cañadas and the Lacandón, populated by migrants not only from Chiapas but also from other states in Mexico, created a new culture more open to different ideas. Uprooted from their native villages, Indians from the highlands mixed with mestizo immigrants from other parts of Mexico. The Mayans' old village relations were shattered, and the Mayan-Catholic religious community broke down. Some of the pioneers in the Lacandón became Protestants, Evangelicals or Mormons. Others created new social and political organizations, among them the Zapatista Army of National Liberation.

□□□

While drawing on the Mayan Indians' long history of struggle, the Zapatista Army of National Liberation was also the product of several other major political currents: Castroism, Chinese communism, the Theology of Liberation, and the Mexican tradition of peasant rebellion.

"Our organization was born after the massacre of the students," EZLN Captain Roberto explained to a reporter.[32] In 1968, the year of the Mexican Olympics, several thousand students demonstrated for democracy at Tlatelolco, the Plaza of three cultures in Mexico City. The government feared the protests would disrupt the Olympics and discredit the regime, so President López Mateos and Minister of the Interior Luis Echeverría ordered the Mexican Army to suppress the demonstrators. The soldiers marched into the plaza and murdered hundreds of protesters—the numbers are still debated—and many bodies were removed, destroyed, or disfigured to prevent identification.

The mass murder of these young people horrified the Mexican people and caused widespread feelings of revulsion toward the government. The 1968 Tlatelolco massacre represented a crucial turning point in modern Mexican history, for it destroyed the state's legitimacy in the eyes of millions. After Tlatelolco, many Mexicans, especially the young, no longer believed in the beneficent state party, the embodiment of the revolution.

These young students and workers were far different from their parents and grandparents. The Mexican youth of 1968 grew up long after the turbulent Revolution of Madero, Carranza, Villa and Zapata, and even long after Lázaro Cárdenas. The young shared no first-hand memories of the distribution of land to the peasants or the nationalization of the oil industry. The Institutional Revolutionary Party's corporate structure of state-sponsored labor unions and peasant leagues seemed to them like Big Brother's controlling hand. After Mexican Army troops attacked and murdered young people like themselves, the PRI's grip on the minds of the young was greatly weakened.

Many young people no longer believed the PRI's "revolutionary nationalist" ideology, and looked for solutions to society's problems elsewhere. Most looked to the left. Mexico had had a Communist Party (PCM) since the 1920s, but few of Mexico's youth found it attractive. The Mexican communists of 1968 were pro-Soviet, Stalinist, and moreover, still supported politically the Institutional Revolutionary Party as a progressive nationalist movement. Fundamentally conservative in so many ways, communism failed to win over the new youth movement.

But a new Mexican Left had already begun to appear even before 1968. Cuba's Revolution in 1959 inspired and enthused young Mexicans just as it did an entire generation of Latin Americans. After years of U.S. Marine invasions throughout Central America and the Caribbean, little Cuba stood up to the United States, fought for its independence, and won. Young Mexicans thrilled at the speeches of Fidel Castro and mourned the loss of his comrade Ché Guevara, when he died attempting to carry the revolution to Bolivia in 1967. When former Mexican President Lázaro Cárdenas came out of retirement in 1961 to form the National Liberation Movement to defend the Cuban Revolution, Mexican nationalism and Cuban communism joined in an enormously influential political current.

While Cuba supported revolutionary organizations in many other parts of Latin America, Fidel Castro hesitated to offend the PRI government in Mexico. Castro, who depended on Mexico both for economic assistance and for diplomatic support in keeping the United States at arms length, was not about to organize either a peaceful or a military opposition to his ally, the PRI. Some small Castroist groups existed in Mexico, but Castroism remained more important as a current of opinion than as an organization.

The other large new left current in Mexico was Maoism. Mexican Maoists knew little or nothing of the horrible truth about Chairman Mao's Stalinist dictatorship in China, but they had enormous illusions in Mao's Great Proletarian Culture Revolution. As the young Mexican radicals understood it, Mao's culture revolution meant the creation of an egalitarian society, free from the bureaucracy which had strangled socialism in the Soviet Union. In that spirit, Mexico's Maoists proposed that student radicals should go to the people, the poor people, the peasantry and urban slum-dwellers, and build a new revolutionary movement.

One of the principal Maoist leaders was Adolfo Orive Berlinguer, the son of Adolfo Orive de Alba who had been the Minister of Hydraulic Works during the administration of President Miguel Alemán Valdés (1946-1952). Later, in the 1980s, Orive Berlinguer would follow his father's footsteps into the PRI-government, serving in President Salinas's National Solidarity Program (PRONASOL).[33] Still, in the 1960s Orive Berlinguer was a radical who would set in motion the forces that helped produce the EZLN.

In 1968, Orive Berlinguer studied in Paris with the Maoist theoretician Charles Bettelheim. Shortly thereafter, Orive returned to Mexico City where he organized the Emiliano Zapata brigades at the National University (UNAM) to resist the military occupation of the campus.[34] In November 1968, Orive wrote a pamphlet entitled "Towards a Politics of the People," in which he argued that the left had to build an organizational base among the common people. The followers of Orive, known as the Popular Politics or later the Proletarian Line tendency, spread through Mexico building grass-roots organizations. Maoist organizers succeeded in establishing political groups in rural communities, urban slums, and labor unions throughout Mexico, but particularly in the northern states of Durango, Coahuila and Nuevo León.

Unlike Marxist socialists, the Maoists defined the proletariat not as the class of wage laborers, but rather as the poor or the people. In the *colonias* (poor neighborhoods), the Maoist groups took up the most pressing needs of the urban poor: demands for land, running water, sewer systems, electricity. In Monterrey, Durango and Zacatecas, Maoist activists led demonstrations and land seizures. The Maoist strategy generally involved an alternation of confrontation and negotiation with the PRI, gradually winning concessions from the state-party.

Orive's Maoist organizing model called for the creation of community assemblies and encouraged the participation of the masses. Maoist community leaders frequently convened assemblies to inform or consult with "the mass base." But participation and consultation did not necessarily mean participatory democracy, or democracy of any kind for that matter. The Maoist leaders generally kept control of the movement in the hands of selected cadres who made the key decisions and carried out negotiations with the PRI. While the majority of community activists were often women, Maoist men dominated the leadership posts. Where the Maoists were successful in winning concessions from the PRI, they attempted to establish their own strict control over a particular *colonia*, peasant organization or labor union. Where they succeeded, the Maoists built a political machine as authoritarian as the PRI itself. Maoist groups fought for the needs of the poor, but the poor themselves generally had little political control over the organization.[35]

In the early 1970s, the Maoist students established one of their bases in the city of Torreón in Coahuila. Working in the slums and shanty-towns, Maoist activists established a community movement they called "*Tierra y Libertad*" (Land and Liberty), the slogan of Emiliano Zapata's peasant movement. The Maoists' community organizing efforts among the poor won the support of the Roman Catholic Bishop of Torreón, Fernando Romo. In 1976 Romo brought his friend Samuel Ruíz, the Bishop of Chiapas, to Torreón to see the Maoists' work. Impressed by the Maoists, Ruíz reportedly invited them to engage in community organizing in Chiapas.[36] Other Maoist Popular Politics organizers had already arrived in Chiapas in the late 1960s and by 1974 they were active in the teachers' union (SNTE).[37] Subcomandante Marcos of the EZLN was reportedly one of the *Torreónistas* who carried Maoism into the Chiapas jungle.[38]

Other left-wing political groups came to Chiapas in the early 1970s as well. The Trotskyists of the Revolutionary Workers Party (PRT) were active in the teachers' union, and the main competitor with the Maoists' Popular Politics Tendency.[39] Mexican Communists also had activists in Chiapas among the peasants and workers. The Maoists, however, were the most influential of the leftist political groups.

The other great intellectual and political influence on the EZLN and its milieu came from an altogether different source: the Theology of Liberation. For 500 years, the Catholic Church in Latin America had been one of the region's largest land holders and the constant ally of reactionary landlords, powerful capitalists, and military dictators. The Roman Church, perhaps more than any single institution in the Americas, kept Indians, peasants, workers and women in subjection. But after the mid-1960s, the advocates of the Theology of Liberation within the Church came to rank among the most important forces for social progress.

These progressive forces within the Church in Latin America burgeoned after the Second Ecumenical Council, or Vatican II, held from 1962 to 1965. At that Council, Catholic bishops began to call for social and economic change. The Council was accompanied by Pope John XXIII's encyclicals *Mater et Magistra* (1961) and *Pacem in Terris* (1963) which argued that human beings had a right to decent living standards, education and political participation. The message from Rome was that the Church was not only concerned with saving people's souls, but also with improving their life on earth.[40] Vatican II led a generation of Catholics to become more active in democratic and socially progressive movements.

The ideas of Vatican II spread throughout Latin America, promoted by the Latin American Episcopal Conference. In 1968, the bishops of Latin America met in an extraordinary conference in Medellín, Colombia. Pope Paul VI himself attended the Conference and told the bishops, "We wish to personify the Christ of a poor and hungry people.'[41] Out of the Medellín conference came the new Theology of Liberation's key ideas: participation and liberation. The Catholic poor should participate in the life of their church, bring it their concerns, and seek their spiritual and physical liberation through it.

Developed at a time when military dictators ruled much of Latin America, the new Theology of Liberation addressed the issue of human rights. The Church began to concern itself about the murder and torture of political dissidents, peasants and workers. Catholic intellectuals and activists began to analyze and criticize, not only the military dictatorships, but also supposedly "democratic" governments such as that of the PRI in Mexico. Priests and lay activists even began to take an interest in Marxism because it provided the intellectual tools for a class and political analysis of the Latin American condition.

The Theology of Liberation also led to social and political activism. According to the Theology of Liberation, the Church had a responsibility to go beyond the walls of the church, to go to the poor in their communities, even in the shanty-towns, slums, and rural villages. Under the influence of the Theology of Liberation, priests and Catholic lay men and women, known as catechists, began to organize tens of thousands of Christian-based communities throughout Latin America. These reforming Catholics became active in the movements of slum-dwellers, petitioning the government for electricity and water, in the fights of workers who went on strike for living wage, and in the organizations of peasants struggling with wealthy landlords over the land. Catholics found themselves working first beside and then together with communists, Castroites, Trotskyists and Maoists.

While the Theology of Liberation was never as influential in Mexico as in Central America and Brazil, it did flourish in some Mexican communities, particularly where it found a sympathetic bishop. The organization of Christian-based communities began in the late 1960s and early 1970s in the Bajío region north of Mexico City.[42] Bishop Sergio Méndez Arceo of Cuernavaca, the most famous of Mexico's liberation bishops, encouraged the organization of Christian base communities throughout the state of Morelos. Samuel Ruíz, the bishop of San Cristóbal de las Casas in Chiapas, encouraged his parishioners to organize grassroots movements. By 1988 the Theology of Liberation church in Mexico had organized 150,000 Catholics into Christian-based communities through the country.[43] While these communities represented only a tiny percentage of the church membership, they came to be an important current among social activists.

Finally, in addition to Castroism, Maoism and the Theology of Liberation, the new Zapatistas appropriated the Mexican traditions of armed struggle. For decades after Emiliano Zapata's death, other Mexican peasant revolutionaries took up his struggle. In 1959 and 1960, Rubén Jaramillo, a Methodist preacher and communist organizer who as a young man had ridden with Zapata, led struggles for land in the state of Morelos. The government negotiated with Jaramillo, made promises—and then sent in the army. At the orders of Mexican President López Mateos, soldiers using machine guns killed Jaramillo on May 23, 1962.

In the 1970s in the state of Guerrero, rural school teacher Genaro Vázquez Rojas organized the Guerrero Civic Association to fight for land and justice for the peasants. Later, after Vázquez's death, another school teacher, Lucio Cabañas Barrientos took up the fight, creating the Party of the Poor, which led peasants in an armed struggle against the Mexican state. Genaro Vázquez supposedly died in a car accident, while the Mexican Army killed Lucio Cabañas.[44] Those revolutionary leaders, martyred to the cause of the peasants' desperate desire for land, left a legacy of armed peoples' movements which Mexico's new radicals appropriated.

During this same period, a real explosion of new indigenous and peasant organizations took place in Chiapas and throughout Mexico. In an attempt to overcome public reaction to the 1968 student massacre for which he had been personally responsible, President Luis Echeverría Alvarez decided to imitate President Lázaro Cárdenas's populist program of the 1930s. Echeverría encouraged peasant land seizures, and administrated one of the largest redistribution of lands in Mexican history.

Echeverría implemented a new Federal Agrarian Reform Law, established a National Fund for Ejido Development, and increased public investment in agriculture. He expanded the National Bank of Rural Credit (Banrural) and created new agencies to purchase the peasants' products including, the Mexican Coffee Institute (INMECAFE).[45] Echeverría hoped that these measures would both revitalize Mexican agriculture and attenuate peasant radicalism. But, the new federal agencies caused a political problem for the PRI because they tended to further weaken the already discredited National Confederation of Peasants (CNC). Since other government agencies were now responsible for agricultural matters, the peasants no longer turned to the PRI's moribund CNC. The peasants, in response, created their own organizations.

At that point, the Catholic priests, catechists, Maoist student organizers, and Communist Party members began to draw the peasants into new community-based peasant organizations. These radical activists proved particularly successful in Chiapas and especially in the communities of Las Cañadas and the Lacandón jungle. In those areas, indigenous migrants from the highlands of Chiapas mixed with outlanders from other Mexican states, both Indians and *mestizos*. In these new villages, traditional religious and political authorities frequently had less influence, and in some cases the PRI's corporative organizations were virtually non-existent. At the same time, these communities were often in need of all the most basic utilities and services, from land, water and sewers to electricity, health care, and schools. In those parts of Chiapas, where Catholics, Maoists and communists joined the peasants in the struggle for land, education, and health care, they gradually succeeded in eclipsing the PRI's National Confederation of Peasants (CNC).

In 1974, Bishop Samuel Ruíz helped to organize the First Indigenous Congress of Chiapas for the Tzotziles, Tzeltales, Choles and Tojolabales. That First Congress represented a real turning point, for it gave impetus to a broad organizing movement throughout Chiapas. The new peasant organizations focussed on three different issues: labor organizing, land reform, and credit. Each of these approaches was pursued by one of the major organizations or political tendencies.

The Independent Confederation of Agricultural Workers and Peasants (CIOAC) founded in 1975, centered its efforts on the organization of rural wage laborers showing them how to use the courts to sue for back pay. CIOAC allied itself with the Communist Party, and supported its political candidates. The Emiliano Zapata Peasant Organization (OCEZ), formed in 1982, concentrated its efforts on land reform. OCEZ eschewed association with any political party, but did join in broader coalitions. The Maoist Popular Politics organizers created community unions which fought for credits for small farmers and helped in marketing crops. By the mid-1980s all three of these tendencies were organizing in eastern Chiapas and the Lacandón rainforest.[46] Many of the Chiapas peasant coalitions also affiliated with the "Plan de Ayala" Coordinating Committee (CNPA), formed in 1979, and which by the early 1980s, brought together peasants and day laborers from 21 organizations in several states.[47]

Even before the peasant organizing began, the school teachers of Chiapas, led by Maoists and Trotskyists, had created a "new labor movement" in the early 1970s. These "democratic" teachers, as they called themselves, succeeded, after years of organizing, in forcing the PRI's national teachers union (SNTE) to recognize their control of SNTE Section 7 in Chiapas. Section 7 fought for an end to wage freezes, opposed the PRI's bureaucratic control of the Ministry of Education (SEP), and fought for the rights of the many indigenous bilingual teachers.

In Chiapas, the democratic teachers actually took over the administration of the state schools and forced the democratic election of school supervisors. Within the Chiapas section, the teachers did away with the SNTE's vertical union structure and created their own horizontal teachers' organization. The democratic teachers also joined in coalitions with peasants. During parts of the 1970s and '80s, the Chiapas democratic teachers movement made a remarkable contribution to the democratization of the union and the schools which, because of their public demonstrations and high visibility, also had an impact on workers, peasants, the poor, as well as, the Left.[48]

The Maoists meanwhile moved into the immigrant communities in the Lacandón jungle where they organized new Ejido Unions (UE). In September 1980, 180 communities from 15 municipalities joined together to form the Union of Unions (UU). Faced with brutal repression by the local authorities, the Maoist "Proletarian Line" organizers often sought to make alliances with the Federal government. The Mexican government eventually gave the new Union of Unions both land and a credit union.

While most of the organizing efforts were both peaceful and legal, during this same period some radicals also attempted to create a guerrilla movement. Headed by César Yañez, also known as Brother Pedro, the Armed Forces of National Liberation (FALN) was established in the Lacandón jungle and recruited from the local villages. In 1974, the Mexican Army succeeded in crushing the young guerrilla movement, although some of the survivors later found their way into the Zapatista Army of National Liberation.[49]

The EZLN was founded in 1983. Marcos argued that the EZLN arose as a self-defense organization to protect the peasants from the attacks of the police, army, and ranchers' *guardias blancas*. "By taking up arms," writes Collier, "the EZLN has attempted to remove the peasants' struggle from the arena of corrupt Mexican law and politics."[50] The EZLN's military appears to be organized in a traditional hierarchy of ranks with soldiers subordinate to officers and ultimately to a military high command. What is not so traditional is the participation of women who make up an estimated one-third of all EZLN soldiers. In theory, the EZLN military is subordinate to the civilian leadership which is itself dependent upon the village communities.

Like other groups, influenced by Maoism, the EZLN built its civilian organization on the village assembly.[51] Above the village assemblies, the EZLN leaders created the Clandestine Revolutionary Indigenous Committee (CCRI) representing both the villages and the various Mayan ethnic groups. While dominated by male leaders, some women also serve on the CCRI.

The EZLN and the CCRI apparently consult with the village councils throughout the region, and have in mind to extend the council system throughout the country. As one Zapatista soldier explained, "We have to consult the people. They have elected us to carry out the work of the revolution....We have great hopes to carry the struggle in this way to the state and the national level."[52] Marcos and the EZLN claim that the Zapatista villages voted for the uprising of January 1, 1994.[53]

Author John Ross in *Rebellion from the Roots* suggests that, through the establishment of the CCRI and the village assemblies, the EZLN has brought about a fusion of Maoism and a "millenium" of traditional Indian communalism, creating a movement which is genuinely democratic.[54] Indian communities, however, are not necessarily models of equality or democracy. Mayan society had a class structure of lords and laborers long before the arrival of the Spanish. While colonial Mayan communities had a communal or closed corporate structure, they were usually hierarchical and not egalitarian or democratic.[55] Modern Mayan societies also seem to have their elites.[56] Collier argues that, Mayan communities in Chiapas have become even more class divided and less democratic in the past 25 years.[57] In any case, it should be remembered that in other contexts, Maoist cadres held the real positions of power in what appeared to be democratic community assemblies.[58] Because of the EZLN's clandestine existence and state repression, we do not know how democratic the EZLN really is.

Whatever the EZLN's organizational practice, the Zapatistas appropriated something of the spirit of Indian communalism in their agricultural program. The rebels demanded the equalization of landholdings in the countryside so that no farmer should have more than 100 hectares. They called for distribution of land to peasant communities and for a renewal of the *ejido*. In a communiqué of June 10, 1994, the CCRI of the EZLN demanded that "Constitutional Article 27 respect the original spirit of Emiliano Zapata: The land belongs to those who work it."[59]

While based in the countryside, the EZLN intends to extend this communalist or socialist approach to the city as well. The EZLN's "Revolutionary Law of Urban Reform," resembling some of Fidel Castro's early legislation in Cuba, calls for tenants to stop paying rents if they have lived in the same place for more than 15 years, and for all other tenants to pay no more than 10 percent of their income in rent. The EZLN calls for the occupation of public buildings and large mansions by the homeless, and for the construction of new dwellings on vacant lots.[60]

The Zapatista communiques are often imbued with a spiritual quality which reflects both the indigenous traditions and the Roman Catholic Theology of Liberation.[61] But within its own movement, the EZLN argues for religious tolerance and pluralism. The Zapatistas assert that they have both Catholic and Protestant members who share social and political equality in the Zapatista movement. Collier suggests that the Catholic Theology of Liberation could not provide the vehicle for a mass social movement in Chiapas because of Catholic rivalry with the Protestant sects. The Maoist Popular Politics tendency made possible "a truly secular movement appealing broadly to pluralism and democracy," which was able to unite the various religious factions.[62]

EZLN women leaders, such as Commander Ramona, reportedly forced the EZLN to take up women's issues creating a kind of indigenous feminism. The EZLN's Women's Revolutionary Law extended to women full equality in both the community and the military. Women were given equal rights, including the right to choose their own partners and spouses. The law gave women the right to decide how many children they will have, though the organization has avoided the issues of contraception and abortion.[63]

But nationalism is, above all, the central tenet of the Zapatistas' ideology. The EZLN has emphasized that while the army is based in the indigenous communities of Chiapas, the EZLN is nevertheless a Mexican movement with national goals. The EZLN pronouncements call for "autonomy" for indigenous communities, but have never suggested separation or independence from Mexico. All of the EZLN's statements attempt to locate the new Zapatista movement within Mexican history, within the mainstream of Mexican populism, and above all nationalist movements.

The EZLN denies the legitimacy of the PRI precisely because it fails to represent the nation and its people. From the beginning, the rebels demanded the resignation of the fraudulently-elected president, Carlos Salinas. The Zapatistas also called upon the Mexican legislature and courts to assume their responsibility to the nation by removing the dictatorial leaders of the PRI. The EZLN called for genuinely democratic elections to create a transitional government which would write a new constitution.

What a revolutionary group rejects is perhaps as important as what it advocates. In keeping with their nationalism, Marcos and the CCRI emphasize that they have no ties to any foreign or communist movements. "We don't want another type of dictatorship, nor anything from anywhere else, no international communism or anything like that," Marcos explained.[64]

While having taken up the armed struggle, the EZLN also explicitly rejects the model of guerrilla warfare as its strategy. The EZLN sees itself as a peoples' movement and a peoples' revolutionary army, not a guerrilla *foco*. Similarly, Marcos explicitly denies the idea that the EZLN forms the "vanguard" of a Mexican revolution, the word traditionally associated with the Leninist tradition. "We don't want to monopolize as a vanguard or to say we are the light, the only alternative and deny the qualifications of 'revolutionary' to one current or another," Marcos explained.[65] Marcos and the CCRI also repudiate the whole Latin American and Mexican legacy of the *caudillo*, the supreme leader who directs the movement. While Marcos attracted enormous attention as the sophisticated and even urbane intellectual spokesman of an indigenous rebellion, he has constantly reiterated that "our leadership is collective."[66]

In sum, the EZLN's strategy can be referred to as armed populism or revolutionary reform.[67] While some of the EZLN officers and soldiers told the press they were fighting for socialism, to the best of my knowledge, the EZLN as an organization has not explicitly called for the destruction of the Mexican state—that is, the break-up of the government bureaucracy and the military—nor for the overthrow of capitalism and the expropriation of the means of production. They are not revolutionary socialists. In many respects, the EZLN's philosophy is a new version of revolutionary nationalism, not that of the old PRI or the PRD, but of some remotely kindred doctrine.[68]

The EZLN's radical nationalist program represents both its strength and its weakness. The EZLN's patriotism and populism situates the Zapatistas within the mainstream of Mexican history and its contemporary social movements. The EZLN's eleven fundamental demands—work, land, housing, food, health, education, independence, freedom, democracy, justice and peace—constitute a devastating critique of the PRI, which after 65 years has proven unable to provide either democracy or economic security. But those words do not add up to an economic and political program for the transformation of Mexico on the eve of the twenty-first century.

In order, to fully comprehend the EZLN's political significance, one has to understand the political and economic system the Zapatistas were fighting. The Mexican one-party state was the most stable in Latin America. The Institutional Revolutionary Party (PRI) represented a unique political organization, remarkably durable and flexible, capable not only of crushing but also of coopting its challengers.

3

FROM MEXICAN
REVOLUTION TO
ONE-PARTY STATE

The Zapatista Army of National Libertion takes its name from Emiliano Zapata, the commander of the Liberating Army of the South. We know Zapata from those famous photos that show him with his big mustache, wearing a sombrero, *bandoliers* filled with bullets across his chest and a rifle in his hands. In those old photos he looks somehow both modest and proud, at once humble and heroic. He is a genuine Cincinnatus: the reticent leader of a farmers' army.

Zapata stood at the very center of the Mexican Revolution of 1910. He and the movement that he led gave the revolution what became its key political demand: land to the peasant community.[1] To understand the Zapatista Rebellion of 1994 and its impact on contemporary Mexico, we have to understand the nature of the Mexican Revolution and the origins of the Institutional Revolutionary Party.

The Mexican Revolution of 1910 to 1920 created contemporary Mexico out of one of the great upheavals of modern history. Massive armies of peasants, ranchers and workers, marching and riding across Mexico, swept away the old regime of the dictatorship of Porfirio Díaz, destroyed the government and the military, and created a new state. The revolution produced the new constitution of 1917, which laid the foundation for the Mexican political system of today. Ultimately, that revolution's impact would destroy the *hacienda* system, by distributing millions of acres of land to the peasants, and reclaim Mexico's oil wealth, by nationalizing the petroleum industry. Of Mexico's population, when was then about 13 million, almost one million perished in the revolution, while tens of thousands of refugees fled to the United States to escape the violence.

The revolution was fought over five great questions, most of which remain central to the political debates in Mexico today. First, would Mexico be a dictatorship run by one man or would the country become a political democracy? Second, would the country's farmland be controlled by a small group of wealthy *hacendados* or landlords, or by the majority of the Mexican people who were overwhelmingly peasants, small farmers or ranchers? Third, would Mexico be dominated economically by foreign powers, particularly the United States, or would Mexicans control their own economy? Fourth, would employers have all power in the workplace, or would workers also have the right to organize unions and strike in order to better their lives? Fifth, would the Roman Catholic Church continue to control education in Mexico, or would education be free, public and secular?

The revolution began in opposition to the dictator, President Porfirio Díaz. Díaz had first been elected president in 1876 as a Liberal, and with the exception of one term, served continuously until 1910. Díaz came to office determined to bring peace, unity, and development to Mexico after years of warfare, rebellion, and banditry. As president, Díaz used the *federales*, or Federal Army, to pacify Mexico, often over the dead bodies of his opponents. To stop the nation's disintegration, Díaz incorporated local political bosses or bandits into the rural police force, the *rurales.*

Díaz's strategy for governing was summed up in the phrase, "*pan o palo*," bread or the club—a loaf of bread for those who cooperated with Díaz and a beating with a club for those who did not. Díaz allied himself with the nation's great landlords, such as the Terrazas-Creel family of Chihuahua, made peace with the conservative bishops of the Catholic Church, and invited foreign businesspeople to invest in Mexico. The thirty-four-year Díaz dictatorship became identified in the minds of the Mexican people with those four forces: the army, the landlords, the Church, and foreign capital.

In Díaz's Mexico, five percent of the population, made up of landlords and industrialists, controlled nearly all of Mexico's wealth, while 95 percent of the population owned little or nothing and worked for wages or as share-croppers. The wealthy landlords' *haciendas* dominated agriculture, producing such crops as sugar for sale on the world market or corn for sale in Mexico. In 1910, some 20,000 landlords employed 80 percent of Mexico's population as agricultural wage earners. While *haciendas* expanded, the indigenous villages and small farmers and ranchers lost their land. By 1910, almost 97 percent of the rural households owned no land at all. Only about 8 to 15 percent of all Mexicans were industrial workers engaged in mining or manufacturing.[2]

Without industry, Mexico remained an underdeveloped country, while President Díaz was intent on modernizing Mexico. To attract foreign investors, Díaz offered spectacular economic concessions including abatement of taxes and guaranteed profits. Lured by these blandishments, foreign capital poured into Mexico from England, France, and, above all, from the United States.

Díaz especially encouraged the British to invest, to counter-balance the influence of the United States. Nevertheless, the United States came to control much of the Mexican economy.[3] Under Díaz, U.S. firms invested in railroads, mining, smelting, and petroleum. U.S. investments mounted to hundreds of millions of dollars by 1910. The American Edward N. Brown controlled the National Railways of Mexico, until Díaz nationalized the railroads in 1914. Colonel Greene, the Guggenheims, American Smelting and Refining Company (ASARCO), and Phelps-Dodge dominated the Mexican copper, silver, zinc and lead mining and smelting industries. Edward L. Doheny, who later sold out to Standard Oil, owned much of the Mexican petroleum industry.[4] Allied with the U.S. industrialists were the great American banks, such as Morgan, which had loaned hundreds of millions of dollars to the Mexican government and U.S. corporations in Mexico.

Mexico also had its entrepreneurs. Probably most important was the Garza Sada family of Monterrey, Nuevo León in northern Mexico, who by the early twentieth century had constructed an industrial complex consisting of bottling plants, glass factories, and even Latin America's first steel mill.[5] But those Mexican entrepreneurs represented only a small percentage of Mexico's economy.

In 1910 through 1911, foreigners—U.S., British, French and German—controlled 130 of the 170 largest firms in Mexico, and held 63.2 percent of the total capital. If one also includes nine other firms in which foreigners had some interest, then foreign investment represented 77 percent of the total capital in the top 170 corporations.[6] Private Mexican capitalists controlled only nine percent of the total capital of the 170 largest corporations.[7] Economic historian José Luis Cecena concludes, "This...'imported capitalism,' did not lead to the rise and consolidation of an independent Mexican bourgeoisie....The Mexican bourgeoisie was weak and almost completely subordinated to foreign capital."[8]

U.S. capitalists also wielded tremendous political power in Mexico. They conferred with the dictator Díaz, distributed largess strategically to the Mexican Congress, and maintained private armies for the defense of their Mexican interests. Because U.S. investors dominated the economy and played a large role in politics as well, Mexico failed to develop an independent capitalist class.

The enormous concentration of political and economic power in the hands of Díaz, Mexican landlords, and foreign investors, combined with the poverty of the peasants of the countryside, and the violent repression by the *federales* and *rurales* form the background to the revolution. The economic recessions of 1902, 1906 and 1908, increased the misery of the lower classes and set the forces in motion.[9]

The first serious attempt at a revolution to overthrow Porfirio Díaz actually came on July 1, 1906, when the Mexican Liberal Party (PLM) in St. Louis, Missouri, issued a revolutionary manifesto. The PLM called for the break up of the *haciendas,* the distribution of land to the peasants, protective legislation for workers, and the closing of Catholic schools.

The PLM, led by the brothers Jesús and Ricardo Flores Magón, was actually an anarcho-syndicalist party which attempted to overthrow Díaz by fomenting strikes. On June 1, 1906, under the leadership of PLM members, workers at the huge Cananea copper mine struck, but their strike was smashed by Mexican *federales* and Arizona rangers from the United States. The anarcho-syndicalist attempt at a worker-led revolution failed, perhaps because the industrial workers had not been able to form their own organizations during the Díaz regime and represented such a small part of the population. But their demands for workers' rights would have to be dealt with in the course of the revolution.

Just two years later, in 1908, Porfirio Díaz gave an interview to an American reporter in which he suggested that he might retire. "Mexico," he said, "was ready for real democracy and the next president should be freely elected." Francisco I. Madero, a wealthy landlord from Coahuila, encouraged by Díaz's statements, published *The Presidential Succession* in which he criticized Díaz as a militarist who had created an absolutist regime. Madero, who had studied at the University of California at Berkeley and was influenced by both American ideas as well as Mexican liberalism, called for reforms in Mexico. Madero demanded free elections, but he opposed a violent revolution to overthrow Díaz.

Meeting with a favorable response from his book, in 1910 Francisco I. Madero ran for president against Díaz. Madero's campaign immediately attracted a broad following, and the dictator Díaz, reneging on his promises of free elections, ordered Madero's arrest. Madero escaped from prison, fled to the United States, and issued his revolutionary manifesto, the Plan of San Luis Potosí, calling for "Effective Suffrage and No Re-election." Madero called upon the Mexican people to rise and overthrow Díaz on November 20, 1910. Madero's plan only mentioned in passing that lands illegally taken from the peasant communities should be returned to them. But those few words proved enough to set off an enormous social explosion as peasants, farmers and small ranchers rallied to the revolution.

In the North, Francisco "Pancho" Villa became the most important leader of the revolutionary forces. When a young man, Villa had killed a man for raping his sister, and, forced to live outside the law, Villa became a bandit. When the Revolution broke out, Villa joined it and organized the Division of the North made up of Chihuahua's miners, railroad workers and ranchers. A military genius, Villa used Díaz's railroad lines to carry his forces south, toward Mexico City, defeating the federal troops at nearly every juncture.

Villa's movement had no clear political or economic program. "More a force of nature than of politics, the Villista party was commotion rampant," wrote historian John Womack. "These northern drifters could give their populism no real point. Cowboys, muleskinners, bandits, railroad laborers, peddlers, refugee peons, the Villistas had no definite class interests or local attachments."[10]

Villa and his supporters mainly wanted to break the power of the *hacendados, caudillos,* and *caciques* who had kept them down. They settled accounts by shooting some of the most obnoxious and running off with the cattle of others. Without changing the property relations, Villa took what he could from the rich, gave much to the poor, and in general attempted to improve the lot of the farmer and the worker.[11] But Villa's movement never provided a political alternative to Madero's—and later Carranza's—political and economic liberalism.

The central programmatic demand of the Mexican Revolution came from Emiliano Zapata's movement in southern Mexico. In 1910, the village council of Anenecuilco elected thirty-year old Emiliano Zapata, a mule driver and horse tranier, to lead the community's fight against the encroachment of the local sugar plantations. Zapata adopted a course of direct action, and led the villagers, arms in hand, to reclaim the lands usurped by local sugar landlords.

When Zapata and the others heard about Madero's revolution and the references in his Plan of San Luis Potosí to returning land to the villages, they too joined the great rebellion. In Morelos, Zapata raised a peasant army and, with overwhelming numbers, crushed the Federal Army at the important town of Cuautla. Zapata then returned to the countryside to carry out the distribution of land to the communities. In doing so, Zapata altered the course of the Mexican Revolution, giving it a radical social dimension which Madero had never intended.

The allied revolutionary forces succeeded in defeating Díaz and driving him out of Mexico, making Madero president in the fall of 1911. But when the conservative Madero failed to carry out the agrarian reform for which the peasants had fought, Zapata and his Liberating Army of the South broke with Madero and declared themselves in rebellion. "I am resolved," Zapata wrote to one of his collaborators, "to struggle against everything and everybody..."[12]

On November 28, 1911, the Zapatistas issued their own revolutionary manifesto, the Plan of Ayala. Zapata's Plan of Ayala demanded the return of stolen lands to the peasant communities, the expropriation of one-third of the *haciendas* for landless peasants, and the nationalization of the land and property of those who opposed the plan. A revolutionary and not a politician, Zapata issued orders that the plan be carried out without further ado by the armed peasants in the areas his army controled.

The Plan of Ayala constituted the core of the Zapatista political program, indeed, it was virtually the entire program. The Zapatistas really . wanted only one thing: community control of the land. But that was the one thing that mattered to millions of peasants in central and southern Mexico, and for that reason it made all the difference.

Madero proved to be not only a conservative president, but also a weak and inept leader who pleased no one. In February of 1913, General Victoriano Huerta, with the connivance of U.S. Ambassador Henry Lane Wilson, overthrew and assassinated Madero, and then attempted to reinstate the old Porfirian order. All the major revolutionary leaders—Venustiano Carranza and Alvaro Obregón, both northern landlords, Pancho Villa and Emiliano

Zapata—declared themselves in rebellion against Huerta, and the revolution continued.

While Carranza led the most important forces, Zapata in nearby Morelos posed the most immediate danger to Huerta. Huerta carried out a scorched earth policy in Morelos, but still the Zapatistas grew in numbers. By the middle of 1914, Zapata and his army had driven Huerta's forces out of the South and were poised to take Mexico City. Huerta, seeing the hand-writing on the wall, surrendered to the more conservative General Venustiano Carranza's Constitutionalist Army.

But the land question remained, and the revolution went on. Having defeated Huerta and reaction, the Mexican revolutionary forces now split into two rival camps: the conservative Constitutionalists and the radical Conventionists. In October of 1914 at the Convention of Aguascalientes, Emiliano Zapata entered into an alliance with Pancho Villa after Villa agreed to support Zapata's Plan of Ayala with its program of agrarian reform. The radical Convention proclaimed the government of Mexico, and in effect declared war on Carranza and his Constitutionalist Army.

But, after having joined together briefly at the Convention, Zapata returned to Morelos and Villa to Chihuahua to continue the local struggle. In effect, they surrendered the national arena to Carranza. As John Womack writes in his masterful *Zapata and the Mexican Revolution*: "In this insistent provincialism was the movement's strength and its weakness."[13] Because the Conventionists proved unable to dominate the national scene, Villa and Zapata soon found themselves on the defensive in their own territories.

Villa and Zapata, remaining inveterate provincials, failed to take control of the cities which were the nerve centers of the society, and failed to win over the urban working class which went over to Carranza and Obregón. Villa and Zapata never succeeded in creating a unified military command or a national army. Zapata and the Morelos peasants fought heroically for communal control of the land. But the peasants had no chance of winning as long as they failed to create a political party, write a program, and take state power. The peasantry proved to be incapable of reorganizing society.[14]

The small Mexican working class, organized in the House of the World Worker, entered the struggle at about this point, but also proved unable to give leadership to the revolutionary movement. Originally mostly anarchists, who theoretically eschewed politics, the workers nevertheless found themselves drawn into the political struggle. Carranza and Obregón offered the anarchists, legal guarantees to labor union organization, the right to strike, and protective legislation, only if the unions would provide troops to fight against Villa and Zapata. The anarchists agreed to Carranza's deal and set about organizing the workers' Red Battallions. Thus Generals Carranza and Obregón captured the working class. After that, the Mexican state would never let it go.

In 1917, Carranza called a Constitutional Convention. In keeping with the deal between Carranza and the House of the World Worker, the convention delegates passed Article 123 which gave workers the right to organize labor unions and strike, outlawed child labor, and provided for-profit sharing. Influenced by the ideas of agrarian reform emanating from Zapata's movement in Morelos, the delegates also wrote into the new Mexican Constitution Article 27, which gave the state the right to distribute land and gave the village the right to hold land. Thus even the enemies in Carranza's camp paid homage to Zapata and his Plan of Ayala in the writing of their new Constitution.

The war between the Zapatistas and the Carrancistas went on for five long years. Though the revolution throughout the rest of Mexico was drawing to a close, the peasants of Morelos fought on. Hoping to decapitate the peasant movement, on April 10, 1919, the Constitutionalists tricked Zapata, lured him into a meeting with false friends, and assassinated him. With Zapata out of the way, Generals Carranza and Obregón finally led the Constitutionalist Army to victory in the civil war.

But the revolution had still not reached its balance point. Carranza, much like Madero before him, was too conservative to resolve what had become the great question of the revolution: the peasants' demand for land. So in 1920, a final fight broke out, this time within the Constitutionalist camp, between Carranza and Obregón. Obregón had long recognized the necessity of incorporating something like the Zapatistas' demands for agrarian reform into the program of the Constitutionalists' revolution, and he welcomed the Morelos peasants' support in the struggle against Carranza. The Zapatistas who had continued to fight on after the death of their leader, quickly moved to support Obregón. With the support of the urban labor movement and peasant rebels, Obregón succeeded in defeating Carranza's forces. Carranza fled and was assassinated in the village of Tlaxcalantongo in the mountains of Puebla. The revolution was finally over after ten long years and nearly a million lives. Obregón became president, and began the reconstruction of Mexico.

What about the peasants and the land? After the revolution, the Zapatistas became a political power in Morelos, and the Liberating Army of the South was incorporated into the new Mexican Army. The Agrarian Party also became a force in the national legislature, pushing the Obregón government of 1920 to 1924 to pass some limited agrarian reform. As a result, the government distributed some land to peasants in Morelos. But for most Mexican peasants the land problem remained unresolved, and was postponed for another decade.

So what had it all meant, this great upheaval called the Mexican Revolution? Some historians have denied that there was any revolution, because unlike the French Revolution of 1789, which brought an end to feudalism, or the Russian Revolution of 1917, which brought an end to capitalism, in Mexico the fundamental economic structures remained unaltered. Mexico remained a capitalist country, and most of the great Porfirian landlords and capitalists survived the revolution with their wealth intact. So, for example, the historian Ramón Eduardo Ruíz, argues there was no revolution and prefers to speak of, "The Great Rebellion."[15] Ruíz and others have a point about the persistence of capitalism. Nevertheless, there was undeniably a political revolution. The revolutionary armies destroyed the old state and army, threw out the old constitution, and created a new regime. And, by 1940, the revolution had also destroyed the *hacienda* system based on debt peonage, and to that extent at least, the Mexican Revolution was also a social revolution.

But what was the nature of the new political regime, how should we characterize it? Could Mexico's revolution of 1910 to 1920 like the revolutions in England in 1640, in the British American colonies in 1776, and in France in 1789, be called a "bourgeois revolution"? Had the Mexican capitalists come to power? Not really. Because the economy had been dominated by foreign investors during the Díaz dictatorship, the Mexican capitalist class had hardly developed. Mexican businesspeople never really organized as a class either under Díaz or during the revolution to put forward their political goals.

The revolutionary solution was what Marx would have called Bonapartist. When all social classes—peasants, workers, landlords and industrial captalists—proved unable to lead the revolution to a successful conclusion, the generals took power, first Carranza and then Obregón. The generals, rising above all the social classes, brought the revolution to a conclusion, which is what gave modern Mexico its authoritarian populist political system: authoritarian because it was dominated by generals, populist because it had to placate the peasants and workers. Over time, the generals would evolve into a bureaucratic caste, still manipulating all the social classes.[16]

Some of the generals who led the Mexican Revolution were rich businessmen. Both Madero and Carranza were wealthy landlords and General Alvaro Obregón, for example, was a successful chickpea farmer. But Obregón came to power not as a leader of the capitalist class, but rather as a general leading a revolutionary army of peasants and workers. The capitalists as a class did not lead the revolution.

At the same time, there was no danger to capitalism as a system in Mexico, primarily because the revolutionary upsurge had produced no alternative. During the revolution, workers created labor unions and cooperatives and some revolutionary peasants established *ejidos*, but neither workers' unions and cooperatives, nor the peasants *ejidos,* were sufficient to challenge the entrenched capitalist system. Neither workers nor peasants created a distinct political party with a program for a state organized around their interests.

The Bonapartist solution to the Mexican Revolution had still other important implications for Mexico's development, many of which are still being felt today. Mexico's Bonapartist Revolution produced no parliamentary democracy. Political parties began to form only after the revolution, and even then remained dependent on the generals, their armies and the state. Mexico's political system became highly centralized and "presidentialist." The president became the country's most powerful figure and the ultimate arbiter of all political conflicts.

At the same time, because the generals and then the bureaucratic caste known as *la clase política* controlled the state, the bourgeoisie continued to play second fiddle. After the revolution, just as before, Mexican businessmen failed to create that panoply of civic organizations which generally accompany the rise of a capitalist class. Without a bourgeoisie and its petty bourgeois train, Mexico failed to create both a civil society and public opinion.

Even after the revolution, foreign capital continued to control much of Mexican commerce and industry. While Mexican nationalism and opposition to foreign domination of the economy played a large role in the ideology of the revolution, the various revolutionary governments were reluctant to nationalize foreign interests for fear of invasion and occupation by European or U.S. forces. Nor were these idle fears. The United States did invade Mexico twice during the Revolutionary period, once in 1914 at the port of Veracruz, and once in 1917 across the northern border. In the period following the outbreak of World War I in Europe, the weakening of European influence in

Latin America actually increased the American capitalists' dominant role in the Mexican economy.

The post-revolutionary Sonoran dynasty of Presidents Adolfo de la Huerta, Alvaro Obregón and Plutarco Elías Calles, believed that Mexico should be developed through private capital, principally through the modernization of agriculture and modest industrial expansion. The Sonoran dynasty suppressed radical labor unions and peasants movements and encouraged private businesses ventures. Under the Sonoran administrations, there was a brief recovery of Mexican capitalism in the early 1920s, as the surviving Porfirian capitalists linked up with the revolution's new bourgeoisie. Revolutionary generals like Calles himself took advantage of their military and political power to acquire land and wealth.[17] Some bankers, like the Legorreta family who owned the Banco Nacional de Mexico (BANAMEX), established a close relationship with the Mexican government.[18] Fortunes were made in the 1920s, yet the military-political class, not the capitalist class, continued to dominate the Mexican government.

In the late 1920s, Mexico passed through a series of political and economic crises. Under the slogan "Long live Christ the King!" Roman Catholic peasants rose against the government in the *cristero* rebellion of 1926 to 1928. The rebellion culminated in the assassination of President Alvaro Obregón in 1928. Then came the Crash of 1929, when the Great Depression wiped out many of the gains that had been made by Mexican businesspeople. In Mexico the depression actually began as early as 1925, and was further aggravated in 1927 by falling oil and mineral prices.[19] The political and economic crises led to increased tensions and factionalism among the revolutionary leaders, as well as the danger of a renewed outbreak of armed conflict.

To overcome the political crisis, in March of 1929, President Calles established the Revolutionary National Party—the future PRI—with the official slogan "Institutions and Social Reform." Although Calles had created the new party, he failed to connect that party to the peasant masses or to resolve their continuing hunger for land. But no stable regime could be established unless it dealt with the legacy of Zapata: the land question. That task fell to General Lázaro Cárdenas.

Lázaro Cárdenas began his military career fighting with the Constitutionalist forces against Pancho Villa's army in Sonora and Chihuahua. He later served as military governor in the oil fields of Veracruz where he saw the wealth and power of the foreign oil companies first hand, and as governor of his home state of Michoacán. In 1933, Cárdenas entered the cabinet of President Abelardo Rodríguez, serving as his Minister of War, and for the first time became a national figure.

That same year, Calles, the *Jefe Máximo* of the revolution and the power behind the throne, chose Cárdenas as the ruling party's candidate for president, intending to use him as another figurehead. Cárdenas, though, assured of victory, traveled 17,119 miles, visiting fields and factories, listening to the grievances of peasants and workers, getting close to the people.

Cárdenas ran for president during the depths of the worldwide depression and widespread unrest in Mexico. "If I am elected president," he told the people, "all the factories which have been closed and whose owners are not able to operate them shall be rented and turned over to laborers organized into cooperative associations....If I am elected president, there will be no one who can stop me until the peasant has received the best lands and the State has given him all financial, moral and material aid possible."[20]

Nationalist, vaguely socialist, and inspired by the communitarian values of the Mexican village, Cárdenas was, as Adolfo Gilly says, a Mexican Narodnik who intended to create an agrarian socialist utopia in Mexico.[21] Cárdenas was an idealist who believed that, under the guidance of the revolutionary state, Mexico could develop its national economy while avoiding the problems of industrial capitalism. Cárdenas believed that it was possible to have capitalist economic development without capitalist control, and capitalist business ventures without exploitation and oppression. This was, as Gilly suggests, his utopia, both an ideal and an illusion.

Once elected, Cárdenas took command of the army, drove Calles into exile, and began to implement the program he had promised. At the center of President Cárdenas's economic program was the agrarian reform. Mexico in 1934 was still deep in a depression, so the Cárdenas administration took over the failing *haciendas* and farms, particularly in central and southern Mexico, and turned them over to Indian villagers and landless peasants. Finally realizing the dreams of Zapata, Cárdenas carried out the greatest land reform in Mexican history, distributing 20 million hectares of land to Indian communities. At the same time, much state-owned land was also turned over to poor peasants as *ejidos*, a corporate form of landholding in collective farms or private plots.

Cárdenas's reforms constituted a social revolution, abolishing the *hacienda* system in Mexico. The land reform caused a rebirth of village life, while an agricultural boom brought cheaper food. Cheap food in turn helped to keep down the price of industrial labor, thus contributing to the renewed industrialization of Mexico. The peasants' sale of agricultural products gave them a cash income, which created an internal market for manufactured goods. In addition to these economic benefits, the agrarian reform strengthened the Mexican village, which Cárdenas saw as the communitarian model for Mexican society as a whole.

The second point of Cárdenas's economic program was the nationalization of the oil industry. Cárdenas believed that it was necessary to reduce the role of foreign capital, and particularly of the powerful petroleum companies, in order to take control of Mexico's economic destiny. Using as a political pretext the very real conflict between Mexican labor unions and the foreign oil companies, in 1938, Cárdenas nationalized the entire petroleum industry.

Cárdenas used his presidential powers and moral authority to establish the state's superiority to Mexican capitalists as well. When Monterrey's capitalists refused to negotiate with their labor unions, Cárdenas personally traveled to Monterrey and told its conservative businessowners: "The industrialists who do not wish to continue to operate because of the demands of the unions can turn over their industries to their laborers or the government for it to operate."[22] Cárdenas put capital in its place, subordinate to the state.

Lázaro Cárdenas's agrarian reform, support for labor unions and nationalization of the oil industry, made him the most beloved president in Mexico's history. Many peasants who benefitted from the land reform referred to Cárdenas affectionately as *Tata*, the Nahuatl word for father. Cárdenas's profound structural reforms aimed at uplifting the peasant and worker in Mexico and at improving the strength of Mexico in the world economy, not only strengthened the ruling party, but also created an enduring populist and anti-imperialist current among the common people that came to be known as *cardenismo*.

But it would be a mistake to believe that Cárdenas was in principle hostile to capitalism in general or to foreign capital and investment in particular. Everything Cárdenas did was intended to promote capitalist development, but development supervised by the revolutionary state. Just as Díaz had built the railroads, Cárdenas built highways which lowered transportation costs and made new markets available, proving a boon to Mexican business. Public works also increased the demand for domestic products like steel and cement and put wages in the hands of consumers.[23]

Cárdenas's economic program was largely dependent upon U.S. capitalism. Cárdenas needed loans from U.S. banks and tax advances from U.S. mining companies to pay for his projects. The Cárdenas government entered into agreements with the Clayton Anderson Company and the Colorado River Land Company to get resources and markets for the *ejidos*. Even as he was nationalizing the foreign petroleum companies, Cárdenas permitted General Motors and Chrysler to establish plants and subsidiaries in Mexico.[24] Ford had already come to Mexico in 1925.[25]

The Great Depression and then the beginning of World War II in Europe in the late 1930s actually created conditions which fostered the development of capitalism in Mexico. Cut off from foreign trade by depression and war, Mexico began to produce goods which it had previously imported from the United States and Europe. Later this "substitution of imports industrialization" would become a policy under Cárdenas's successors who used tariffs and quotas to protect infant industries. Cárdenas's policies were largely successful, making industry "the engine of growth in the 1930s."[26]

□□□

But the very success of Cárdenas's economic program of promoting capitalist industrialization posed a problem: if the capitalists became powerful enough, they might attempt to change the course of Cárdenas's revolutionary state. Cárdenas thought that if capitalists participated in politics they would eventually come to control both the economy and the government. So, while he promoted both Mexican and foreign business in Mexico, Cárdenas also reorganized the state and the ruling party to prevent direct capitalist involvement in politics.

In March of 1938, Cárdenas changed the ruling party's name to the Party of the Mexican Revolution (PMR), and adopted a new slogan: "For a Workers' Democracy." Cárdenas's new PMR was based on four institutional pillars: the labor unions, particularly the Confederation of Mexican Workers (CTM); the peasantry, organized in the National Peasant Confederation (CNC); the popular sector of the self-employed, government employees and bureaucrats, joined in the National Confederation of Popular Organizations (CNOP); and finally the military. (Cárdenas's successors gradually phased out the military as one of the party's sectors.) Membership was not individual or voluntary, but "corporate," that is, by group. The party directly incorporated the mass memberships of organizations of workers, peasants and government bureaucrats.

Cárdenas's scheme also explicitly excluded capitalists from the party. While the name of the party was changed in 1946 to the Institutional Revolutionary Party (PRI) with the new slogan "Democracy and Social Justice," the organizational scheme of the party remained the same. In this scheme, businesspeople and business organizations were not permitted to participate in the life of the party either as members or as political candidates. By and large businessmen were also excluded from the cabinet, the direction of government agencies, and the state bureaucracy, with the exception of the involvement of bankers in the Treasury Ministry. Exclusion from participation in the ruling party was, to all intents and purposes, exclusion from participation in political life.

Yet, Cárdenas recognized that even if the party excluded businessmen from politics, the state still must have on-going contact with business interests in order to develop the nation's economic policies.[27] So, just as he had created mass organizations that incorporated workers and peasants into the party, Cárdenas and his successors also chartered organizations that tied businessmen directly to the state. The National Federation of Chambers of Industries (Concamin), the National Chamber of Commerce (Concanaco), and the National Chamber of Manufacturing Industry (Canacintra or CNIT) became the official business organizations, while bankers belonged to the Mexican Bankers Association (ABM). By law, businessmen were required to join the appropriate association. While business thus maintained contact with the government, it did not necessarily wield any great influence there. The initiative always remained with the state-party and above all with the president.

Cárdenas retired from the presidency in 1940, and Mexico moved in a more conservative direction under his successors. But the political institutions and the mixed economy which Cárdenas established proved enduring and gave Mexico the most stable government in Latin America. Mexico's relative success was based upon the fact that it had carried out a genuine agrarian reform, had incorporated organized labor, and had curbed the power of the petroleum companies.

After 1940, The Mexican state-party, now known as the PRI, became a leviathan that dominated all social classes and many aspects of Mexican life. Politically, the PRI won virtually every election for every important office in the country, with the exception of a handful of mayors and deputies.

State corporations and the mixed economy established by Cárdenas laid the basis for the success of Mexico's substitution of import industrialization program and for the "Mexican miracle" of the 1950s and 1960s. Cárdenas's successors viewed the agricutural problems as solved and turned to the building of industrial infrastructure. During the next three decades, Mexico built dams, hydroelectric plants, gigantic irrigation projects, and expanded the railroad and highway network.[28] Government control of workers' and peasants' unions helped to keep both wages and food costs low, while the government's enormous state-sector (petroleum, electricty, railroads) subsidized privately owned foreign and domestic manufacturing firms.

During the middle decades of the century, it seemed possible to many that Mexico's solid one-party state would succeed in urbanizing and industrializing, and leading the nation into the twenty-first century.

□□□

From the very beginning back in the 1930s, Cárdenas's corporate state had had its opponents. The National Action Party (PAN) had its origins in a middle-class backlash against Lázaro Cárdenas's administration.[29] A Protestant banker, Manuel Gómez Morín, and a Roman Catholic ideologue, Efraín González Luna, founded the PAN on September 16, 1939. The membership in the early years consisted of Roman Catholic militants who saw in the PAN the Christian alternative to the Mexican Revolution; landlords and small ranchers who feared Cárdenas's agrarian reform; merchants and businessmen—including some major industrialists—who opposed labor unions; and Catholics who feared Cárdenas's program of socialist education. The PAN's leaders attacked Lázaro Cárdenas and the Party of the Mexican Revolution (PRM, the future PRI) as crypto-communists. According to the PAN, "Mexico needed Catholicism and capitalism," and on the basis of that reactionary program, the PAN elected its first four congressmen in 1946.

The PAN began as a regionally based political party, strongest in the northern states such as Nuevo León, Chihuahua, and Baja California, and in the historically conservative states like Guanajuato. In 1949, ten years after its founding, the PRI government recognized the PAN as a legal, national party, and in 1952 the PAN founder Efraín González Luna became the party's first presidential candidate. González Luna received only 7 percent of the vote, but the campaign established the PAN as the nation's second party. By 1964, when the PAN ran José González Torres for president, the party received over one million votes or 11 percent of the total. The PAN was strong by 1967, enough to present candidates in every electoral district and in every state in Mexico.

During the 1960s, under the impact of liberal currents in the Roman Catholic Church and the rising social conflicts in Mexico, the PAN surprisingly underwent a major ideological shift. Influenced by thinkers like Jacques Maritain, Efraín González Morfin argued that the PAN should represent a "third way" between capitalist individualism and communist collectivism, based on a religious conception of social solidarity. The PAN condemned the PRI's repression of the student demonstrators at Tlatelolco and General Pinochet's overthrow of Salvador Allende's government in Chile. The PAN's presidential candidate in 1970, the liberal González Morfin won nearly two million votes or 13 percent of the total votes cast.

◻◻◻

That year, the PRI candidate Luis Echeverría Alvarez became president, bearing the burden of his role as Minister of the Interior in violently suppressing the student movement. Echeverría recognized that he had to solve Mexico's growing economic and social problems, and rebuild the social support for the PRI. He set out to do so by returning to the style, if not the substance, of Lázaro Cárdenas. Echeverría encouraged peasant land seizures, the organization of new labor unions, and the formation of new socialist parties—all controlled by the PRI.

Immitating Lázaro Cárdenas, Echeverría distributed over 12 million hectares of land to *ejidatarios* and also vastly expanded Mexico's state sector. Yet Echeverría's populist, state capitalist program failed to resolve either the social or political problems of the society, and in many respects, exacerbated them. Class conflict led to increased opposition from both the left and the right, and for the first time in decades the PRI began to face a real and growing political challenge.

Very often some dramatic event serves to galvanize one sector or another of society into opposition. On September 17, 1973, Eugenio Garza Sada, was gunned down in the streets of Monterrey by leftist urban guerillas of the "23 of September" Communist League during a failed kidnapping attempt. Garza Sada was the head of the powerful Monterrey Group whose holding companies were responsible for 20 percent of Mexico's total industrial production.

Shocked by the assassination of Garza Sada—and infuriated by the continuing waves of government supported strikes and land seizures—in May of 1973, COPARMEX, the conservative industrial association backed by the Monterrey group, succeeded in uniting nearly all of the major employ-

ers associations in Mexico to form the Business Coordinating Council or
CCE. The creation of the independent Business Coordinating Council represented a turning point in the history of Mexican business and its relations
with the state. For the first time in Mexican history, businesspeople had organized themselves self-consciously as the capitalist class.

In 1976—to the delight of big business—Echeverría retired to be succeeded by José López Portillo. In his first message to the nation on December
1, 1976, López Portillo asked for a "treaty" with business, and invited business to join the government in an "alliance for production." The new president called for government austerity and a rationalization of government
agencies. Conservative businesspeople could not have been more delighted.

López Portillo and Jorge Díaz Serrano, the director of the state's Mexican Petroleum Corporation (PEMEX) hit upon a new development strategy.
They decided to use Mexico's oil wealth to finance the country's industrial
and social development. Díaz Serrano expanded enormously the rate of petroleum production, the resulting oil boom dynamized the rest of the economy.
The oil money and foreign loans often ended up in the hands of private construction contractors and manufacturers who supplied the needs of the state.
Business thrived.

López Portillo and Serrano pumped more oil and more quickly than
any government in Mexican history. During López Portillo's presidency, oil
production rose astronomically, from 165 million barrels of oil per year in
1973 to over one billion by 1982. Selling for nearly $30 a barrel, Mexican's
oil production served as collateral on $60 billion in public sector foreign
loans. The Mexican private sector loans brought the country's total indebted-
ness to the enormous figure of $99 billion. The huge loans paid for every-
thing from steel mills to new schools. López Portillo believed that, with oil,
Mexico could create the infrastructure that would make it possible for Mexico to become an industrial manufacturer and exporter and leave the third
world behind.

In 1980, however, oil prices began to fall, first slowly and then precipi-
tously. In August of 1982, Mexico found itself unable to make the interest
payments on its $100 billion foreign debt, most of it owed to New York
banks. López Portillo dispatched Jesús Silva Herzog, assistant Minister of Finance, to New York to explain to the bankers that Mexico was bankrupt.

Foreign capitalists hestitated to invest in a country clearly headed for
disaster. Mexican businesspeople did what any capitalists would have done,
and withdrew their money from the failing Mexican economy and socked it

away or invested it elsewhere. Mexicans put $25 billion in U.S. real estate, $14 billion in foreign banks, $12 billion in foreign currency deposits in Mexico. By mid-1982 Mexico was hemorrhaging, bleeding away its capital.[30] On September 1, 1982, President José López Portillo, frustrated by the continuing unraveling of the economy and the state's inability to stem the flow of cash out of the country, nationalized the Mexican banks.

The 1982 bank nationalization brought about the final and decisive step in the class organization of Mexican capitalists. Business was horrified at the nationalization of the banks fearing that Mexico was moving toward communist totalitarianism. If the government was moving toward totalitarianism, then the role of business was to defend the private sector, the firm and the family which formed the basis of society. If the state was swallowing up civil society, then business had to organize civil society to defend itself against the totalizing state.

"Society is all that really counts," José María Basagoiti Noriega, the president of COPARMEX, said at a 1983 meeting of the Chamber of Commerce. With that remark, Mexican capitalism crossed a great ideological and rhetorical divide. Entrepreneurs began to speak of "democracy, and liberty." In a radical new turn, Mexican businessmen now proclaimed themselves the defenders of civil society.[31]

The Business Coordinating Council and other business organizations had in the course of the fights with Echeverría and López Portillo evolved into a self-conscious capitalist class, fighting not merely in its own selfish interests, but now—as they saw it—in the interests of society as a whole. By the early 1980s, Mexican businessmen, particularly those organized in COPARMEX and the CCE, were beginning to play a larger role in politics, offering their views on every important issue.

The next logical step in class organization should have been the political organization of business, either through the formation of a new political party or through the movement of business into the existing National Action Party. Yet, while the PAN should have been a likely home for big business, most corporations and business executives were reluctant to make the move. Businessmen feared that if they supported the PAN, the PRI would use its regulatory powers and its labor unions to destroy them. Only the largest and most secure corporations of the Garza Sada family's Monterrey Group were able to defy the PRI with impunity.

Moreover, from the mid-1970s through the 1980s, the tumultuous social conflicts and deep ideological differences led to intense factional struggles in the PAN. Internal dissension paralyzed the PAN, which did not even field a candidate, in 1976. By the early 1980s, the PAN had divided into two main currents: the "fundamentalists," representing Catholic liberalism, small business and hostility to the PRI, and the "modernizers," or "*neo-panistas*" representing big business interests and a desire to cooperate with the PRI. With the backing of business associations such as COPARMEX and CON-CAMIN, the modernizers succeeded in defeating the fundamentalists and taking control of the PAN. The PAN emerged from the 1980s with a strong organization and a more conservative ideology.

The victory of the *neo-panistas* paralleled the technocrats' coup in the PRI led by Miguel de la Madrid. Throughout the 1980s, both the PAN and the PRI leaderships drew closer to big business and adopted a free market philosophy, developments which laid the basis for their future cooperation. One could say that by the 1990s Mexican business had two parties.

In the 1980s, the National Action Party (PAN) made impressive political gains at every level. In 1982 the PAN ran Pablo Emilio Madero for president, and the party won 52 congressional seats. But the biggest breakthrough came in the 1988 elections when Manuel J. Clouthier, the president of CO-PARMEX, ran at the head of his party's ticket, winning the PAN 101 congressional seats. Equally important, the PAN became the first opposition party to win gubernatorial races: in Baja California in 1989, in Guanajuato in 1991, and in Chihuahua in 1992. By 1994 the PAN governed 15.4 percent of the population of Mexico.[32]

□□□

While the PAN had been growing in influence and political power throughout the 1980s, so too were left-wing opposition movements. The left opposition to the PRI had developed during the Cold War, when the state-party turned in a more conservative direction. The Mexican Confederation of Workers (CTM), the PRI's "official" union, purged itself of its founder, labor leader Vicente Lombardo Toledano, a long-time Stalinist. He then organized Peoples Party (PP) in 1948, and then in 1949 organized the General Union of Workers and Peasants (UGOCM) to challenge the PRI's new conservative direction. The PRI, however, effectively isolated the Peoples Party, which later reconciled itself to the PRI-government, and ironically became its staunchest defender.

The Tlatelolco massacre of 1968 created a new generation of political activists and a Mexican New Left. Throughout the late 1960s and early 1970s this New Left organized new social movements of peasants, workers and the urban poor throughout the country. At the same time, peasants seized land in the states of northern Mexico, while a guerrilla movement appeared in the state of Guerrero. Poor people in Mexico's shanty-towns organized militant demonstrations for water, electricity and other services. Rank and file workers rebelled against the "official" labor unions of the PRI, carrying out strikes and organizing independent unions, particularly in the manufacturing sector. The high-point of these movements was the Democratic Tendency (TD) of the mid-1970s, led by electrical worker Rafaél Galván. In 1976, when the TD began to emerge as a grand alliance of rank and file workers, peasants and the urban poor, the PRI used the Mexican Army to crush the movement.

In an attempt to channel the discontent on the left, in 1977 the PRI passed a political reform law that legalized the Communist Party and other leftist parties, permitting them to stand in elections. By the early 1980s, three left political parties had emerged: the Mexican Communist Party (PCM, later PSUM, then PMS); the left nationalists of the Mexican Workers Party (PMT); and the Trotskyist Revolutionary Workers Party (PRT). Taken together, in 1985 these three independent left parties were receiving a little over 6 percent of the vote in national elections. The PRI's puppet, pseudo-socialist parties, the People's Socialist Party (PPS) and the Socialist Workers Party (PST), together received 4.5 percent of the vote in 1985. All of the left parties together then received about 11 percent of the vote. That same year the PAN received 15.6 percent.

Because of Mexico's authoritarian political system and fraudulent elections, the vote totals are suspect. Nevertheless what remained clear was that even with coercion and fraud, by the late 1980s, over a quarter of the population regularly voted against the state-party. In the late 1980s, left and right sometimes even joined together in common protests against the state-party's fraudulent elections.

By the 1980s, the PRI was being challenged by both the Left and the Right. The corporate system built by Lázaro Cárdenas was in crisis. The Tlatelolco massacre in 1968 and the economic crisis of 1982 had undermined the system. Throughout the 1970s and 1980s mass movements began to appear fighting for social justice. Citizens demonstrated for electoral reform. Yet the PRI refused to grant democracy and civil rights. Only a political earthquake could shake the PRI from power.

4

OUT OF THE RUBBLE:
THE RISE OF CIVIL
SOCIETY

The earthquake began at 7:19 A.M., luckily before most of the children got to school and before most workers arrived at their factories and offices. First there was the trembling—and then the earth shook. Within a few moments many of Mexico City's landmark buildings had collapsed: The National Medical Center, Juárez Hospital, the Ministry of the Navy, the Regis Hotel, and many, many others. Several public schools were reduced to rubble. Entire districts and neighborhoods were severely damaged, among them glorious Colonia Roma and poor Tepito.

More than 10,000 victims lay dead under the ruins. In the Tlatelolco public housing development, the collapse of one multi-family unit alone killed hundreds of people—many just sitting down to breakfast. In the San Antonio Abad garment district, some women who had gone to work early were crushed as they sat at their sewing machines, the cloth clenched in their hands. Thousands more victims remained trapped under tons of steel and stone, or, in older or more modest neighborhood, pinned under piles of wooden beams. Screams came from the ruins, and in other places, whispers from the rubble.

The earthquake of September 19, 1985 was the greatest natural disaster in the history of Mexico City. Not only were there at least ten thousand dead, but there were also tens of thousands injured, while hundreds of thousands found themselves homeless. Most of Mexico City's millions still had shelter, but hundreds of thousands had no water, electricity or gas. In the ruins, the rescue workers listened for the broken gas lines, like snakes hissing among the stones.

Then out of the rubble, and out of their own fear, came the people of Mexico City. Though the PRI-government told them to stay home, the people went forth, and set about rescuing the victims. In the midst of tragedy, the people of Mexico City lived their finest moment, and in doing so, said writer Carlos Monsiváis, they created a new way of being and a new way of seeing themselves. The earthquake gave birth to a new phenomenon, which Monsiváis called "civil society."

"Civil society" was an utterly new idea, virtually unknown in the Mexican political lexicon before 1985. The notion of voluntary activity, civic associations, ordinary people doing for themselves without party leadership was a practical and theoretical novelty.[1] Yet in 1994, civil society would become a major force in Mexican society, and one which the Zapatistas' Subcomandante Marcos would call upon to reform Mexican society. One has to understand something about Mexican political history and theory to appreciate what a psychological and political shift the earthquake created.

From the revolutionary convention of 1917 until 1985, there was a remarkable continuity of political ideology and rhetoric in Mexico. Mexican revolutionaries and later politicians talked about the struggles of the "people" for "social justice" through "the revolutionary state." Later during the Lázaro Cárdenas years in the mid-1930s, the revolution was institutionalized, the theory somewhat modified, and its language codified. The Cárdenas administration combined the revolutionary rhetoric of 1917 with the language of the Communist Popular Front. The struggle was one of the whole "people," but the people were made up of "sectors": workers, peasants, and the "sector popular," of the self-employed and state employees. The government was national and democratic, but democratic in the sense that it incorporated the lower classes into the ruling party and the state, not in the sense that either social classes or individuals enjoyed civil liberties or political rights.

The revolutionary party's organizational forms coincided with its ideology. In an organizational structure borrowed from Mussolini's "corporate state," the various sectors of the people were directly incorporated *en masse* into the party, to ensure that their interests found representation there. For example, the state-party pledged its "historic commitment" to the workers, and the workers' sector reciprocated with its support for the state-party. When one got a job one automatically joined the labor union or the peasant league which was affiliated to the ruling party. If one were a businessman, one's firm was affiliated to the proper commercial or industrial chamber created by the state. The party and its corporations included almost everyone, and, most importantly, there was in theory no political space outside the official structure. Independent or autonomous organizations had no juridical status and no legitimacy in the political system. In a sense, neither individual citizens nor autonomous organizations existed.

The idea of citizenship, as that word is used in France, Britain or the United States was completely alien to Mexican politics. Democracy, the idea that the people should be able to control their own destiny through voice and vote, did not figure into the system in an important way. Political and civil rights had little or no place in Mexican politics. One might say that the system was about social justice, not political liberty—except that, as it turns out, without freedom there was not much justice.

According to this concept of politics, then, "the people" sought "social justice" through the revolutionary state, or later, through the Institutional Revolutionary Party. Both the ruling party and its leftist opposition tended to share this view. Mexican parties from the old Left such as the Communist Party (PCM) and the People's Socialist Party (PPS), which had grown up during the Popular Front period of the 1930s, supported the PRI, indeed, they were almost more loyal to the Mexican system than the PRI itself.

Even after the Tlatelolco massacre and the appearance of the new social movements of the late 1960s and early 1970s, there was almost no break with the earlier revolutionary rhetoric. Perhaps this was because so many radical leaders of those years tended to be inspired and influenced by the revolutions in Cuba and China. But those revolutions too had created one-party states, and even more monolithic states than Mexico's. Consequently, the new radicals of the 1970s had no more democratic tradition on which to draw. Most Mexican leftists possessed no alternative to the theory of the one-party state.[2] Most left groups merely wanted to substitute their party in the place of the PRI, and to carry out a more thorough statification of the economy.

The most important labor and popular reform movement of the 1970s, the Democratic Tendency, shared the revolutionary nationalist conception of

67

the Mexican state. The Democratic Tendency, a broad movement of workers, peasants and the urban poor, could be called a "Cardenist" organization. Rafaél Galván, a leader of one of the electrical workers' unions (SUTERM), and a workers' sector senator for the PRI, argued in the mid-1970s that working people had to support the revolutionary state and push it to the left. Galván believed that it was possible to recreate a situation such as had existed in the Cárdenas era, when workers and peasants allied themselves with the government and pressured the government to stand up to both Mexican capital and U.S. imperialism. In 1976, as Galván's Democratic Tendency began to burgeon into a broad national movement, the government stepped in and used the military to break the electrical workers' strike and demoralize the broader democratic movement, calling Galván's theory into question in the most decisive way.

These movements of the 1970s were no challenge to the PRI's corporatist regime for two reasons. First, while they began to question and criticize elements of corporatism, they often remained revolutionary nationalists with illusions in the Mexican state. Second, they failed to develop their own vision of democracy, including a vision of how democratic institutions would function. At the same time it is also true that the great peasant and labor upheavals of the 1970s, with their developing criticism of corporatism, anticipated the emergence of civil society in the 1980s.

The most important anticipation of civil society was the urban popular movement. The urban popular movement first began in the early 1970s as student organizers, mostly Maoists, worked with local community groups, particularly in the northern states of Chihuahua, Nuevo León, Durango, and in the southern state of Oaxaca. The new community groups, often made up of urban squatters, fought for land, housing, water, sewers and electricity using a combination of confrontation and negotiation. A second wave of community organizing led to the establishment of new local groups in the late 1970s and early 1980s in Baja California Norte, Guerrero, Jalisco, the Valley of Mexico, and Sinaloa.

Soon the local groups began to coalesce. In the late 1970s and early 1980s, groups in the valley of Mexico joined together in regional coalitions. Most importantly, in 1981 the local and regional urban popular movements came together as the National Coordinator of Urban Popular Movements (CONAMUP).

The urban popular organizations represented a tremendously important phenomenon, but they still operated in the old political context. These urban groups were often dominated by clandestine Maoist cadres who were frequently engaged in traditional deal-making with the PRI. Consequently, the urban popular movement organizations fell short of a democratic ideal. When in the early 1980s the urban popular movement began to acquire a more independent and democratic character, it still failed to transform the national political consciousness or to create a new national discourse.[3]

Only with the September 19, 1985 earthquake, did a new outlook and rhetoric appear. The popularization of the new political view can be largely attributed to the writer and social critic Carlos Monsiváis. In a series of eye-witness reports and essays written for Mexico's left-of-center magazines— *Proceso, Cuardernos Políticos,* and *El Cotidiano*—and later collected in the book *Entrada Libre: Crónicas de la sociedad que se organiza,* Monsiváis interpreted the Mexican people's response to the earthquake, and in doing so described a new force for social change, and perhaps most importantly, described that force in a new political discourse.

The 1985 earthquake revealed a great deal besides the structural weaknesses of some of Mexico's skyscrapers. Roads and schools collapsed because of the corrupt practices of contractors. The police headquarters broke apart, revealing the secret torture chambers. The army moved into industrial zones at the request of manufacturers to protect machinery while citizens remained buried under the rubble. At the same time, the president and other officials appeared on television and called upon citizens to remain in their homes, do nothing and await instructions.

The people of Mexico City defied their government's plea to remain at home and set about helping each other. By the thousands, and then by the tens of thousands, Mexicans poured into the streets. "They're organizing brigades of 25 to 100 people, little armies of volunteers," wrote Monsiváis on the first day. Many of the organizers of the brigades were leftists, leaders of community organizations or women's groups, who, cut off form their organizations, were acting on their own initiative.

These volunteer brigades, forming themselves in the midst of the chaos of the earthquake, literally moved mountains. The brigades shifted tons of rubble to save a life, or in the end only to remove a body. Volunteers built temporary shelters to house the survivors. The people of Mexico City performed miracles, but the greatest miracle of all was that they had done it themselves without the party or the state. And, "for the moment," wrote Monsiváis, "everything crystallized in this word, an act of *solidarity.*"

Monsiváis, in his very first essay on the earthquake, wrote a few phrases which summed up the significance of the heroic work of the volunteers and at the same time created a new political outlook and discourse: "Civil society exists as a great latent necessity, even in those who don't know the term, and its first and most insistent demand is a redistribution of power....On the 19th of September—in the face of the tragedy—Mexico experienced a *taking of power*, one of the most noble in its history, which went far beyond mere solidarity, which was the conversion of a people into a government, and of official disorder into civil order."[4]

The earthquake proved, said Monsiváis, that there was "a greater civic and national spirit than anyone had supposed." The sources of this were to be found in "Christian attitudes and civic generosity." Because of the earthquake, for a brief time "society had become a community." For a whole week, due to the extraordinary circumstances, people simply went far beyond the state's official institutions, the parties, the Church, and virtually all other organizations. The centralized state which could not or would not act, forced people to act for themselves. "A universal solution is discovered," wrote Monsiváis: "decentralize."

"By the beginning of October," Monsiváis wrote, "practice has become dominant: *civil society* is the communitarian effort at self-organization and solidarity, the space which is independent of the government, or more exactly, a zone of antagonism to it. And the theoretical objections, however well founded they may be, don't matter, they came too late. Each community, if it really wants to be one, makes up, as it goes along, its own definitions, and so the Marxist academy condemns them."[5]

The earthquake of September 19, 1985, the peoples' response to it, and the interpretations of that response created an entirely new way of thinking about politics in Mexico. The essays of Monsiváis, and of other political commentators, created a new political discourse at the center of which were two words: "solidarity" and "civil society." The new discourse rejected the old revolutionary language of both the Mexican state-party and of Marxist parties and academics. The new political discourse did not speak in terms of the people's struggle for social justice through the revolutionary state, but rather in terms of the volunteers joining together in acts of social solidarity and of citizens struggling for democracy against the state-party.

Monsiváis was not the inventor of the idea of "civil society," of course, nor was Mexico its state of national origin. The contemporary idea of "civil society," was first developed in the struggles against the communist one-party state in Eastern Europe and the military dictatorships in Latin America.[6] Jacek Kuron and Adam Michnik in Poland developed the concept in the 1980s as they attempted to strategize a struggle against the communist party-state. "Society organizes itself in the form of a democratic movement and becomes active outside the limits of the institutions of the totalitarian state," said Kuron in 1980.[7] Later Guillermo O'Donnell and Francisco Weffort, among others, appropriated the idea of "civil society" in conceptualizing the struggle against the military usurpers in Latin America. In Mexico, those on the Left came to the idea of civil society through the writing of the Italian communist Antonio Gramsci.[8] In all of these countries "civil society" came to refer to the new social movements and the political space they created in struggling against authoritarian political systems.

The idea of a "civil society" in struggle against a controlling state clearly resonated in Mexico, where by the 1980s, there was a kind of ideological and intellectual vacuum. Many Mexicans had distrusted their government since the 1968 massacre. After the crisis of 1982, when Mexico was unable to pay its debt to the New York banks, the PRI's nationalist economic development program was also discredited. Mexico appeared to be the perfect political dictatorship presiding over a collapsing economy. Mexico shared with communism the domination of a one-party state, and with capitalism, the recurrence of economic crises. Mexicans, seemed to partake of the worst of both worlds. The PRI appeared to be both a moral and an economic failure.

But what were the alternatives? Communism, a political ideology which was so attractive to many Mexicans in the 1960s and '70s, also seemed to have failed by the 1980s. For Mexicans, the failure of communism was not only the collapse of the communist regimes in Eastern Europe and later the former Soviet Union, but also the unending agony of Cuba. While many Mexicans remained sympathetic to Cuba's revolution, Castro's communism was clearly being starved into submission by the United States. Communism seemed impossible in a hemisphere dominated by the United States, its banks, and corporations. In Mexico itself, the Communist Party of Mexico (PCM), founded in the 1920s, gave up its Stalinist theory, and after passing through a Eurocommunist phase, merged with the nationalist Mexican Workers Party (PTM). Mexican communism was gradually losing its ideological and organizational identity, but without posing a really new alternative.[9]

Finally, the National Action Party (PAN), established in the 1930s, was also trapped in the past. The PAN participated in the same political discourse as the PRI, only as its diametrical opposite. The PAN, in the minds of many Mexicans, both its supporters and opponents, was still the anti-PRI, the party of conservative Roman Catholic priests, reactionary bankers, and northern industrialists which had opposed Lázaro Cárdenas in the 1930s.

Consequently, when the quake shook Mexico on September 19, all the old idols fell from their altars and were shattered. Mexico was ready for a new movement and, equally important, for a new way of thinking about and describing that movement. When Monsiváis wrote that the earthquake had produced this new thing called "civil society," everyone else saw it too. Civil society in Mexico came to mean a non-partisan, multi-class movement fighting for human rights, civil rights, political reform and social justice against the domination of the one-party state. The earthquake had created civil society, and now civil society would create its own political earthquakes.

First, the Mexico City earthquake set off an "unprecedented" wave of neighborhood organizing and a vast expansion of the "urban popular movement" throughout Mexico.[10] In Mexico City, the Victims Coordinating Committee (Coordinadora Unica de Damnificados or CUD) made up of 20 neighborhood groups was formed in October 1985, and called a demonstration of 30,000 to join in presenting a petition to President Miguel de la Madrid. Two years later, in April 1987, dozens of neighborhood groups in Mexico City created the *Asamblea de Barrios* or Neighborhood Assembly, represented by the masked wrestler Superbarrio. Superbarrio, with his mask and cape was a superhero who fought for Mexico City's slums and shantytowns, but he also soon became a symbol of the new civil society movement. Scores of other neighborhood groups formed throughout the country to take up the struggle for basic services for the urban poor.

After the earthquake, the new civil society movement appeared, appropriately, among the young, in the form of a new student movement. In April of 1986, Jorge Carpizo, the rector of the National University (UNAM), undertook the reform of the largest university in Latin America. UNAM had grown enormously during the 1960s and '70s, from 55,000 students in 1960 to over 300,000 in 1980. By 1986, UNAM had more than 325,000 college students, over two millon associated secondary and preparatory students, and over 25,000 faculty members.[11]

UNAM had once been one of Latin America's most prestigious institutions of higher learning, and the training ground for Mexico's political elite.

But in the quarter century between 1960 and 1985, the University's character had changed significantly. With the urbanization and industrialization of Mexico, and with the tremendous growth of the government bureaucracy, a university degree became the passport into the Mexican middle class. As Mexico City's population exploded, so did the demand for higher education.

During the social upheaval of the Echeverría administration in the early 1970s, students fought for and succeeded in winning open admissions and automatic passes, while preventing the imposition of tuitions and fees. A free university which accepted virtually everyone who applied gave working class Mexicans a chance for some upward social mobility, and the students tenaciously defended their democratic university. As the university became inundated with many poorly prepared students, state support for the university declined, and the quality of education deteriorated.

The economic crisis of the 1970s and early '80s also affected the University. Between 1981 and 1986, while the university continued to grow, its budget was cut by 44 percent. The professors' real salaries, that is their wages in terms of purchasing power, fell by 67.5 percent. The academic budget fell by a third—though the administration budget doubled. The student body also reflected the economic crisis. As the quality of education at Mexico's once great public university declined, the political elite began to remove their sons and daughters from UNAM and to enroll them instead at private institutions. About 75 percent of UNAM's students came from low income working-class families, and out of the 325,000 students, over 80,000 worked to support themselves while attending school.

Jorge Carpizo distributed his document *The Strengths and Weaknesses of UNAM* on April 16, 1986. Carpizo principally criticized the university bureaucracy, pointing out that between 1973 and 1985, while the student body had grown by 73.8 percent, academic personnel had grown by 95.5 percent, and the administration by 150.1 percent. Carpizo pointed out that despite the large growth in administration, there was little accountability. The faculty was demoralized and there existed a high rate of absenteeism among the professors. Carpizo wanted to revamp the university, reduce the bureaucracy and improve the quality of teaching and research. However, he also wanted to impose fees, stop open admissions, and end the automatic pass. UNAM's students, mostly from lower middle class and working class backgrounds, saw those measures as an attack on their birthright. Entrance exams, fees and other requirements would drive them out of school. As word spread so did the realization of what was at stake, the students decided to fight back. Carpizo's document touched off the biggest student movement in 20 years.

As in all other areas of Mexican life, the PRI party-state had its corporative organization on campus, the University Student Federation (FEU). Students were expected to take their grievances to this official organization to negotiate problems with the PRI. But since the student movement of 1968, the FEU had been held in low esteem and few students belonged to it.

Leadership for the new student movement initially came from student members of left groups such as Punto Crítico, Communist Convergence, the Communist Party (PSUM) and the Trotskyist Revolutionary Workers Party (PRT). But leadership soon passed into the hands of other young men and women, who proved to be talented political leaders but closer to the mass of apolitical working-class students: Carlos Imaz, Imanol Ordorika, Leyla Méndez, Andrea González, Antonio Santos, Oscar Moreno, Luis Alvarado, and Guadalupe Carrasco. Unlike the male-dominated student movement of 1968, there were several women leaders; and perhaps 25 percent of the movement was made up of women.

After several months of discussions, organizing and small protests, on October 13, 1986 the students organized the CEU, the University Student Council. The CEU argued that Carpizo and the university administration were acting illegally, contrary to the Constitution, and that they had no right to carry out the proposed reforms. The CEU demanded the resignation of Carpizo and his administration. The students called for a democratic reform of the universty from below, rather than a top-down reform. The CEU demanded that a congress be held on campus to discuss the role of UNAM in the national project, the university's internal organization, and the question of academic standards. Throughout the many months of organizing, the CEU put itself forward as the defender of student rights and democracy.

The CEU movement grew throughout the fall of 1986. On November 6, the CEU organized a march of 10,000 students on the campus. By November 25, somewhere between 10,000 and 50,000 students marched from the Parque Hundido to the University. On December 11, more than 50,000 students marched from the Parque de los Venados to the University. The University workers' union, STUNAM, declared its support for the CEU on January 6. With each of these developments there was a growth in the confidence and combativity of the students.

For five days, beginning on January 5, CEU leaders and the university administration debated Carpizo's reforms in the Humanities Auditorium. The debate was broadcast by Radio University to all of Mexico City, and listened to by the students' friends and families, and millions of other Mexicans. The student leaders impressed much of the Mexican public with their demands for a democratic reform of the university, and their explanation of needs of the university's working-class student body.

Still the struggle continued and, on January 21, some 200,000 students marched to the Zócalo, the national plaza. On February 3, the CEU declared a strike at the university, and six days later, for the second time, the CEU again occupied the Zócalo, only this time with a quarter of a million students. Finally, in mid-February 1987, after months of protests, dialogue and negotiation, the CEU reached an agreement with the Carpizo administration. The students won the right to a more democratic debate over university reform and prevented the impositions of the most onerous changes such as entrance exams and fees.

The CEU movement exemplified certain features of what Mexico had begun to call civil society. First, the students argued their legal rights and democracy, and fought for these rights in the public arena, both in broadcast radio debates and on the streets. The students did not make appeals to class, but rather, appeals to the citizenry—the public. The students did not seek a general confrontation with the Mexican government or the capitalist system, rather, the students attempted to expand their own political elbow room, to create a democratic space for debate and negotiation.

While the student movement became larger, stronger and more combative, there was no general political radicalization of the student body such as occurred in the 1970s. The PSUM and the PRT, the parties of the old left, hardly grew at all out of the new student movement. Those prominent student leaders who did become interested in party politics, later joined Cuauhtémoc Cárdenas's Party of the Democratic Revolution. For instance, student leader Antonio Santos left the Trotskyist PRT to join Cárdenas's PRD. The CEU student movement of 1986, in its emphasis on legality, democracy, and reformist politics, expressed the new civil society movement Monsiviás had described.

The Mexican anti-nuclear movement of the 1980s also clearly exemplifies the new movements of civil society, and helps to explain why those movements often arose as both anti-PRI and sometimes anti-leftist movements. In order to understand the anti-nuclear movement, it is necessary to know something about Mexico's nuclear energy industry.

The idea of creating a nuclear energy program in Mexico was first proposed to the Mexican government in the mid-1950s by the United States Atoms for Peace program. Atoms for Peace and the Mexican Light and Power Company arranged for scholarships for several Mexican students to study nuclear engineering in the United States. The commercial nuclear energy program began during the presidency of Gustavo Díaz Ordaz. In 1967, Mexico's Federal Electric Commission joined with the Stanford Research Institute to develop plans for a commercial nuclear facility in Mexico.

It was the new group of technocrats in the Luis Echeverría Alvarez administration, however, who really pushed Mexico into the atomic age. Echeverría's leadership planned to create 15 nuclear reactor plants throughout Mexico. The technocrats believed that in the course of building and operating a nuclear industry, Mexico could accomplish a real technology transfer, creating its own nuclear scientists and technicians. In this way Mexico would end the twentieth century as part of the first world, no longer dependent on foreign capital.

In 1970, with the assistance of the International Atomic Energy Agency, the Mexican government chose Laguna Verde, 50 miles from the Gulf port of Veracruz, as the site for its first nuclear reactor. Financing for the reactor was arranged through the World Bank, the U.S. Export-Import Bank, the Japanese Export Bank, and the Wells Fargo Bank. In 1972, General Electric won the contract to build the boiling water reactor, and Mitsubishi got the contract for the turbines. The New York-based Ebasco Corporation won the contract for overall engineering design. Laguna Verde was supposed to be completed by 1976, though construction work did not even begin until 1977.[12]

Meanwhile, the Mexican anti-nuclear movement had appeared.[13] The movement actually began in 1981 with a struggle over the creation of a Reactor Engineering Center (CIR) at Santa Fé de la Laguna, Michoacán. The Mexican government proposed to build the center on Lake Pátzcuaro, the home of the Purepecha Indians. The proposed engineering center was an important component of the government technocrats nuclear energy program, and they were firmly committed to it as a key element of Mexico's modernization. The Three Mile Island incident had occurred in the United States only two years before and had made many people throughout the world more leery of nuclear power, however. So from the beginning, the center was opposed by a number of scientists, environmentalists, and eventually, by an incipient anti-nuclear movement. In this movement one already begins to see the emergence of civil society of the mid-1980s.

Kunguarekua Purhecheri, a Purepecha Indian organization, denounced the proposed center before the Russell Tribunal in Rotterdam, Holland. Later the Supreme Council of the Purepechas issued a manifesto opposing the project. Local residents formed the Committee for the Ecological Defense of Michoacán (CODEMICH), one of Mexico's first environmentalist groups. One of the members of this organization was Carolina Escudero, the widow of General Francisco J. Múgica, a close collaborator with former President Lázaro Cárdenas.

These organizations opposed the Reactor Engineering Center on the grounds that radioactive emissions would harm human beings, as well as the fauna and flora of the lake. In addition they feared that the reactor would raise the lake's temperature, killing micro-organisms, wiping out the base of the food chain, killing the fish and eventually destroying the ecological balance of the lake. Such damage to the lake would destroy the economy of the area which was based on the Purepecha fish trade and on tourism.

This anti-nuclear and environmental movement found itself in a fierce confrontation not only with the PRI, but also with the communist-led Nuclear Workers Union (SUTIN) which was the foremost advocate of the project. In the public debate over the center, SUTIN attacked the anti-nuclear movement as "reactionaries," and claimed for itself the banner of revolutionary nationalism. Mexican environmentalist and author, Hugo García Michel, wrote that "all of those who dared to oppose the plans of the Nuclear Workers Union (or better, of its leaders) suffered the risk of being condemned before the sacred tribunal of the Mexican left of the time, more Stalinist than Stalin himself."[14] The more important point might be that the leaders of SUTIN were also more nationalist than the PRI, and that they shared the PRI's revolutionary nationalist ideology and rhetoric.

In any case, the movement against the Engineering Research Center on Lake Pátzcuaro continued to grow, with many public pronouncements and demonstrations. Under the pressure of the burgeoning movement, Cuauhtémoc Cárdenas, an important leader in the PRI, the son of the former president, former senator, and at that moment governor of Michoacán, decided to come out against the Center. Cárdenas met with the Secretary of National Patrimony and it was finally agreed in May of 1981 that the Center would not be based on Lake Pátzcuaro. The Mexican anti-nuclear movement won its first victory, and then became dormant until the struggle over Laguna Verde began in earnest, after the Chernobyl incident in 1986.

The first serious criticism of the Laguna Verde reactor project arose in 1977. The criticism came from SUTIN, which strongly criticized the project for abandoning its goal of attaining technological autonomy. Arturo Whaley, director of SUTIN, argued that foreign corporations, mainly U.S., and their employees, were supervising the work, while Mexicans had little responsibility. Whaley and SUTIN criticized the PRI and the Federal Electrical Commission for lack of nationalism. SUTIN later suggested that Mexico might do better with the Canadian natural uranium reactor design (CANDU).

The point here is that SUTIN exemplified the old style of political struggle in Mexico which always took place within the framework of an ideology of revolutionary nationalism. Whaley and the communist leadership of SUTIN, while they seriously differed with the PRI over nuclear policy, struggled over the policy within the same political and ideological framework as the PRI.

Such was the debate over Laguna Verde until the Chernobyl disaster of 1986, when a really new anti-nuclear and pro-environmental movement appeared and became a major constituent of the new Mexican civil society. The Anti-Nuclear Committee of Xalapa, the state capital of Veracruz, was formed on May 15, 1986, just 15 days after the Chernobyl incident. The near melt-down in the Soviet reactor, and the release of nuclear contaminants into the atmosphere, created new fears about nuclear power in countries around the world. Equally important, the Chernobyl incident occurred less than a year after the Mexico City earthquake. The new anti-nuclear movement that developed in Veracruz, and then throughout Mexico in 1986, was built on the experience of the earlier movement against the Pátzcuaro Center in 1981, and on civil society's response to the earthquake in 1985.

The new movement was qualitatively different. The anti-nuclear movement of 1986 and 1987 was the political debut of civil society, the mobilization of the people against the state. Unlike older social movements in Mexico, the Left played little role in its initial organization. The anti-nuclear movement's appeal was to all Mexicans as citizens, regardless of class or other social characteristics, and its members had few illusions about the ability or desire of the Mexican state to solve the environmental problems.

The people of Veracruz reacted to the Chernobyl incident by forming scores of anti-nuclear groups throughout the state. Two of the founders were Genaro Guevara and Rosalba Lomelí, both students in the Humanities Department at the University of Veracruz. They and others traveled throughout the state in 1986 organizing local support, and on August 31, 1986 three thousand persons participated in the First National March Against Laguna Verde.

The new anti-nuclear movement appealed to all of the people of Veracruz, regardless of social distinctions. For example, Genaro Guevara, one of the student founders of the movement, travelled to the Panpanteca Sierra, a mountainous region inhabited by indigenous people, where he helped to organize the Coxquihuense Common Front. The front was made up of Totonaca Indian peasants from Chumatlán, Coxquihui and Zozocolco. A Catholic priest and a Protestant minister joined together to help bring the Totonaca Indians for a meeting with the anti-nuclear activists. Guevara and other anti-nuclear leaders held a meeting with the Indians in the Chumatlán cathedral, a church that had been built on top of an Indian pyramid. They explained the dangers of nuclear energy as their presentation was translated into the Totonaca language. The Totonaca Indians decided to join the anti-nuclear movement, but they did so not as an indigenous group affiliated to the National Indigenous Institute (INI) controlled by the PRI-government, but as Mexican citizens, part of the new movement of "civil society."[15]

Women made up another important component of the new anti-nuclear movement and of the new civil society. In January of 1987, a group of women, many of them middle or upper class, formed the Mothers Group of Veracruz and joined the struggle against Laguna Verde. They organized meetings, issued statements, and participated in demonstrations like other anti-nuclear groups, but their most important contribution to the movement was a campaign to get citizens to hang red ribbons on their doors or in their windows to protest the construction of the reactor. In Córdoba and Xalapa, hundreds of houses were bedecked in red ribbons, a testimony to the growing power of anti-nuclear activists and the growing political space being created by civil society. During the next several years, women would be at the forefront of every movement of civil society, and frequently, the most prominent leaders.

The Roman Catholic bishops of Tuxpán, Papantla, San Andrés Tuxtla, Xalapa and Veracruz also came out in support of the anti-nuclear movement and in opposition to the reactor. "Not all technological advances can be categorized as authentic human progress," was the bishops' statement, indicating that the Church too was part of the new movement of civil society in Mexico.

The leftist parties, by and large, did not join the anti-nuclear movement, and some actually opposed it. The Mexican Left, says García Michel, could never understand what the new movement was all about. "They didn't understand," he writes, "that an inter-class movement could exist in which, united in one cause with one objective, students, professors, lawyers, housewives, ranchers, peasants, fishermen, professionals, workers, public employees, taxi drivers, artists, journalists, and so on, could all participate. Where was the class struggle? Where was the vanguard of the proletariat? There, they said with their fists raised on high, was a real insult to the immutable laws of historical materialism."[16]

On January 24, 1987, some 15,000 people carrying red ribbons marched to the entrance of the proposed nuclear installation. On April 26, 1987, the first anniversary of the Chernobyl disaster, 20,000 people marched. The continuing growth of the movement forced the PRI's Minister of Urban Development and Ecology, Manuel Camacho Solís, to meet and negotiate with its leaders on July 7, 1987. Camacho proposed that the International Atomic Energy Agency be brought in to certify the safety of the Laguna Verde site. Camacho was furious when the environmentalists rejected his proposal, and told him he should be "the first ecologist to defend our cause."[17]

The fight over Laguna Verde continued on into the presidential pre-election period in 1988. The environmentalists called upon the people of Veracruz and of Mexico to vote against the PRI unless the state-party gave up its plan for the Laguna Verde reactor. The PRI held on stubbornly to its position, and on October 10, 1988, President Miguel de la Madrid authorized the loading of the first two reactor units at Laguna Verde. Though Laguna Verde went into operation, the anti-nuclear movement had really won on the question of Mexico's nuclear future. Faced with the experience of Three Mile Island and Chernobyl, with its own economic crisis, and with the Mexican anti-nuclear movement, the PRI abandoned its ambitious plans for a dozen or more nuclear reactors. Civil society had its first major victory.

What were the politics of this new civil society? While in other parts of the world civil society sometimes had conservative implications, in Mexico, civil society remained a radically democratic theory and was associated with the pratice of grassroots organizations. The new civil society in Mexico was made up primarily of non-governmental organizations (NGOs) and the new social movements, particularly human rights groups, voluntary social service organizations, women's groups, indigenous people's movements, and environmental organizations. The new civil society also came to encompass many of the independent organizations created by the Left in the 1960s and 1970s, such as independent peasant organizations, autonomous organizations of the urban poor, and independent labor unions. The Catholic Church was also involved, or at least some of its bishops, priests and lay activists were.

Certainly upper- and middle-class people were involved and often played leadership roles in the new organizations of civil society, yet no one could characterize this as a movement self-consciously organized and led by the wealthy or by business. The leaders of the movement were often middle-class intellectuals, professionals, and students. But frequently they shared the leadership with independent unionists, indigenous leaders, or the urban poor.

Politically, this was a movement opposed to the existing order. In the case of the anti-nuclear movement, this was a movement against the PRI's atomic energy policy, but it soon became a movement against the PRI itself, against Mexico's one-party state. While civil society opposed concentrated, centralized power, it often declined to analyze or describe the powers that it opposed. The problem for civil society was simply the PRI's one-party state. Civil society seldom analyzed the power of capitalism, the role of the Mexican bourgeoisie or U.S. economic involvement.

In Mexico, the theory of civil society tended to minimize class differences, both within the opposition and within Mexican society taken as a whole. The implication was that in times of crisis, acts of social solidarity could overcome class differences and conflicts. The differences between the interests of the middle classes, the workers and the poor tended to be overlooked.

Because of its character as a citizens' movement for democracy and its cross-class composition, civil society seldom concentrated its attention on the economic and social matters that most affected workers, peasants and the poor. Civil society as a whole tended to take up the environmental issue or political reform, while its grassroots member organizations fought for sewers in the slums or workers' rights on the job.

Yet Mexican civil society tended to take the side of the underdog, to side with peasants and workers, poor people and Indians. The new civil society gradually absorbed parts of the disintegrating old left, and the Left brought a greater awareness of class issues to civil society. These things were never very clearly defined, and within this new civil society various political ideologies seemed to be jostling against one another: Mexico's traditional populism and *cardenismo*, a developing political liberalism, and a grassroots democratic socialism. Civil society itself was a congeries of contradictions, even as it was a powerful new source of idealism, energy, and organization.

The first great test for this new civil society and its incipient political theories came at once in the campaign of Cuauhtémoc Cárdenas for president in 1988.

5

CUAUHTEMOC CARDENAS:THE SON OF THE GENERAL

The peasants stood by the side of the road, sometimes for hours, waiting to get a glimpse of the man. Families stood together. Thousands of peasants—whole villages, men in their sombreros, women in their shawls, and the children beside them—lined the side of the roads for mile after mile, sometimes tens of thousands of them standing under the hot sun, or at times waiting in the rain.

When the campaign bus passed, they raised their hats or waved their handkerchiefs, in one way or another saluting the tall, dark man with the somber face, and the uninspired demeanor. Or perhaps it would be more correct to say they saluted the name, the memory of the man's father. In their remembrance of the past lay their hope for the future.

So it was, in 1988, along the rural roads and highways whenever Cuauhtémoc Cárdenas entered one of those areas where his father, President Lázaro Cárdenas had distributed land to the peasants in the 1930s. In the Bajío, in the Laguna region, in Michoacán, the peasants lined the roads for miles to salute the man they called, *"El hijo del General,"* the son of the General.

When Cuauhtémoc arrived at the town Zócalo, the people crowded into the plaza. As the candidate finished his speech, and looked up from his text, the men raised their sombreros in the air and cheered. Everyone pressed forward to see the General's son, to wish him well, or to cheer him on. Occasionally, at that moment some man or woman stepped forward and pressed a note into Cuauhtémoc's hand, or gave a letter to one of his assistants. A school teacher from Michoacán wrote, "I am ready to take up arms whenever you say, Mr. Cárdenas. My family is very poor, and we are prepared to fight for you."[1] There were many notes like that, pledging—if it should be necessary—to rise up in arms. The revolution never ends in the Mexican countryside.

In Mexico City, another bastion of strength for Cárdenas in 1988, his supporters were the educated middle classes, the public employees, and the public school teachers. Cárdenas also struggled to break the factory workers and the urban poor from the control of the PRI, and often succeeded. In the cities there also was an outpouring of support for Cárdenas among all of those elements who had begun to see themselves as part of this new thing called "civil society." Middle class intellectuals and academics, activists in non-governmental organizations, environmentalists, and feminists were all likely to be supporters of Cárdenas.

That the Cárdenas campaign of 1988 was somehow simultaneously both a throwback to the past and an anticipation of the future, an atavistic organization of Mexico's poorest peasants, and a progressive movement of the urban intellectuals is the oddest thing. It was at once the last expression of the old radicalism, and the first political expression of the new civil society. No doubt it was the confluence of these two elements that gave the Cárdenas campaign of 1988 its tremendous energy.

Who would have really expected that Cuauhtémoc Cárdenas should have led such a movement? There was nothing charismatic about him. Both in private and in public he was somewhat reserved and soft-spoken. Cárdenas made one feel comfortable, but he was not charming. He was certainly intelligent, but he did not have the quick wits of a debater. His speeches were as thoughtful and serious as the man himself, but he read them. Still the people liked him well enough, and Cuauhtémoc Cárdenas became the leader of the most important electoral campaign since Madero ran for president against the dictator Porfirio Díaz in 1910.

Why was there such a tremendous wave of support? In part it was because he was Lázaro's son, and as Adolfo Gilly has suggested, there was something mythic about the return of the avenging son of the dead king, coming to right the wrongs in the kingdom and put the usurpers to flight.[2]

But perhaps more important was the fact that in 1988 people felt that Cuauhtémoc could be trusted. In a country where no one believed in politicians, or in the political parties, that was the highest possible compliment. Even though he had spent his political life in the corrupt Institutional Revolutionary Party, and even though he came out of the PRI arm-in-arm with Muñoz Ledo, a man who was seen by many as the epitome of the cynicism and hypocrisy of the Mexican political system, still the people believed in Cuauhtémoc or in the name Cárdenas. In that regard perhaps Cuauhtémoc's stolid style was a positive asset for it made him appear to be modest, and, indeed, he was. Or at least he was as modest as a man can be who, above all, wants to be president.

Cuauhtémoc Cárdenas was born a month early on International Labor Day, May 1, 1934, the year his father became president of Mexico. Cuauhtémoc passed his first six years in Los Pinos, the presidential residence, running through the grounds with his playmates as his father distributed land to the peasants, encouraged the organization of the labor unions, and national-' ized the petroleum industry. Cuauhtémoc was too young to remember much of it. There remains, however, a famous photo of Cuauhtémoc, as a little four-year-old boy, carrying his piggy bank to a government office to make his contribution. Like millions of other Mexican citizens, little Cuauhtémoc had taken his pennies to help pay the indemnification to Standard Oil and Royal Dutch Shell for the expropriation of their oil wells and refineries in Mexico.

Lázaro Cárdenas left the presidency in 1940, and a year later took responsibility as a General in the Mexican Army for the Pacific military region during World War II. As his father moved from place to place on the west coast, Cuauhtémoc followed, attending elementary schools in the towns of Jilquilpán, Pátzcuaro, Mazatlán and Ensenada. After 1943, Cuauhtémoc returned to Mexico City and attended school there into the 1950s. His life would always be divided between Michoacán and Mexico City.

While still a teenager, Cuauhtémoc Cárdenas participated in his first political campaign. Lázaro Cárdenas and others in the left-wing of the PRI, broke away from the party briefly in 1951 to support the presidential candidacy of General Miguel Henríquez Guzmán against the PRI's candidate Adolfo Ruíz Cortines. Cuauhtémoc, still in high school, became a student supporter of Henríquez.

The Henríquez campaign was one of the few real political contests in modern Mexico since José Vasconcelos's campaign of 1929. The PRI dissidents criticized the out-going Miguel Alemán regime and PRI presidential candidate Ruíz Cortines for conservatism and corruption. There were scurrilous attacks on both sides. The PRI distributed *pulque* and barbecue to the all-male electorate in rallies around the country. (Women could not vote in Mexico until 1958.)

On election day in 1951, the government called out planes, tanks, and troops, and to ensure its own victory, the state-party engaged in widespread fraud, carrying off some ballot boxes to be burned and stuffing others. The opposition organized protests against the fraud, but the government put down the demonstrations, and in the aftermath, several Henriquistas were murdered. After the election, both Lázaro and Cuauhtémoc Cárdenas returned to the PRI.

After finishing preparatory school, Cuauhtémoc studied at the National Engineering School. One of his teachers there was Herberto Castillo, though Cuauhtémoc knew Herberto better outside the university as a leftist political activist. In 1988, Herberto Castillo would, after much soul searching, step down as the candidate for president on the ticket of the Mexican Socialist Party (PMS) in favor of Cuauhtémoc Cárdenas.

Cuauhtémoc's first experience as the leader of a protest political movement came as the result of political developments in Guatemala. "We formed a committee at the university against foreign intervention in Guatemala in 1954," he later remembered. "The committee denounced the coup carried out by the CIA and the military against Arbenz, and decided to take action. They chose me as the president of the committee, and we began to become involved in activities, protests. We carried a funeral wreath to the U.S. embassy to mark the death of the good neighbor policy."[3]

In 1957, Cuauhtémoc graduated with a degree in civil engineering, and went to Europe to continue his studies. He worked at the Ministry of Reconstruction in Paris, France from 1957 to 1958, and subsequently received a Bank of Mexico fellowship to work for the famous Krupp armaments company in Germany in 1958. He also spent some time in Italy. His *Wanderjahr* over, in 1960, Cárdenas returned to Mexico to begin work as a private engineer.

Cuauhtémoc Cárdenas again became involved in a political movement through his father. In 1961, Lázaro Cárdenas came out of semi-retirement to help organize the Latin American Conference for National Sovereignty, Economic Emancipation, and Peace. The conference, which was held in Mexico in March of that year, was intended to support the new revolutionary government that had come to power in Cuba in 1959 under the leadership of Fidel Castro.

Lázaro Cárdenas also took advantage of the conference to launch a new Mexican organization, the National Liberation Movement (MLN). Lázaro Cárdenas founded the MLN to push the PRI-government to the left and to defend the Cuban revolution. The MLN brought about a regroupment of the Mexican Left, including "Cardenists," communists, the People's Socialist Party (PPS), and many independent labor and peasant organizations. The MLN was a pale reflection of the Cárdenas coalition of the 1930s, but the most important regrouping of the Mexican Left of the 1960s. Cuauhtémoc served for two years on the MLN national committee, and several of his MLN comrades would later become involved in his 1988 election campaign.

Beginning in the mid-1960s, Cárdenas entered upon a rather traditional career in the PRI, and spent 20 years rising through the ranks of the bureaucracy and the Party. First, from 1964 to 1969, Cárdenas oversaw the construction of the José María Morelos Dam on the Balsas River, in what was then Melchor Ocampo, Michoacán. Then, during the period from 1970 to 1973, he was an assistant director involved in the creation of the Las Truchas steelworks (also known as SICARTSA) in the same town, but now renamed Lázaro Cárdenas, Michoacán, after his father. While working as an engineer on the construction of the plant, Cuauhtémoc also served as trust manager of the steel mill community, overseeing the region's urban and economic development.

Cárdenas's involvement in the PRI began back in 1966 when he became part of the technical council of the National Peasant Confederation (CNC), the peasant sector of the PRI. Cuauhtémoc's first experience in electoral politics came in 1973 and 1974 when he became a "pre-candidate," that is one of the contestants within the PRI, for the office of governor of Michoacán. But President Echeverría chose another candidate, and Cuauhtémoc was out. "Despite promises to the contrary," said Cárdenas, "undemocratic procedures were followed which I publicly denounced."[4]

Nevertheless, two years later, in 1976, Cárdenas went to Echeverría and asked to be permitted to run for the Senate. With the president's approval, Cárdenas's election was automatic—at the time, the PRI had never lost a Senate seat—and Cárdenas became the PRI Senator for the family's home state of Michoacán. Within a few months, Cárdenas resigned his senate seat at the request of the new president, José López Portillo, in order to serve as his assistant secretary for Forestry and Wildlife.

Cuauhtémoc sought office again in 1980, and, with the approval of President López Portillo, was elected governor of Michoacán. Like his father, who had shut down the gambling casinos in Mexico in the 1930s, Cuauhtémoc was a moral reformer. As governor, Cuauhtémoc made prostitution a criminal offense and denied permits for cockfights. But he was also a political reformer and a progressive. He created a state-owned public transportation system in the state capital of Morelia, established rent-control legislation, and opened the state university campus to more low income students. Cuauhtémoc also dealt with the proposed Nuclear Engineering Center in the Purepecha homelands on Lake Pátzcuaro, and—under the pressure of the new environmental movement—Cuauhtémoc helped negotiate an alternative. Throughout the years, from his entry into party work in 1966 until his break with the party in the late 1980s, there was nothing in Cárdenas's career to suggest his future role as leader of a national opposition to the PRI. Like his father, Cuauhtémoc was clearly on the left of the PRI, but he was certainly not a dissident. Cuauhtémoc made no public protest when the Mexican Army crushed the railroad workers in 1959, murdered the students in 1968, or smashed the Democratic Tendency in 1976. Throughout all of those years, Cuauhtémoc said "it still seemed possible to reconstruct the revolutionary movement from within," that is, from within the PRI.[5]

Even in the 1980s, Cuauhtémoc Cárdenas never really changed his position—it was rather that the party changed around him, until, with the election of de la Madrid, it became clear that the technocrats had carried out a palace coup and had seized the leadership of the Party. Cuauhtémoc strongly opposed the technocrats' economic plans, and was disgusted by their servile behavior before the International Monetary Fund (IMF) and the New York bankers. Cuauhtémoc believed that the technocratic group led by de la Madrid and Salinas wished "to give away the country and to dismantle the Mexican economy and subject the masses to ever-greater levels of exploitation."[6] As a nationalist—and as his father's son—Cuauhtémoc felt obligated to resist the tearing apart of Mexico's nationalist economic order.

When Cuauhtémoc attempted to oppose the technocrats, however, he found all avenues to change within the party were closed. The technocrats had seized control of the party's key organizational and ideological structures, and were gradually squeezing out the old political leadership. Only at that point, driven primarily by his concern over changes in economic policy, did Cárdenas take up the issue of democracy within the PRI. And then, for Cárdenas, the fight began at the top, within the the PRI's leadership.

Looking for allies within the party, Cuauhtémoc soon found the man who would become his principal partner in the struggle to reform the PRI: former PRI-president Porfirio Muñoz Ledo. As former president of the PRI and a top official in the administrations of four presidents, Muñoz Ledo was an inveterate insider, and a sophisticated operator. Muñoz Ledo, felt he had been passed over for president, and resented the wealthy, privileged, young technocrats who were taking over the leadership of the party. In the mid-1980s, moreover, Muñoz Ledo stood on the left of the PRI, and, like Cárdenas, was deeply disturbed by the new economic and social policies of the technocrats. Together in 1985, Cuauhtémoc and Muñoz Ledo organized the "Democratic Current" as a reform movement within the PRI.

The first informal meetings among PRI dissidents took place in June 1985 in Mexico City. When in October of that year Muñoz Ledo returned home after his six year stint as Mexico's representative before the United Nations, he too joined the discussions. The dissidents continued their quiet meetings for nearly over a year before any public declarations or activity. Knowledge of the group's existence stayed within a small circle of the PRI's elite, most of whom were prominent in the state-party or the foreign service.

The first sign that something might be happening in the PRI was a demonstration for national sovereignty held on May 21, 1986. Muñoz Ledo led the group which included a number of prominent intellectuals, artists, labor officials, and several thousand demonstrators on a march through downtown Mexico City. A few months later, on August 14, the leftist newspaper *Unomasuno* carried a story mentioning the formation within the PRI of a new democratic tendency led by Porfirio Muñoz Ledo, Cuauhtémoc Cárdenas, and Rodolfo González Guevera. Two days later, in what was clearly a coordinated campaign, a number of PRI congressmen, senators, and governors expressed their support for such a democratic movement within the party.

The Democratic Current was formally founded by Cuauhtémoc Cárdenas on August 22, 1986 in a meeting before several hundred peasants in Michoacán. At the same time, Porfirio Muñoz Ledo held a meeting with Adolfo Lugo Verduzco, head of the PRI, at which he announced the Democratic Current's formation to the party leadership. "The PRI leadership did not accept our proposal to form a *corriente*," said Muñoz Ledo, "Adolfo Lugo Verduzco, then party president, told me that the the PRI was a 'pluriclassist' party but not 'pluri-ideological.'" "The response," said Muñoz Ledo, "was Stalinistic and papal." "The PRI," he said, "denied freedom of thought within the party, including the right to interpret party doctrine freely."[7]

Nevertheless, the PRI did not explicitly ban the faction and the Democratic Current continued organizing. Among the party's regional leaders and members, the Democratic Current became the subject of a debate. Leaders of the CNC, the National Peasant Confederation, in which Cuauhtémoc Cárdenas had begun his political career, expressed support for the idea of a democratic movement within the party. The PRI's youth organization also backed the new democracy movement. Fidel Velázquez, head of the Confederation of Mexican Workers, the most important labor federation in Mexico, predictably attacked the reformers as threatening the unity of the official party. Throughout the country, in every state, PRI leaders began to take sides on the new reform movement, and the political pressure mounted.

The tension between PRI technocrats and the Democratic Current's reformers eventually errupted at the Thirteenth National Assembly of the PRI, held in Mexico City in the first week of March of 1987. The PRI leadership had brought in former presidents Luis Echeverría and José López Portillo to bolster opposition to the reformers. Cuauhtémoc Cárdenas and 25 other Democratic Current leaders presented proposals at the party conference, calling for a democratization of the party and rejecting the technocrats' free-market economic program. The PRI leadership ignored the proposals, and at the closing of the Assembly, on March 4, the new PRI president Jorge de la Vega lashed out at the Democratic Current. "If you are unhappy with the PRI, leave the party," said de la Vega.

The attack both surprised and offended Cárdenas who responded a few days later with a letter in which he denounced de la Vega's authoritarian and anti-democratic position. The struggle now broke into the open at all levels of the party. Throughout the spring of 1987, Cuauhtémoc Cárdenas and other Democratic Current leaders traveled the length and breadth of Mexico organizing the new movement. On June 22, the PRI, threatened by this new wave of organizing, published a declaration signed by Jorge de la Vega and other leaders of the PRI officially condemning Cárdenas, Muñoz Ledo, and the Democratic Current. Nevertheless, the party was still reluctant to discipline the dissidents.

The inner circle of the Democratic Current had decided some time before that it would run a candidate for president, which made Cárdenas the natural choice. Muñoz Ledo remembered, "I visited with Cuauhtémoc, the

Laguna District in northern Mexico, where General Cárdenas distributed land in the early years, and was witness to the amazing devotion that Cuauhtémoc commands there....Several of us quickly realized Cuauhtémoc's capacity to gather support, because he became a national figure rather than a mere ex-governor in just a few weeks."[8]

On July 3, 1987, several thousand Democratic Current supporters drafted Cuauhtémoc Cárdenas for president. In announcing his candidacy, Cárdenas explained that he wanted to reorient Mexico's political economy and social policies. He emphasized the creation of jobs, the raising of wages, the strengthing of the Mexican domestic market. Cárdenas, while rejecting a moratorium on the payment of foreign debt, called for renegotiating the debt's terms. Finally, Cárdenas suggested that the government's conservative economic policies, and the public disgust with those policies, could lead either to outbreaks of violence or possibly even a right-wing coup.[9] Without saying so, Cárdenas suggested that, with the support of the United States, the PRI was becoming fascist. Fascism was an issue that has never been far from Cuauhtémoc's mind, and that may have its origins in his father Lázaro Cárdenas's struggles against his predecessor Calles and the right-wing General Cedillo in the 1930s.

The Democratic Current launched a campign throughout the country to gather signatures to register Cárdenas as a pre-candidate within the PRI, and within several weeks some 780,000 signatures were collected. The Democratic Current also petitioned the party asking it to hold a party primary election, something unheard of within the PRI.

"All of this was denied, of course," said Muñoz Ledo. "No one paid any mind to us; they acted as if we didn't exist. Our supporters began to feel the pressure too. Government employees who were seen with us were fired. Peasants who supported us by attending our meetings found that their credit requests were denied. When members of a fishing cooperative showed up at our meetings, their boats were denied access to the port."[10]

At the same time, the PRI responded in its way to the growing demands for democracy in the party. PRI leaders announced the names of six pre-candidates for the presidency, who then proceeded to appear in various venues making political speeches. While hardly a primary, or even a party nominating convention, it was a novelty. Nevertheless, the final choice of the next president remained in the hands of out-going President de la Madrid who chose his former student and protegé Carlos Salinas de Gortari. Both Cuauhtémoc and Muñoz Ledo immediately issued statements proclaiming that the choice of the PRI's presidential candidate had been conducted without regard for democracy, and declared it illegal. While Muñoz Ledo, Cuauhtémoc Cárdenas and their supporters were never formally expelled from the PRI, they gradually moved away from the state-party, eventually establishing their own independent organization.

The PRI had split, opening a new era in Mexican politics. "The split was a watershed," wrote Jorge Castañeda, "it broke the back of Mexico's famous elite consensus and mass acquiescence which had provided stability and continuity since the late 1920s."[11] If the PRI could split, then anything could become possible. Maybe the opposition could even turn the PRI out of power.

Cuauhtémoc and the Democratic Current were determined to go ahead with his presidential campaign. However, since he was no longer a member of the PRI, Cuauhtémoc would have to find a legally registered party that would permit him to run for president as candidate on its ballot line. The National Action Party or PAN—a conservative party originally created in a struggle against Lázaro Cárdenas—was out of the question. Nor did Cuauhtémoc, who was not a socialist, wish to run as the candidate of leftists parties such as the Mexican Socialist Party (PMS), Socialist Workers Party (PST) or Socialist Peoples Party (PPS).

Cárdenas wanted to remain in the nationalist center of Mexican politics and with that consideration in mind, Cárdenas and Muñoz Ledo secretly carried out hurried negotiations with Carlos Cantú Rosas, the leader of the Authentic Party of the Mexican Revolution or PARM. The PARM had been founded by former military men who left the PRI in 1954. Like the PRI, it had a revolutionary nationalist ideology, and it stood in the center of the Mexican political spectrum. Organizationally, the PARM was extremely weak, and had little power to mobilize the vote. Some referred to it as a "dummy" party. Acting quickly, Cárdenas and Muñoz Ledo got the PARM leadership to agree to let Cárdenas run on its ballot line before the PRI could thwart the plan. The PARM membership was never consulted on the nomination.

The moment Cárdenas launched his independent campaign as a PARM candidate, the effect was like an electric current creating a magnetic force, and polarizing Mexican society. The magnetic pull was strongest on the left which immediately gravitated toward Cárdenas's new movement. In order to facilitate an alliance with the various leftist groups and parties, Cárdenas and Muñoz Ledo established the National Democratic Front (FDN).

The FDN was an electoral coalition which permitted the various parties to retain their separate identities while supporting Cárdenas's presidential campaign. The Socialist Workers Party (PST), which had recently changed its name to the Cardenist Front of National Reconstruction Party (PFCRN), joined the front and supported Cárdenas's candidacy. A group of parliamentarians and intellectuals, led by Ricardo Pascoe and Adolfo Gilly, left the Trotskyist Revolutionary Workers Party (PRT), formed a group called the Movement to Socialism (MAS), and then joined the new National Democratic Front. Finally, dozens of local and regional leftists groups around the country, Maoists, Castroists, and radical nationalists, also rallied to the Cárdenas campaign. Many of these leftists led significant organizations of the urban poor or rural peasants. The Democratic Current's alliance with the various socialist groups provided a network of talented writers, speakers and organizers with connections to social movements throughout the country.

Cárdenas and Muñoz Ledo negotiated entrance into the front with the heirs to Mexico's communist tradition who were members of the Mexican Socialist Party (PMS). The PMS had held a national primary for the 1988 elections in which Herberto Castillo had been selected as the party's presidential candidate. Castillo and many leaders of the PMS were reluctant to withdraw his candidacy. There was a heated debate within the PMS, but in the end, Castillo stepped down in favor of his former engineering student. While Cárdenas originally intended to run as a centrist candidate, the formation of the National Democratic Front quickly shifted the campaign to the left.

But equally important was Cárdenas' influence over the new movement that Carlos Monsiváis had called "civil society." Many of those who had joined the volunteer brigades of rescue workers after the September 19, 1985 earthquake formed Cuauhtémoc's base of support in Mexico City. The leaders of non-governmental organizations, social service volunteers, environmental activists, feminists, and many others gradually identified with the campaign and soon became enthusiastic supporters.

Following in his famous father's footsteps, Cárdenas traveled throughout Mexico, visiting nearly every state and major city, speaking in small towns and half-forgotten hamlets. Particularly in the rural areas where his father had distributed land, the peasants came out by the thousands to greet him. In the big cities, there was tremendous support as well. Tens and hundreds of thousands crowded the plazas in cities across Mexico. As election day, July 6, 1988 approached, Cárdenas was riding a wave of political support that washed over the plaza of Mexico City, depositing half a million supporters at the final rally.

Speaking at his final rally on June 25, 1988, Cárdenas told the crowd, "Our proposal is very clear: we fight to retake the abandoned and rejected road of the Mexican Revolution, whose principles, and objectives, we believe, remain valid: the importance of the vote with which Madero launched his struggle in 1910; economic emancipation, a condition of political autonomy and the full exercise of national sovereignty; the eradication of poverty, ignorance, injustice and exploitation; an equitable distribution of wealth; a position of equality in the world order." Cárdenas denounced "the breaking of the social pact of the Mexican Revolution and the assumption of real power by a new governing group, the representatives and bearers of the economic and political doctrines of a new reaction."

What Cárdenas had once hinted at, he now said openly: "The modernization of the political center is nothing other than the up-to-date face of fascism: the strengthening of one-man management and the centralization of all decisions, the state's subordination of the masses, the collusion of the government with the great corporations, the triumphalism and spectacles which obscure and distort reality, the authoritarianism and vertical control used to impose decisions, the repression." "In the face of this modern fascism", said Cárdenas, "Mexico was rising up." "The people of Mexico decided to use the electoral path in order to ensure a peaceful change of government and to return to the direction of the Revolution."

The Cuauhtémoc Cárdenas campaign of 1988 had been the greatest electoral contest in Mexico since Madero ran against Porfirio Díaz in 1910 in a campaign that sparked the Mexican Revolution. How did he do it? What did it mean for Mexico? Carlos Monsiváis and Adolfo Gilly offered two interpretations of events, each of which got at an important aspect of the phenomenon.

Carlos Monsiváis, who had introduced the term "civil society" in his descriptions of the reaction to the earthquake of 1985, was sure that the Cárdenas campaign was a continuation of the same phenomenon. In July 1988, Monsiváis wrote, "The closing of Cuauhtémoc Cárdenas's campaign is, among other things, an extraordinary synthesis of the democratizing process in Mexico that, crushed with homicidal fury in 1968, began again with expressions of solidarity in 1985, and organized itself with the elections of 1988."[12]

"In a brief lapse of time," wrote Monsiváis, "new words have been energetically appropriated to the national vocabulary, terms previously only used rhetorically: *the need for change, the democratic will, civil society, participation.* Now you hear them wherever you go, and respect for the vote is, for the first time, a real national cause....What began as a mere verbal demand ('the urgency of change'), even though it may still be part of a nebulous goal, has lead to a great national novelty: the exercise of the consciousness of rights."[13] Monsiváis was delighted with the change in the vocabulary of the Left: "the Left opted for a change in terms, and where it once said *revolution* today the word *democracy* appears."[14]

With the experience of the Cárdenas campaign, Monsiváis modified and broadened his idea of civil society to include the end of the PRI's political monopoly and the creation of genuine political parties and real citizens. Alluding to Franz Kafka's famous story "The Cockroach," Monsiváis wrote, "Now on the seventh of July, the instantaneous common place has become the national truth: this is a new country. Something unforeseen and magnificent has happened here. Gregory Samsa woke up and was surprised to find that he had been transformed into a citizen, and all his neighbors had as well." Monsiváis continued, "If the PRI is defeatable, then citizens can really exist." But now that the PRI appeared to be vulnerable, the organization of political parties became all important. "What was looked upon with indifference becomes urgent: the existence of real political parties."[15]

In his short essays on the Cárdenas campaign, Monsiváis seemed to argue for an expansion of the idea of civil society to include the organization of political parties. Cuauhtémoc's campaign thus became simultaneously the expression of civil society, the movement of the political opposition, and the birth of a genuine political party. Insofar as civil society became an appendage of a political party, however it would lose its legitimacy as the social basis for a democratic political life. The tension or sometimes contradiction between civil society and the opposition political party would continue through the 1994 election.

Adolfo Gilly, a veteran of the revolutionary left, offered a different interpretation of the meaning of the Cárdenas campaign in an essay he wrote as the introduction to a collection of letters written to Cuauhtémoc Cárdenas by his supporters. Gilly, who left the Trotskyist PRT to join the leadership of the Cárdenas campaign, had both a political and psychological need to justify his own presence as a leftist in the nationalist camp. Gilly's appreciation of the Cuauhtémoc Cárdenas campaign was based on his understanding of the government of Lázaro Cárdenas in the 1930s. In Gilly's view, Lázaro Cárdenas's government in the 1930s was seen by the Mexican people, particularly by the rural people, as an expression of their own struggles during the period of the revolution and afterwards. The Cárdenas government was, in the minds of the Mexican people, the expression of an ideology of universal liberation, of socialism. In fact, of course, the Cárdenas regime was not socialism or anything of the kind. Rather it laid the basis for the development of Mexican capitalism and the authoritarian, corporativist state. Nevertheless, argued Gilly, though it was an illusion, many poor, rural people subjectively believed that Lázaro Cárdenas was fighting for a democratic, even socialist society.

Gilly said "the Left is correct that in that way Cardenism legitimated the Mexican state." "But the Left," said Gilly, "is wrong if it thinks that was only a top-down manipulation." In fact, the legitimation of the Cárdenas regime "came from the bottom-up," from the people.

Throughout the following years, as the Mexican state became more authoritarian and conservative, the Cardenist ideology survived among the people, particularly the rural people, according to Gilly. At the center of this ideology was peasant ownership of the land. "But not just the land by itself as a material reality, but also as a social reality: land, the *ejido*, the community as the center of a democratic-peasant reorganization of social life in its totality." Cardenism was a "rural Arcadia," a peasant utopia.

"That ideology of the poor," wrote Gilly, "was in effect a time bomb within the heart of the PRI." Cardenism, said Gilly, was a kind of Theology of Liberation within the state-party. "During this whole long period," wrote Gilly, "which covers five decades of this century, Cardenism was a kind of secret and hidden political identity of the masses."

When Cuauhtémoc Cárdenas launched the Democratic Current, and later the National Democratic Front, he struck the chord that resonated so deeply within the Mexican people. His very name spoke to that communitarian, democratic, socialist utopia which still inspired so many Mexicans after so many years. The Cárdenas campaign blew on the embers of the old Mexican Revolution of 1910-1940, and Cuauhtémoc's breath brought forth flames of discontent. Cuauhtémoc set off the time bomb.

Gilly claimed that the Left had never been able to understand Cardenism. He said that Cardenism, "acted as a vaccination against the penetration of lefist socialism, from which the Left deduced, on the one hand, that Cardenism was its competitor, and on the other hand that the poor did not want socialism. When, in fact, what they did not want was the doctrinal socialism that the left brought them, or they did not want that socialism expressed as a break not founded on their experience, with their earlier political identity."[16] So, when the Left—including Gilly himself—entered the Cárdenas campaign, for the first time in 70 years, its politics coincided with the latent socialist intuitions of the masses.

These two interpretations, Monsiváis's view of the Cárdenas campaign as the burgeoning of civil society and Gilly's understanding of the Cárdenas campaign as the rebirth of a political ideal rooted in a rural, democratic, socialist utopia, both get at certain elements of the Cárdenas phenomenon. In the Cárdenas campaign of 1988, peasant discontent joined with the modern demand for civil rights and political democracy to create a powerful political movement.

Still, there are other elements that both Monsiváis and Gilly fail to discuss that are equally important. First is the role of Cárdenas as a traditional *caudillo*, a political leader who derived his power from his father's name and a lifetime spent in the political establishment. Cárdenas exercised an enormous influence over the peasants not only because he represented the tradition of the *ejido* and peasant communalism, but also because he was the kind of political boss to whom, for decades and centuries, peasants have been forced to defer.

This is not to say that Cuauhtémoc was a hypocrite or a manipulator, for he appears to have been sincere in his populist views. Rather the reality is that the two aspects of Cárdenas' influence, his role as the embodiment of the peasant ideal and his role as *caudillo* are inseparable. *Caudillos*, even reactionary *caudillos*, have often appealed to the peasants' communal values and put themselves forward as representatives of the peasants' own collective traditions. One might even say that the lesson of the Mexican Revolution is that *caudillos* are capable of leading plebeian, democratic, and even quasi-socialist movements, but do so to install in power a ruling class whose interests are altogether different from those of the peasants they lead. Peasants, by virtue of their rural existence and diverse economic roles, seldom exercise an independent role in politics. If the peasants had to wait 50 years for the appearance of Cuauhtémoc, it is because they were unable to create their own political leadership or to find a better leadership in the form of a working-class, socialist movement.

The second and even more important point about the Cárdenas campaign of 1988 is that, with the exception of the petroleum workers—the working-class sector was virtually absent. Certainly millions of workers supported and voted for Cárdenas, the employed and the unemployed, from school teachers to factory workers. Those workers, however, supported Cárdenas as citizens, not as workers, union members, or activists in working class political parties. By and large, the Cárdenas campaign did not organize or appeal to the electorate as workers, but rather as democratic citizens.

Nor did the working class demand an independent voice. The technocratic counter-revolution begun in the de la Madrid administration had savaged the workers. Since the summer of 1982, Mexican workers had been beaten down in fight after fight, their factories closed, their unions destroyed, their contracts ripped up or rewritten. The police had been used to attack unions, occupy workplaces, attack and break strikes. The Mexican labor movement, which had never been very independent politically, had by the 1980s been almost completely subjected to the PRI.[17]

The attacks on the labor movement had had momentous political repercussions. The Mexican socialist parties never found a strategy to lead the labor movement as it was demolished by de la Madrid. Nor were they ideologically well prepared to defend and preserve an independent role for the workers. The working-class parties had a long tradition of subordination of the old Cardenism. It had taken the Left years to begin to struggle free of its Stalinist and Cardenist subordination to the Mexican state. When 1988 came, the Left was utterly unprepared to sort out the meaning of this new Cardenism. Consequently, when the Mexican Socialist Party (PMS) entered the National Democratic Front, it did not represent an independent working class attitude toward the electoral contest, but rather tended to dissolve itself into the Cardenist movement, a process which became complete a year later with the formation of the Party of the Democratic Revolution.

Cárdenas's name and Muñoz Ledo's cadres became the crucial factor in leading and organizing the opposition, in part because the working class failed to present any alternative. It would not be far wrong to suggest that the absence of the working class as an important factor in the election, was largely responsible for both the importance of the peasantry and civil society.

Cárdenas's name proved, in any case, to be enough to create the biggest electoral movement in modern Mexican history, and as most observers agreed, on July 7, 1988 Cárdenas won the presidential election. But he would not become president.

The results of the July 6, 1988 election were supposed to be posted almost immediately, thanks to a new computer system. But there had been a glitch, said the election authorities. Technical problems. The computers went down, and when they came back on-line Carlos Salinas de Gortari had won with just over 50 percent of the vote.

The "alchemists," the local PRI officials charged with counting the vote and "getting it right," worked hurriedly to bring local polling place results into line with the official computers' national results. PRI loyalists, desperately worried about their jobs, stayed up all night, dumping ballot boxes, marking ballots and stuffing new boxes. The next morning, election officials, also PRI members, quickly announced that local counts coincided with the national results. Immediately, the ballot boxes and ballots were impounded and placed under Mexican Army guard.

For months after the July election, Mexican citizens stumbled upon the ashes of burned-up ballot boxes and ballots in back alleys, or came upon bags of blank ballots left in garbage dumps. A few years later, as a result of a deal reached between the PRI and the PAN, the Mexican Congress permitted the impounded ballots to be burned. The evidence of fraud went up in smoke, an offering to the ancient gods in the Mexican heavens who protect *caciques*, *caudillos* and one-party states.

The National Democratic Front (FND) and the rest of the democratic opposition in Mexico denounced the election as "cybernetic fraud." The Mexican people themselves expressed tremendous anger and resentment. From one end of the country to the other, angry voters organized protest demonstrations, marched through the streets, seized city halls, and blocked highways. In many areas there were violent conflicts between protesters and the police, leaving a number dead. For a few days in mid-July of 1988 Mexico seemed on the brink of a national upheaval.

6

CARLOS SALINAS AND THE TECHNOCRATIC COUNTER-REVOLUTION

As president, Carlos Salinas was a kind of Zapata in reverse. Salinas took from the poor and gave to the rich at an unprecedented rate. The rise to power of Carlos Salinas represented a kind of counter-revolution within the Mexican government and the Institutional Revolutionary Party (PRI).[1] Between 1982 and 1994, Miguel de la Madrid, Salinas, and their followers, transformed the state-party and its relations with Mexican society. Under their leadership, the PRI abandoned its revolutionary nationalist ideology, revamped its old corporativist structure, and gave up its protectionist economic development model for the panacea of free trade. Some have argued that the counter-revolution of the 1980s was as important as the reorganization of Mexico under Cárdenas in the 1930s.[2]

How did this counter-revolution take place? The process has little of the romance of rebellion. There are no Pancho Villas here. It is the story of the victory of number-crunchers and pencil-pushers over more traditional politicians. The hothouse of the technocratic counter-revolution was the Ministry of Programming and Budget, Secretaría de Programación y Presupuesto (SPP), which during the 1970s and 1980s succeeded in taking control of the Mexican government. State bankers carried out the revolution from above,

101

over the heads of the old style *políticos* and local *caciques*. The colorless bureaucrats and planners of SPP gradually extended their influence until President de la Madrid succeeded in taking power in 1982.

President Echeverría actually laid the basis for the technocratic counter-
revolution, a development he did not intend or foresee, and would certainly
have opposed. In the early 1970s, he bought up and nationalized a variety of
firms and industries, vastly expanding the state sector. To administer the state
corporations, he found he needed global economic plans and he turned to the
PRI's think-tank, the Institute of Political, Economic and Social Studies
(IEPES), to develop them. IEPES thus became an incubator of the technocratic elite, and many of the future cabinet members and cadres of the de la
Madrid and Salinas administrations developed there.

President José López Portillo inherited from Echeverría the state industries and the new need for economic planning. To carry out this function,
López Portillo created a powerful new agency, the Ministry of Programming
and Budget (SPP) in December 1976 under social democrat Carlos Tello.
López Portillo also created a National Planning System to produce plans for
economic and social development. In 1979, future president Miguel de la Madrid became head of SPP and responsible for drawing up its plans. He also
brought on board his former student Carlos Salinas to create the National
Planning System.

De la Madrid, Salinas and the other planners who inhabited IEPES and
later SPP, constituted a distinct technocratic elite which differed from earlier
generations of Mexican government officials. The technocrats came almost
exclusively from upper-class backgrounds, and were often of European de-
scent. They had been born in the Federal District, and their parents were involved in business, the professions, or the higher levels of government. Most
of the members of this group were young men, and a few women, who had
done their undergraduate studies at the National Autonomous University of
Mexico (UNAM), or increasingly, at private schools such as Autonomous
Technological Institute of Mexico (ITAM) or the Colegio de Mexico. After-
ward they went to the United States to do their graduate work at elite private
universities such as Stanford, Princeton, Yale or Harvard. While a number of
the technocrats were lawyers, their preferred areas of study were economics
and administration. After studying management or banking in the United
States, these young men and women had become convinced by business
schools of the wisdom of the free market and free trade.

Unlike many earlier PRI leaders, this new generation of technocrats did not work their way up either through the mass political organizations, such as unions, or through the technical organizations of the party, but rather came into the party at the top, working in the IEPES think-tank or in the shadow cabinet of the president-elect.[3] Half of the de la Madrid and Salinas cabinets had worked in IEPES.

These technocratic counter-revolutionaries who worked within the government, primarily as financiers or economic planners, came to share fundamental social values. They believed in neoliberal—that is conservative—capitalist economic values such as privatization of the economy and integration into the world market. They had faith in technocratic methods, in state "rectorship" or regulation of the economy to help achieve capitalist success. The technocrats were extremely elitist and inherently undemocratic. They believed that the science of economics was the basis of decision making, and that they as the scientists should make the decisions. They knew what was best for the people. The technocrats were committed above all to bureaucratic and economic efficiency as the highest goals.[4] Finally, the technocratic elite was also a political vanguard which aimed to take control of the Party and the state in order to transform their own society and their relations with the world order.

Precisely because of the debt crisis of the 1980s, the technocrats had been in regular contact with New York bankers and international organizations, such as the World Bank and the International Monetary Fund (IMF). The Mexican planners had come to share, with the metropolitan financiers, the program of privatization which the bankers advocated and their institutions demanded. The Mexican planners were convinced of the benefits of an industrialization program led by foreign investment and committed to production for export.

When the time came, the technocrats acted. De la Madrid, Salinas and their *camarillas* used the SPP, and the Ministry of Programming and Budget, as the power base for their conquest of the Mexican state. With the support of President López Portillo, the technocrats cut off the funds of their rivals in other ministries. In doing so, they debilitated patronage powers of their opponents and thereby destroyed their political machines.[5]

Salinas, who became head of SPP in 1982, was prototypical of the technocrats in his background, education and political experience. Salinas was born into the Mexican power elite. His father, Raúl Salinas Lozano, had served as Minister of Industry and Commerce in the Adolfo López Mateos administration and as a Senator from Nuevo León. His mother, Margarita de Gortari Carvajal, was a co-founder of the Mexican Association of Women Economists. Carlos Salinas himself grew up on the family estate in Agualeguas, Nuevo León, and would have had an idyllic upbringing, except for a horrible childhood incident. At the age of three, while playing with his father's shotgun, Salinas accidentally shot and killed the family maid.

From adolescence on, Salinas prepared himself for power. Unlike his bohemian brother Raúl, who hung out with the Mexican Maoists, Carlos relentlessly pursued his career. He entered the National University (UNAM) in 1966 and wrote his 1969 undergraduate thesis on "Agriculture, Industrialization and Employment: the Case of Mexico," receiving an honorable mention in the economics contest. While at UNAM Salinas became a favorite student of law professor and future president, Miguel de la Madrid.

De la Madrid was one of the leaders of the new generation of technocrats, who adopted American capitalism as their religion and Harvard Business School as their Mecca. A ready convert to the new faith, Carlos Salinas did his graduate work at Harvard, earning two master's degrees, one in administration and another in economics, as well as a doctorate in economics. While at Harvard, Salinas established contacts not only with American academics, but also with a future generation of U.S. politicians and corporate leaders.

As part of his graduate studies, Salinas lived briefly with a peasant family in the village of Tetla and studied social welfare and political control in the Mexican countryside. While finishing his doctorate, Salinas worked as professor of economics at the National University, at the conservative Autonomous Technological Institute (ITAM) and then at the Center for Latin American Monetary Studies.

Bypassing a long and tedious governmental career, Salinas used his family connections to begin his professional life near the top of the political pyramid. In 1971, his father's friend, Treasury Minister Hugo B. Margain, made Salinas director of public finance. Later, when Salinas's former professor Miguel de la Madrid became treasury minister, Salinas became his right-hand man. Next, President de la Madrid appointed Salinas, then only 34 years old, to head the Ministry of Planning and Budget (SPP). By the early 1980s, Salinas was the head of his own *camarilla* or political clique, known as the "SPP group" or the "Harvard group."

The Mexican Constitution prohibits presidential re-election, and as his six-year term came to an end in 1988, de la Madrid chose his protegé Salinas as his successor. But the PRI split, and Salinas found himself, surprisingly, running in a real election against Cuauhtémoc Cárdenas. While Salinas attended the usual rallies of party loyalists bussed in by political bosses, Cárdenas filled the streets and plazas of Mexico in what was perhaps the greatest political campaign in Mexico since Francisco Madero's in 1910.

Cuauhtémoc Cárdenas won a plurality in the election, but the PRI and de la Madrid installed the usurper Salinas in the presidency. The PRI had never lost an election, and de la Madrid, Salinas and the technocratic elite did not intend to let the voters' unfortunate decision turn them out of power. The PRI-government declared Salinas the winner, and in January 1989, Salinas assumed office.

The election results made it clear that while de la Madrid and Salinas had taken over the PRI, the state-party had been losing its hold on the electorate. The 1988 election was a debacle for the PRI, a crushing and humiliating defeat for Salinas. In Mexico City, Salinas and the PRI suffered a rout at the hands of Cuauhtémoc Cárdenas of the National Democratic Front.

Installed in office by fraud, Salinas recognized the immediate necessity of rebuilding the base of the Party, particularly among rural communities and the urban poor. As Salinas said at that time, "We must seek new bases of support for the Party…We must convince them to participate."[6] Salinas had given a great deal of thought to the problem of revamping the PRI's system of political support among the poor. In his doctoral dissertation, later published as a book titled *Production and Political Participation in the Countryside*, Salinas criticized the Mexican social welfare system for its failure to work with and develop local leaders. He pointed out that lacking local support, the PRI's political organization had been severely weakened. Salinas argued that if the state worked with natural leaders in the countryside it could both carry out more effective social welfare, and build a base of political support.[7] In that idea was the germ of the organization that Salinas decided to call *Solidaridad*.

Salinas's first official presidential act, on December 2, 1988, was to outline the design and goals of the Programa Nacional de Solidaridad or PRONASOL. The word "solidarity" gained currency in Mexico after the earthquake of 1985 when the citizenry organized to carry out rescue and reconstruction in the face of the state's ineffectiveness. Volunteer organizations, which sprang out of that experience, used the word "solidarity" in their names. By appropriating the name *Solidaridad*, Salinas had reached into civil society and snatched away its identity. At the same time he attempted to create for *Solidaridad* the image of an extension of civil society.

Salinas said that he wanted PRONASOL to reach the 48 percent of Mexicans who lived below the official poverty line, and especially the 19 percent who lived in extreme poverty. Salinas claimed to reject "paternalism, populism, clientelism, or political conditionality in the improvement of the welfare of the population in poverty." Salinas promised that all PRONASOL projects would be managed honestly and efficiently. "PRONASOL would lead to justice and democracy."[8]

In the past, in keeping with its revolutionary nationalist ideology and its corporatist structure, the PRI had created national programs aimed at entire social classes, programs such as the Mexican Institute of Social Security (IMSS) which was the national workers' health plan, or the workers' housing program (INFONAVIT). PRONASOL, however, rejected mass or class programs and redefined the Mexican people: they were no longer members of social classes but rather citizens and consumers.[9] Under PRONASOL, social welfare was targeted to specific groups, supposedly the neediest.

Salinas's PRONASOL appealed to the civil society's desire for autonomy and independence. The emphasis in PRONASOL was on self-help, and PRONASOL officials claimed that the new social welfare program would lead to decentralization thus furthering democracy and citizen involvement. Through a process called co-participation, PRONASOL projects were to be organized and managed jointly by local communities and the state. From early on, Salinas and PRONASOL officials made it clear that they were not only willing to bypass PRI state organizations, but also willing, and even anxious, to work with independent community and peasant organizations. In 1989, PRONASOL showed a desire to work with the leftist organizations and their community and peasant groups, who would be permitted to keep their own organizations. By 1990, however, those who wanted to continue to receive PRONASOL funds had to form local PRONASOL groups.

As president, Salinas personally oversaw the creation and development of PRONASOL, together with the head of the PRI, Luis Donaldo Colosio. Salinas originally put PRONASOL under the control of SPP, the technocrats' headquarters, but he chose ideological leftists to administer the program. The first coordinator of the Consultative Council of PRONASOL, the organization's think-tank, was Carlos Tello, a nationalist and a social democrat. He was followed in that position by Rolando Cordera, a former member of PSUM. Carlos Rojas, a former Maoist with many contacts in the Left and so-

cial movements, became PRONASOL's director. The technical director of
the program was Raúl Salinas, the older brother of the president, who had
spent his youth consorting with Maoist radicals. Adolfo Orive Berlinguer and
Gustavo Gordillo, two of the leaders of the Maoist Popular Politics tendency,
were also recruited by PRONASOL.[10]

Within the first few years, PRONASOL created a wide variety of organizations designed to provide funds for and involve various groups: from
businessmen to Indians and women. PRONASOL distributed most of it
funds as federal block grants to state and municipal governments; negotiation
over the control of these funds provided the basis of PRONASOL's power.
PRONASOL used that power both to build its own political base of support,
and to discipline PRI governors, mayors and other officials.

PRONASOL's personnel represented a remarkable fusion of bureaucrats and social activists. While SEDESOL's program officers tended to be
typical government accountants, PRONASOL's *promotores*, or community
leaders, were frequently former leftists from the Mexican Communist Party
(PMC, PSUM, PMS) or from former Maoist groups, such as Mass Line or
the Organization of the Revolutionary Left.[11] Not since Lázaro Cárdenas'
government of the 1930s, had a president succeeded in incorporating so
many leftists into the government.[12]

The leftist organizers had worked for years in labor unions, poor urban
neighborhoods and in the countryside with indigenous peasants. They had
shown a willingness to endure hardships and had won the confidence of local
communities. The radical organizers had a familiarity with the social conflicts in the community as well as the political sophistication to sort them out.
The leftists were invaluable in identifying the "natural leaders" of the communities and linking them with PRONASOL.

Through the leftists, PRONASOL was able to make connections to the
myriad non-governmental organizations that had appeared in 1985 and
which had come to identify themselves as civil society. "Those NGOs that
overwhelmed the government after the 1985 earthquake and during the 1988
elections became the basis of PRONASOL," explained one of its local organizers. "We turned these organizations into instruments of change, into an engine driving our efforts."[13] Some non-governmental organizations and
grassroots organizations maintained their independence, but Salinas succeeded in capturing many through PRONASOL.

When PRONASOL negotiated an agreement with a local community,
it generally created *comités de vecinos* or neighbors' committees, in which

women played a major role.[14] While PRONASOL talked about co-participation, this generally meant that SEDESOL and PRONASOL officials controled the budget, while local community leaders did the actual work. Ostensibly created as a poverty program, PRONASOL's funds did not go to the poorest neighborhoods or rural communties. Money generally went to communities deemed politically crucial to the rebuilding of the PRI. In particular, PRONASOL targeted areas where Cárdenas and the FDN had beaten Salinas and the PRI in the 1988 election.

The experience of the Committee for Popular Defense (CDP) in northwestern Durango provides the most important example of the way Salinas built PRONASOL, because it set a pattern for PRONASOL's work with other leftist and independent organizations over the next several years.[15] Founded by Maoist student activists in the 1970s, the CDP sent colonists to a number of cities and states, mostly in northern Mexico. The Maoist organizers worked with urban squatters to organize land seizures, and then negotiated with the PRI. The government conceded land on which the CDP eventually organized over a dozen *colonias* or poor, suburban neighborhoods of the city of Durango.

A Maoist cadre made the principal decisions for the CDP, which was never a democratic organization or movement. Those decisions were handed down to local leaders who had the job of convincing the residents of the *colonias* and eventually producing a concensus. During the 1970s and 1980s the CDP both organized protests and negotiated agreements with local, state and federal governments for loans and services such as running water, sewers, and electricity. The CDP in the 1980s had 1,100 community activists in the city of Durango and was the dominant political force in several neighborhoods with over 70,000 residents. The CDP also had a peasant organization and a street vendors' union.

When Cuauhtémoc Cárdenas ran for president in 1988, the CDP joined his campaign. But when Cárdenas lost the election, the CDP quickly moved away from him. Meanwhile Salinas and Rojas, then the heads of PRONASOL, began making overtures to the Maoist Left. In February 1989, the CDP became one of the first leftist community-based groups to sign an agreement with Salinas and PRONASOL, only a few months after the new president took office. The agreement was the first in a series of deals between PRONASOL and the CDP providing millions of *pesos* for a variety of social services, public works projects and CDP-owned businesses.

After signing on with PRONASOL, the CDP publicly broke with the PRD and stopped criticizing the PRI. A few months later, Salinas and Rojas helped the CDP and other Maoists form a new political party, the Labor Party or PT. The PT, while ostensibly independent, became another one of the PRI's puppet leftist parties.

Salinas personally, or sometimes his brother Raúl, or Rojas or Colosio, negotiated deals with leftists and local community groups in dozens of other cities in which they exchanged economic resources, usually basic social services, for political support mostly inside the PRI, but sometimes through the PT or some other puppet party.

As PRONASOL proved successful, Salinas increased its budget and its power. These resources were not enough to end poverty in Mexico, but were sufficient to rebuild the PRI's political base. PRONASOL's budget rose from US$680 million in 1989 to over US$2.5 billion in 1993. The total budget for PRONASOL programs, both state and federal, was about US$12 billion in its first five years. By November of 1993, Salinas claimed that PRONASOL had 150,000 committees, and that they were operating in more than 95 percent of Mexico's 2,378 municipalities. Hundreds of thousand of Mexican children received PRONASOL scholarships to attend primary and secondary schools. Tens of thousands of deeds were handed out to urban and rural squatters. Thousands of kilometers of local roads were paved. Telephone and postal services were extended to thousands of isolated villages. In Cárdenas' home state of Michoacán, PRONASOL established 10,000 committees encompassing 80 percent of the state's population.

In his third State of the Nation address, Salinas proclaimed, "Solidarity is the democratic reform of the popular bases throughout our country that gives a new dimension to our nationalism. It provides the stability and social peace that we deserve; it has created new ties between institutions and public officials, ties that are part of the state reform that I proposed to bring government closer to the people."[16] In truth, Salinas had overhauled the PRI machine.

In no way was this new Mexican state more democratic, and in many respects it was less so. Under Salinas, Mexican presidentialism was strengthened, for it was Salinas, and Colosio who controled the resources of PRONASOL, bypassing the governors and mayors, and overriding the PRI and its mass organizations when necessary. PRONASOL succeeded in recapturing many—but by no means all—of the independent groups which had grown up in the 1970s and 1980s. Salinas' slogan might have been: Where civil society is—there the state shall be.

But Salinas' long-term political objective was the implementation of the Harvard group's economic program: privatization of state-owned industry, encouragement of foreign investment, and the creation of an industrial export platform for the multinationals and a new Mexican corporate elite. The North American Free Trade Agreement (NAFTA) would simply ratify that project. To carry out that program, Salinas realized he would have to break the power of the labor unions.

The PRI had controled Mexico's labor unions for decades. Since the 1940s, Fidel Valázquez, the ninety-odd-year-old head of the Mexican Confederation of Workers (CTM), had cooperated with the state and employers to crush independent union movements, and could be expected to continue to do so under normal circumstances. But Salinas was proposing to sell off virtually all of the state industries and put them in the hands of private Mexican or foreign investors. Such a vast reorganization would threaten both the union bureaucrats' political power and perquisites of office; the new management could be expected to break unions, rewrite contracts, and possibly layoff workers or cut wages. If the officials began to organize politically, or if the workers began to strike in defense of their jobs and wages, they could create economic or political problems which would jeopardize Salinas' plan.

Salinas struck first, against the Petroleum Workers Union (STPRM). The move was partly motivated by politics. The Petroleum Workers Union leader, Joaquín Hernández Galicia, known as "La Quina," had supported the Cárdenas campaign in 1988. Salinas feared a continued alliance between Cárdenas and the powerful La Quina. But much more was involved.

Since Lázaro Cárdenas nationalized Royal Dutch Shell and the Standard Oil Company in the 1930s, PEMEX had not only been a state firm but also a symbol and shrine of Mexican nationalism. Salinas dared not raise the issue of privatizing PEMEX because the oil company held a sacred place in the national consciousness. PEMEX was the core of the whole complex of about 1,500 state firms, and constituted the foundation of Mexico's national industries. As long as PEMEX resisted, they would all resist, and Salinas would be stymied.

Oil meant everything in Mexico: wealth, power, history, and national identity. Oil paid the bills in Mexico. Oil was Mexico's most important export, and Mexico depended upon petroleum production to pay off its huge debt to U.S. banks. Salinas could not afford any interruption in oil production, or his plans would be ruined. At the center of all of these matters was the Petroleum Workers Union (STPRM), historically the nation's most important labor organization. In order to carry out his economic plans, Salinas decided he would have to break the Petroleum Workers Union. The union's leader, La Quina, notorious for his corruption, provided Salinas with a justification for repression.

In a sudden raid on January 10, 1989, police and soldiers, blasting away with bazookas and automatic weapons, attacked the offices and homes of the leaders of the Petroleum Workers Union and arrested over 30 top officials, including La Quina. The state accused La Quina and the other union leaders of weapons trafficking and murder, because of the death of one policeman in the raid. The dead police officer turned out to be a man murdered two days before in Chihuahua, whose corpse had been deposited at La Quina's doorstep by the police. The weapons trafficking charge came from the union's recent purchase of a number of automatic weapons. La Quina and dozens of other union officials were subsequently tried, convicted, and jailed.[17]

With La Quina out of the way, Salinas imposed on the Petroleum Workers Union a new leader, Sebastián Guzmán Cabrera. Guzmán Cabrera was a former associate of La Quina's who was also implicated in all the former corruption, but he was a man loyal to Salinas. Guzmán Cabrera and PEMEX subsequently negotiated a new contract which resulted in tens of thousands of permanent layoffs, the elimination of the old labor union agreement and the writing of a new "more flexible" contract. In addition, PEMEX removed many technical and professional workers from the union.

A month later, apparently to give the impression of evenhandedness, Salinas also arrested Eduardo Legorreta Chauvet, chief executive of Operadora de Bolsa, Mexico's largest brokerage house, for fraud in the 1987 Mexican stock market crash. The Legorreta family had been the state-party's bankers since the 1920s, and the arrest of Eduardo came as a shock to business. Salinas might be a pro-business conservative, but he evidently harbored no sentimental affections for the old-line Mexican bankers and businessmen. Unhappy with the capitalist class he had inherited, Salinas would proceed to build a better bourgeoisie through privatization.

When a teachers strike broke out in April of 1989, Salinas removed the old union boss, Carlos Jongitud Barrios. Co-opting the feminists' demands for more visible female leadership, Salinas awarded PRI-loyalist Elba Esther Gordillo top spot in the teachers' union.

111

Next it was the miners. On August 20, 1989 the president sent 5,000 Mexican Army troops to occupy the mining town of Cananea, Sonora to prevent protests over the privatization of the copper mine. The courts simultaneously declared the state-owned company bankrupt and sold it to private Mexican and foreign investors. The miners courageously resisted, but in the end, Salinas won. Many miners were laid off or had their contract rewritten along more flexible lines to please the new private management. The last president to send the army to Cananea had been Porfiro Díaz when he crushed the anarchist strike there in 1906.

The attacks on the Petroleum Workers Union and the Metal and Mine Workers Union at Cananea were powerful blows against Mexican workers, and their impact went far beyond those unions and workers immediately involved. Much like Ronald Reagan's destruction of the Professional Air Traffic Controllers (PATCO) in the United States, the attack on the miners and petroleum workers was also meant as a warning to other unions. Salinas' actions demonstrated that he would not tolerate resistance either from the unions and their officials nor from workers in the public sector.

Salinas' assault on the state workers' unions also served as an example. Private employers in a variety of industries immitated the president and attacked the unions which represented their employees. In some cases, unions were destroyed and labor union contracts were eliminated. In others, the contract was rewritten, destroying many of the workers' historic gains. Job descriptions, seniority, and protection of working conditions were replaced by new, more "flexible" language.

Workers at Modelo Brewery, Tornel Rubber Company, Ford, Volkswagen, and at many other workplaces stood up and fought back against their employers in really heroic strikes. But the Salinas government and the employers crushed the union movement unmercifully. In the most notorious case at the Ford Plant in Cuautitlán, Mexico, the state-controled CTM union and Ford joined together and put 200 armed thugs in the plant to rough up the Ford workers. Many workers were beaten, and one worker, Cleto Nigno, was assassinated. At the Volkswagen plant in Puebla, the company fired the entire workforce of more than 10,000 workers.

Salinas did not always use violence against the labor movement, and in many instances he preferred to proffer the blandishments of power. For example, in the case of the Telephone Workers Union (STRM) at the state-owned Mexican Telephone Company (TELMEX), Salinas preferred flattery to force. The force already exerted against the petroleum workers and the miners made clear the possible repercussions of non-cooperation.[18]

In the 1980s, the PRI's technocrats saw telecommunications, including satellites and cellular phones, as key to the integration of Mexico with the United States and world economy, and also crucial for the creation of a modern national economy. Telecommunications linked not only the telephones and faxes, but also the computers of international banking and manufacturing networks. As presidential candidate Salinas asserted in October 1987, "Telecommunications will become the cornerstone of the program to modernize Mexico's economy."[19]

Salinas intended to sell off TELMEX, the state-owned Mexican Telephone Company, but he was worried about possible opposition from Francisco Hernández Juárez, the leader of the Mexican Telephone Workers Union. The union had a reputation for being relatively democratic and historically militant. Opposition from the union could scare off Mexican and foreign investors, or create political problems that might impede Salinas's broader plans for privatization. Rather than sending in the army, Salinas courted Hernández Juárez.

Hernández Juárez, reportedly a member of the Maoist Proletarian Line, had become the leader of the telephone workers back in 1976. In April of that year, a strike by women telephone operators led to the ousting of the old *charros*, as well as the election of a more militant and democratic leadership headed by the young radical Hernández Juárez. With the leadership of Hernández Juárez and the militancy of the young women operators, between 1976 and 1987, the STRM carried out five strikes at TELMEX, mostly for higher wages. On each occasion, the government invoked Article 112 of the Federal Law of General Routes of Communication, under which federal troops occupied the telephone facilities and forced the striking telephone workers to return to their jobs.[20]

Unable to make gains through the use of the union's economic power, Hernández Juárez, the Telephone Workers Union, and other leaders, turned to politics, and attempted to use the workers' political power to win concessions from the state-management of the industry. Because of the historic weakness of opposition parties, Hernández Juárez began a process of negotiation with the PRI. The Telephone Workers Union had some leverage because of the centrality of their industry to the PRI's development plans.

Salinas had wooed Hernández Juárez even before the presidential election with promises of making him an important figure in the coming period.

Hernández Juárez, formerly a political independent, declared himself "a PRI supporter by conviction and after consideration," and supported Salinas de Gortari in the 1988 election. For its support the union was given two federal deputy seats in the Mexican Congress. Hernández Juárez's support for Salinas represented a significant shift toward incorporation into the new administration and the PRI.

By early 1989, Salinas was vaguely suggesting that TELMEX should be privatized. The STRM, at first, resisted suggestions of privatizing the corporation, as well as management's attempts to modify the collective bargaining agremeent. The examples of the police attack on the Petroleum Workers Union and the Mexican Army's occupation of Cananea, however, must surely have been intimidating to Hernández Juárez and the Telephone Workers Union, and must have succeeded in helping Hernández Juárez to make a decision about the union's future policies.

We may never know exactly what happened, but at some point in early 1989, President Salinas seemed to have made a deal with Hernández Juárez. Hernández Juárez would insure that the STRM would not oppose privatization and would accept changes in the contract. In exchange, Salinas would guarantee that TELMEX would not layoff employees. Moreover, Salinas would praise Hernández Juárez as an exemplary modern union official, and put him foward as the leader of a new union federation. At the same time, Hernández Juárez and the STRM would work closely with the government's new National Solidarity Program (PRONASOL or Solidaridad), the anti-poverty program headed by Luis Donaldo Colosio. In any case, that was how the agreement worked out in practice.

After April of 1989 when Salinas and Hernández Juárez reached agreement, the path was smoothed for both privatization of TELMEX and the writing of a modern flexible labor agreement. The new flexible labor agreement came first. On April 14, 1989, the STRM leaders signed the first "Cooperation Agreement," (*Convenio de Concertación*), in the industry, which accepted changes in working conditions and permitted management greater flexibility: workers could be assigned to different steps of the production process, in many cases, transferred to different departments and jobs, and the company could hire temporary employees as it needed. "As a result, 57 departmental agreements were replaced with one single pay-scale set for 40 levels, 31 specialties and 134 categories."[21] TELMEX and the union also reached agreement on a reduction in force through early retirements, voluntary resignations and termination of temporary employees. But TELMEX remained a state enterprise.

Salinas moved obliquely toward the privatization of TELMEX, concentrating the discussion on a program for the modernization of the company, which he linked to the modernization of Mexico, to social justice, and to political reform. The nationalization of TELMEX could not be justified on the grounds that the company was unprofitable. Unlike some nationalized industries, TELMEX was not an economic failure by any means. TELMEX sales in the 1980s exceeded one billion dollars annually. In 1988, TELMEX earned more than 200 million dollars, and its net profit was over 20 percent, but because the state used TELMEX's profits for its general operating expenses, sufficient funds were not set aside for modernization, a process that would require billions.

Salinas never claimed the company was a failure. Rather, he argued that the only way to modernize the telephone company was to privatize it. On September 18, 1989, Salinas laid out plans for a vast expansion and modernization of the telephone service involving new technologies. The changes would require an investment of $10 billion from 1989 to 1994. The Mexican press interpreted this goal as indicating that Salinas intended to privatize TELMEX, since both economically and technically the changes were beyond the capacity of the state-owned company.

Two days later, on September 20, 1989, Minister of Communications and Transport, Andrés Caso Lombardo, accompanied by Hernández Juárez, announced the decision to privatize TELMEX. Hernández Juárez, who had once opposed privatization as detrimental to his union members' interests, now supported it, provided that workers not be fired and that the collective bargaining agreement (which had already been modified to make it more flexible) remained intact. Hernández Juárez said that it was better to accept this privatization, "than to wake up and hear the news that the company has already been closed or already sold, and we are terminated."[22]

The privatization plan ceded TELMEX to the private sector for 30 years, allowing foreign investors to control 49 percent of the capital. TELMEX was sold on December 9, 1989 for US$3.9 billion to a consortium made up of Grupo Carso, headed by Mexican Carlos Slim Helu, and also including: Southwestern Bell, the St. Louis based U.S. corporation, and France Cable et Radio, a subsidiary of France Telecom, Inc. That consortium acquired 51 percent of the voting shares of TELMEX for US$1,757.6 million. As part of the deal, the STRM, the Telephone Workers Union, acquired 4.4 percent of the non-voting shares of the new privatized TELMEX. The union was only able to finance its purchase of 466 million shares at 70 cents per share thanks to a loan from the Mexican Development Bank, NAFINSA, arranged by President Salinas. The government and the union advertised that telephone workers were now also "co-owners." In reality, the workers owned almost nothing.

For TELMEX stockholders, things generally went well, at least in the first year or two. Widely promoted in the United States by brokers and mutual funds, TELMEX stock became the most important stock traded on the Mexican stock market, and rose in value, at least until the crises of Chiapas in January 1994 and the assassination of Luis Donaldo Colosio in March of that year. For the public, service remained poor, prices went up and Mexico's phone service became the most expensive in the world.[23]

But Salinas' cooptation of Hernández Juárez and the Telephone Workers Union was not just a maneuver intended to carry out an economic program. The partnership between Salinas and Hernández Juárez had equally important political implications. With presidential patronage, Hernández Juárez became the leader of the "new-unionism" (neo-sindicalismo), which accepted privatization and flexibilty. With the encouragement of Salinas, Hernández Juárez led the telephone workers to join with the Mexican Electrical Workers Union (SME), the Teachers Union (SNTE), the Airline Pilots Union, and three smaller unions to form a new labor federation known as FESEBES (Federación de Sindicatos de Empresas de Bienes y Servicios Púbicos—The Federation of Unions of Firms of Public Goods and Services). As head of FESEBES, Hernández Juárez argued for a "closer connection between employers and workers through the unions."[24] Salinas and Hernández Juárez apparently hoped that FESEBES might displace the Confederation of Mexican Workers (CTM) as the dominant labor federation, but it never did.

Within a year or two, Salinas, through force, fear and flattery, had broken the spirit of the unions. The petroleum workers and the miners had been defeated, the government had kept control of the tumultuous teachers' union, and the telephone workers had been hoisted on to the privatization band wagon. Salinas turned then to his primary project, the transformation of the Mexican economy through privatization, foreign investment, and the creation of an export platform for the multinationals.

In many respects, the model for Salinas' economic policies could be found in Mexico's own *maquiladora* or border industry program. Mexico established the border industrialization zone in 1965, granting special tax breaks and other incentives to foreign corporations to establish businesses in Mexico. The zone took off in the 1970s, and by 1994, half a million workers were laboring for about $US4.50 per day in the 2,000 manufacturing and assembly plants along the northern border. Most of these *maquiladora* plants either have no labor unions or have unions controlled by the PRI, which mainly serve to control workers and keep wages low.

Multinational corporations such as General Motors, Zenith, and Sony own the majority of these plants. In some cases the *maquiladoras* were runaway shops, which fled the United States to seek lower wages in Mexico. In other cases, the plants were constructed in Mexico to avoid the more stringent enforcement of environmental or occupational health and safety laws in the United States or Canada. Often these plants were key to industrial production for U.S. corporations, particularly in electronics and auto parts. Zenith was the largest electronics employer in 1990 with about 13,800 workers at plants in Juárez, Reynosa, Matamoros, and Agua Prieta. But other electronics companies included Goldstar, Hitachi, Matsushita, Murata Erie, Philips, Sanyo, Sony, Thompson, Tocabi, and Toshiba.[25]

A key element in this kind of economic development program obviously was low wages. The 1982 devaluation of the peso cut Mexican workers' wages by nearly half, to about one-tenth of U.S. wages, with government determined to keep them there. In November of 1987, President de la Madrid had negotiated the Economic Soldarity Pact, which was supposed to stop inflation. The effect of the pact was to freeze workers' wages at the 1982 level. Salinas renewed the pact in August of 1988 and thereafter several more times, though now with the name Pact for Stability and Economic Growth (PECE).[26] The longevity of the PECE, testified to the weakness of the state-controlled labor movement and the strength of the government.

Low wages made Mexico extremely attractive to U.S. investors. Even four years before NAFTA, the U.S. investment in Mexico for 1990 reached $9.4 billion, the largest U.S. investment in any single Latin American country. U.S. investors were attracted by rates of return of 20.3 percent, the highest rate outside the Asian industrializing countries, which earned 25.9 percent.[27] For those making portfolio investments, the Mexican stock market brought "extraordinary rewards: in 1991, values on the stock exchange rose an average of 118 percent in dollar terms; two years later, they rose almost 49 percent."[28]

According to the Secretariat of Commerce and Industrial Promotion of Mexico (SECOFI), cumulative foreign investment in Mexico rose from about 10 billion in 1980 to over 50 billion in 1992.[29] U.S. corporations were not the only investors in Mexico by any means. There was also significant involvement by European, Japanese, and Korean companies. For example, in the early 1990s in the auto industry, Japan's Nissan Corporation, Germany's Volkswagen, United States' Ford Motor Company, each invested several hundred million in Mexico.[30] Through these billions of dollars worth of investments, foreign and particularly U.S. corporations, began to dominate the Mexican economy. By 1994, General Motors had a complex of 40 plants with 40,000 workers, making it the largest private employer in Mexico.

At the center of the whole project, however, was privatization and foreign investment. Salinas' great auction of the Mexican economy rapidly transformed Mexico's mixed economy into a model of private enterprise. In 1982, Mexico had 1,555 state-owned firms, but by 1992 only 217 remained.[31] The state industries which Salinas sold included TELMEX, the state telephone company, Aeromexico and Mexicana, the state airlines, and Altos Hornos de Mexico, a state steel mill.

In many cases, the state-owned firms were bought by foreign investors. Frequently, Mexican state-owned corporations were sold off to the close friends and political supporters of President Salinas. TELMEX, today estimated to be worth about one billion U.S. dollars, was sold to Salinas's friend, Carlos Slim.

Salinas and the technocrats in the PRI would also have liked to sell off PEMEX, the state-owned oil company, however, political opposition was too great. Yet under Salinas, Mexico began openly to invite foreign firms to invest in new petrochemical plants owned and operated by PEMEX. U.S. corporations became involved, as well, in oil exploration and drilling in Mexico.[32]

Salinas also changed Mexican agriculture. He pushed through Congress the changes in Article 27, which ended agrarian reform and permitted the privatization of *ejidal* lands, clearing the path for Mexican and foreign agri-business to create a modern agriculture system using chemical fertilizers, pump and pipe irrigation, tractors and combines—and without the trouble-some peasant. The changes in the *ejido* would speed up the break-up of small Mexican farms and drive former farmers into the labor market. Multinational agricultural corporations such as Anderson-Clayton, DeKalb, Northrup-King, and Pioneer had already moved into Mexican agriculture.

To raise the money to take advantage of Salinas' privatization program, Mexican capitalists had to combine their resources into new holding companies, conglomerates, and corporations. They created new stock brokerage houses, and expanded old ones. Mexican capitalists also sought new loans, including loans from U.S. banks. Morgran Guaranty Trust, for example, loaned $850 million to the Monterrey group's VISA holding company to purchase Bancomer. In many of these arrangements, Mexicans ceased to be the dominant stockholders, and control passed into the hands of U.S. corporations.[33]

Through the process of privatization, Carlos Salinas fundamentally reshaped the Mexican economy and its capitalist class. By selling off the state's copper mines, steel mills, airlines, and telephone company, Salinas virtually eliminated the once huge government sector. Rather than spreading the wealth among a broad layer of Mexican businessmen, Salinas promoted economic concentration by unloading the state industries on a handful of very wealthy people. Those individuals, and the corporations in which they were involved, formed monopolies which came to dominate the Mexican economy. Those investors were, moreover, a group closely associated with Salinas himself, and with other leaders of the dominant technocratic current within the PRI.

Under Salinas, Mexico experienced its gilded age of captains of industry and robber barons. Salinas' privatization not only led to an enormous concentration of wealth, but also brought about tremendous new economic inequalities. By 1994, Mexico had 24 new billionaires whose wealth was equal to that of the 24 million poorest Mexicans.[34]

By selling off the state-owned industries and inviting in foreign investors, Mexico lost whatever degree of national economic independence it once had. The Mexican economy became closely integrated into the economy of the United States, both through the *maquiladoras* and through other foreign investment and loans. Under Salinas, Mexico returned to the days of Porfirio Díaz: a nation ruled by a small elite tied to foreign banks and corporations.

The crowning achievement was Salinas' negotiation of the North American Free Trade Agreement, or NAFTA, uniting Canada, Mexico and the United States in one huge economic market. Ostensibly a free trade agreement, in reality NAFTA really gave multinationals the freedom and security they desired to combine U.S. capital, Canadian natural resources, and cheap Mexican labor. Remarkably, Salinas had done it all without a major upheaval. Despite the stolen election on which his presidency was based, Salinas ruled a stable Mexico, which was free from the kind of social turmoil that plagued Central and South America —until the Chiapas Rebellion.

7

PARTY OF THE DEMOCRATIC REVOLUTION: MEXICAN SOCIAL DEMOCRACY

Cuauhtémoc Cárdenas faced a difficult choice in 1988 when the PRI stole the election he had won. He might have attempted to lead a national movement to throw out the Institutional Revolutionary Party and put himself and the National Democratic Front (FND) in office. Cárdenas must have asked himself: What were the chances of a successful struggle to turn the PRI out of office? Such a movement could easily have become a full-scale rebellion. Cárdenas could, for example, have called for a national general strike to force the PRI to recognize his victory in the election. But such an action would have placed him on a collision course with the Mexican government and the PRI. When the railroad workers called a national strike in 1959, the state used the army to crush them.

Since 1986, Cuauhtémoc Cárdenas had led a growing movement for political change in Mexico. He had enormous support among a wide variety of groups, from peasants to school teachers, from factory workers to the urban poor. However, the Democratic Current and the National Democratic Front had never set those groups in motion outside of the electoral arena. As opposition candidate, Cárdenas had called no strikes, led no peasant land seizures, condoned no poor peoples' food riots. Some of those things had happened in the shadow of the FDN, but Cárdenas had not led them. While the FDN appeared to have the whole-hearted support of at least a third of the country's population, Cárdenas and the FDN had never tested the peoples' strength as a social force. If Cárdenas called for a general strike, would the FDN be able to break the PRI and the CTM's hold on the Mexican workers?

Without having tried to mobilize those forces in the past, there was no way of knowing. Would the Mexican people have been capable of standing up to the military and forcing that crack in military authority which is essential to a popular victory over the state? Again, without a previous history of mobilization and confrontation, there was no way of knowing.

Cárdenas conferred with his closest advisors, but ultimately, responsibility for a decision rested on his shoulders. Would he accept the official results of the election and Salinas' victory? Or would Cuauhtémoc give the signal for a national movement of resistance, which might become a rebellion, and perhaps even a revolution?

In the end, Cuauhtémoc Cárdenas chose a middle course. He continued to claim victory and refused to acknowledge Salinas as the legitimate president of Mexico. Wherever possible, Cárdenas encouraged his supporters to engage in acts of civil disobedience against the authorities. But, at the same time, Cárdenas and the FDN leadership restrained their supporters when they engaged in armed conflicts or when they threatened to raise local conflicts to a national level. Cárdenas never gave the signal for the kind of massive civil resistance which might have led to a national rebellion and a violent confrontation with the state.

The inevitable result was that the enormous, vibrant, turbulent movement, which Cárdenas and the FDN had led through July, began both to retreat and to contract. The Cárdenas campaign of 1988 had represented a peak of power and influence for the political opposition in Mexico. For a few months in 1988, everything seemed to come together in an effervescent political movement that believed it could carry all before it. But when Cárdenas allowed himself to be counted out, the inevitable result was a demoralization and disorientation of the opposition, the Left, and civil society. The Cárdenas movement lost much of its political momentum and consequently its attractive force, and from the beginning it was clear that not all of the parties in the FDN would enter the new Party of the Democratic Revolution (PRD).

The leaders of the PARM, PPS, PST-FCRN were aghast when they realized that they had backed a loser. They were appalled to think that they might find themselves outsiders in Mexico's insiders' political game. Salinas would become president in a few months and the PRI would still rule Mexico. Those political leaders and parties which failed to reach a *modus vivendi* with Salinas would find themselves politically isolated and perhaps crushed. As inauguration day in January 1989 approached, splits began to appear in the Front.

The first betrayal came from Aguilar Talamantes, leader of the Socialist Workers Party-Cardenist Front for National Reconstruction (PST-FCRN), one of the three original founders of the FDN. Talamantes recognized the PRI as victors in the fraudulent state elections in Tabasco, invited a PRI speaker to the annual celebration of the nationalization of the oil industry, and eventually met with Salinas, recognizing his legitimacy. The PST-FCRN assumed its former role as one of the PRI's pseudo-socialist puppet parties. The Popular Socialist Party (PPS) also returned to the arms of the PRI.[1]

Again Cárdenas faced another momentous decision. He could remain the leader of a broad movement, or he could form a new political party. After much deliberation, he and his closest collaborators decided on the latter course. Two months after the election, in September of 1988, Cárdenas announced the establishment of a new political party, the Party of the Democratic Revolution (PRD), to continue the struggle for democracy and social justice in Mexico.

To become a legally registered party the PRD would have to pursue one of two courses. One path was to convene assemblies of 300 members each in half of Mexico's 300 congressional districts and prove it had 65,000 members nationwide. The alternative route was to persuade some existing party to give the PRD its registration. In order to avoid dilatory challenges from the federal electoral authorities, Cárdenas and other PRD leaders decided on the second course and asked the Mexican Socialist Party (PMS), the successor to the old Mexican communists, to give up their party registration for the PRD.

The leaders of the PMS agreed. The Mexican Socialist Party met for the last time in May 1989; the old comrades stood, fists raised high in the communist salute and sang *The Internationale*. They then voted themselves out of existence, 1,079 to 18, turning over their party registration to the PRD. Mexican communism had been born shortly after the Russian Revolution, and now it died as the Soviet government collapsed. With the absorption of the PMS into the PRD, the largest part of Mexico's independent left went out of existence and socialism ceased to exist as a mass political movement in Mexico.

The demise of the communist government in the Soviet Union and the disappearance of the last vestiges of the Mexican Communist Party had profound implications. The disappearance of socialism in 1988, both as a political current and as a mass phenomenon, dramatically altered the landscape of Mexican politics. Without the Left, there no longer existed an alternative to capitalism in Mexican politics. Without the existence of the PMS, groups like the Trotskyist PRT were simply too small and marginal to make socialism a genuine option.

When the PMS voted itself out of existence, it sawed off the left end of the political spectrum at the same time. Mexican politics necessarily shifted to the right, so the center also moved to the right. The collapse of the left parties made politics in general more conservative. The collapse of the Left also reduced the political options for the independent labor unions, peasant organizations and other social movements. In part, the suicide of the Left in 1989 helps to explain why the Zapatista Chiapas Rebellion of 1994 would not, or could not, explicitly place socialism on the agenda. By 1994, that alternative had become politically unthinkable. By default, the PRD had become the Left.

The PRD held its Founding Congress on November 20, 1990, the anniversary of the Mexican Revolution, and Cuauhtémoc Cárdenas was elected its first president. Without the other parties which had made up the FDN, the new PRD was fundamentally a marriage of Mexican nationalism and what remained of Mexican communism. The PRD defined itself as pluralistic and welcomed into its ranks "democrats and nationalists, socialists and Christians, liberals and ecologists."[2]

With little controversy, the new political party adopted a nationalist and social democratic program. The PRD demanded the democratization of the Mexican government and society. In economic matters, the program called for cooperation between government, business and labor, as well as a mixed economy. The PRD sought to raise workers' wages and farmers' prices in order to strengthen the internal market. The new party called for the preservation and the expansion of Mexico's social welfare state. Finally, the PRD accepted the necessity of both foreign investment and foreign trade, but called for government regulation to prevent undue foreign influence in Mexico. Octavio Rodríguez Araujo noted, "The PRD does not propose any form of socialism; rather it proposes a less virulent, more friendly form of capitalism."[3]

The PRD suffered from the very beginning from a number of intrinsic problems. The new party's birth resulted from a defeat, the inability of the Cárdenas forces to defend their victory at the polls and to create a new government in 1988. The defeat had tended to demoralize, disorganize and divide the Cárdenas campaign forces. The National Democratic Front that came together in January 13, 1988, had attracted virtually all of the social movements that made up civil society, however, the new Party of the Democratic Revolution appeared much more like a traditional Mexican political party. Many of those from the movements hesitated to join what they feared would become a bureaucratic organization controlled by former PRI leaders.

At the same time, the PRD reproduced many of the earlier problems of the FDN. Like the earlier Front, the new party depended to a large degree on Cárdenas' name. Whether he willed it or not, Cárdenas was the *caudillo* of the PRD, even if he was not necessarily the ideal leader of such a party. Cárdenas himself often remained aloof from the problems of the Party, and frequently arrived at his own positions at variance with party program and policy.

While Cárdenas looked down on the Party from on high, the Party leadership remained divided into several factions: the PRI's Democratic Current, the Communist Party, the Castroite Commmunists or the former Trotskyists. Some of these groups maintained their own networks within the PRD, while others attempted to establish strongholds in one or another party office, such as, the trade union commission, the office of press and publications or foreign relations. At the same time, the PRD often remained somewhat distant from its own bases of power among peasants, teachers, factory workers, the urban poor, and university students. The PRD never succeeded in coordinating its work in the social movements and remained primarily an electoral organization held together by Cárdenas' name.

Yet, in many respects, the PRD represented an important new development in Mexican politics. The PRI had produced other oppositional political campaigns before, but now, for the first time, a split from the PRI created a permanent political party. Whatever else one might say about him, Cárdenas refused to give up and return to the PRI. He would not go away. Perhaps because he felt an obligation as the son of the General, Cárdenas resolved to struggle on against the Technocrats and the PRI.

Throughout the country, FDN/PRD supporters carried out militant struggles to defend the vote. They blocked highways, seized town halls, organized parallel governments, and even engaged in gun fights with PRI officials and the police. These tactics both cohered a core of PRD cadres, and raised the spector of violence, which frightened off potential new members. In any case, Cárdenas and his supporters in the PRD were far more intransigent in their struggle against the PRI than the leaders of the National Action Party (PAN). For this very reason, Salinas and the PRI technocrats loathed the PRD and were determined to destroy it.

Jorge G. Castañeda, in his book *Utopia Unarmed,* has suggested that the determination to form a new party rather than to remain the leader of a movement "was probably an unfortunate choice."[4] Yet Cárdenas did not want to become the gadfly of Mexican politics. He wanted to be a future contender for political power, and to do so he needed a party, moreover, a legally recognized party. Given that the FDN coalition was in the process of disintegration through the defection of the PRI's old satellite leftist parties, the PPS and PST, Cárdenas had little choice but to create a new party. As the son of the General, a former leader of the PRI, a practical politician, and a genuine reformer, Cárdenas realized that the movement would not suffice and that a political challenge required a national political party.

Cárdenas, however, remained aloof from the actual tasks of party building, consequently, the leadership of the party often fell to Muñoz Ledo, the man who had helped Cárdenas found the Democratic Current. If there was any figure within the PRD who would give it organizational and political continuity over the next few years, it was Muñoz Ledo. Nearly the same age as Cuauhtémoc, Porfirio Muñoz Ledo had been born in Mexico on July 23, 1933, the son of two schoolteachers. He attended the public schools in a lower-middle-class neighborhood and won a Ministry of Education fellowship, which made it possible for him to attend private preparatory schools. Upon graduation, he studied law at the National University (UNAM), later taking a job as a clerk in a government office.

While at the university in the early 1950s, Muñoz Ledo joined a student group called the Midcentury Generation, which also included the author Carlos Fuentes and the future president Miguel de la Madrid. At the age of 17, Muñoz Ledo became executive secretary of the group's magazine, *Medio Siglo* (Midcentury). A joiner, Muñoz Ledo also became president of the Law Students' Association, and then organizer of the Federation of Student Societies. Intelligent, ambitious and affable, wherever Muñoz Ledo went he made friends and contacts that furthered his career. Typical of future PRI leaders of his era, Muñoz Ledo followed up his education at UNAM with study in Europe. In 1956, Muñoz Ledo went to France to do post graduate work at the Political Studies Institute. He also attended the Law School of the University of Paris, where he took a doctorate in constitutional law and political science, writing a dissertation on the Mexican political system.

Mexico's political system is based on *camarillas*, pyramids of political patronage. Within the big pyramid topped by the PRI president, are many little pyramids each headed by a patron. Mexican ambassador, Jaime Torres Bodet, became Muñoz Ledo's patron, helping him up the ladder of success within the PRI. Through Torres Bodet, Muñoz Ledo was appointed to teach courses on Latin America and the history of the Mexican Revolution at the University of Toulouse. Torres Bodet also introduced Muñoz Ledo to other influential PRI leaders.

While living in Europe, Muñoz Ledo became a convinced Social Democrat. Social democracy had much in common with the PRI in terms of its social program. At that time, both were committed to politically administering a capitalist government and economic system, while attempting to create a comprehensive social welfare system. The PRI had longstanding informal ties to the Socialist International, which led Muñoz Ledo to see his personal mission as strengthening the bonds between the Institutional Revolutionary Party and European Social Democracy.

Muñoz Ledo was still only 26 years old when President Adolfo López Mateos offered him a job in his administration. López Mateos had declared his government to be "the administration of the constitutional left," and Muñoz Ledo felt he would fit in. "I entered government service," said Muñoz Ledo, "because the president of the republic wanted me to organize progressive teams." Meanwhile, Torres Bodet had become Minister of Education, and again acted as patron, appointing Muñoz Ledo to the position of assistant director of higher education.

When the more conservative administration of Gustavo Díaz Ordaz came to power, Muñoz Ledo wanted out of Mexico and took a position as cultural counselor of the Mexican embassy in France under Ambassador Dr. Ignacio Morones Prieto. When he returned to Mexico, Dr. Morones Prieto became director of the Social Security Institute, which at the time trained many of Mexico's physicians, and appointed Muñoz Ledo as one of his assistants. Later, Muñoz Ledo served as secretary-general of the Institute from 1966 to 1970.

In 1972, Echeverría, the new president, invited Muñoz Ledo to join his cabinet as Secretary of Labor, a step into the highest echelons of the Party and a particularly important post during that period. After the 1968 massacre and the tremendous political disaffection which it had engendered, Echeverría realized that it was necessary to give the opposition some political space, and more necessary even, to co-opt the new radical social movements which had begun to appear. Echeverría adopted the posture of a populist and encouraged the organization of new labor unions, approved peasant land seizures, and even fostered the creation of new socialist parties. At the same time, Echeverría wanted to keep all of those new movements under control.

Muñoz Ledo's job as Minister of Labor was both to encourage new currents within the labor movement and to keep them from becoming genuinely independent. When really democratic, independent and militant labor unions appeared, the administration quietly suffocated them, or if necessary crushed them. As Secretary of Labor, Muñoz Ledo was responsible, for example, for coordinating the government's campaign to crush the strike by the Authentic Labor Front (FAT) at the Spicer autoparts plant in 1974 (though he left office before the final blows were struck).[5]

During the Echeverría years, Muñoz Ledo attempted to bring the PRI into closer relations with the Socialist International, possibly into actual membership. Muñoz Ledo invited a stream of European Social Democrats to visit Mexico, and in May 1976, Mexico hosted a major conference of European and Latin American Social Democrats. Echeverría addressed the conference and suggested that the Institutional Revolutionary Party's social program had much in common with social democracy.[6] In the end, however, Echeverría declined to lead the PRI into the Socialist International.

In 1975, Muñoz Ledo's name was mentioned for the Mexican presidency, instead, Echeverría chose López Portillo to be the next president, appointing Muñoz Ledo to head the PRI. Muñoz Ledo served as the campaign manager for the López Portillo campaign, and then as López Portillo's Minister of Education and Mexican representative to the United Nations, as well as member of the U.N. Security Council. Resentment at having been passed over and denied the presidency may have helped to drive Muñoz Ledo into the opposition.

While Muñoz Ledo was serving in New York at the United Nations, de la Madrid and Salinas de Gortari succeeded in taking control of the PRI. Muñoz Ledo was appalled at the technocrats' economic policy, which, as he said, "consists of opening up Mexico and tying it to the decision of the great financial and international centers of the world."[7] By the mid-1980s Muñoz Ledo had decided that the time had come to take a stand against the technocrats. When Cárdenas approached Muñoz Ledo about creating an opposition within the PRI, the wily politician was ready. Muñoz Ledo threw himself into the organization of the Democratic Current, played an important role as a leader of the National Democratic Front, and became one of the key leaders of the new Party of the Democratic Revolution.

There was an irony in Muñoz Ledo's role as an organizer of the new reform movement for he never protested publicly. Muñoz Ledo stuck with the López Mateos administration through the crushing of the 1958 teachers' movement and the 1959 railroad workers' strike. If he was critical, he kept his own counsel. Again Muñoz Ledo remained silent when President Díaz Ordaz and his Minister of the Interior, Luis Echeverría, murdered the students at Tlatelolco in 1968. If Muñoz Ledo later disagreed with Echeverría's use of the army to crush the Democratic Tendency in 1976, we know nothing about it, for he never protested publicly.

Like many PRI leaders of his era, Muñoz Ledo espoused lofty humanistic and even socialist values in public pronouncements, while serving presidents who used the state to crush the labor movement. He shared with much of Mexico's political elite, the cynicism and hyprocrisy which inevitably accompany a betrayal of youthful ideals and the perversion of revolutionary slogans. But the youthful technocrats' palace coup had cut off Muñoz Ledo's political possibilities and drove him into the opposition. Once in the opposition, Muñoz Ledo became one of its driving forces. Over the next six difficult years, when a political crisis arose, more often than not, it was Muñoz Ledo who stood up as leader of the Party of the Democratic Revolution, pointedly challenged the PRI and criticized the PAN.

In the aftermath of the 1988 election, the National Democratic Front/Party of the Democratic Revolution faced the immediate task of winning local and state elections. A real political party had to be able to get elected to office even in Mexico's corrupt and fraudulent election system. Salinas hoped to strangle the new party in its cradle. Would the infant party survive or succumb? The tests came at once, and in one state after another the PRI crushed the PRD.[8]

The key struggle was in Cuauhtémoc Cárdenas' home state of Michoacán. The 1989 elections for 18 legislative seats tested Cárdenas and the FDN/PRD on their own turf. Cuauhtémoc Cárdenas had been governor of Michoacán and had won about two thirds of the vote there in 1988. It was the one state where the FDN/PRD had a real party organization and where the new party even chose its candidates through primaries. The PST-FCRN and PPS, however, refused to participate; another indication of the break-down of the 1988 coalition. Still, once its candidates were chosen, the PRD's campaign "was almost invisible."[9] The Cárdenas supporters in Michoacán may simply have been exhausted after the 1988 presidential election.

The PRI, on the other hand, mobilized its machine. Again, PRI President Colosio led the assault. The state-party sent in scores of advisors, held hundreds of meetings and mobilized tens of thousands of supporters. The PRI dominated the media, particularly television. Throughout the state, the PRI conducted a massive red-baiting campaign, equating Cárdenas with communism, while the government mobilized the army ostensibly to keep the peace, but in actuality to intimidate the populace.

The PRD organized 5,000 vote watchers to cover the 2,330 polling places, but they had little success. On voting day, the PRI engaged in massive fraud and considerable violence, and in the end, the State Electoral Commission awarded victory to the PRI in 12 of the 18 districts, giving six to the PRD. In reality, the PRD probably won more than a dozen of the districts, but, as in the 1988 presidential election, there was no way to enforce the victory short of civil war.

Throughout the first two years, the PRD did poorly in local and state elections, in part because the old coalition was in disarray and the new party was just getting organized. Gradually the PRD's functioning improved, but the PRI continued to mobilize the powerful machine to crush the fledgling party. When denied victories it had won, the PRD engaged in massive civil resistance to protest the PRI's voter fraud. In Michoacán, Guerrero and other states, PRD activists seized town halls, organized parallel municipal governments, blocked the principal highways, held demonstrations, and participated in protest marches. Frequently, conflicts between PRD protesters and the PRI authorities led to violence. PRI officials, policemen and gangsters beat and murdered PRD activists, while the state and federal police arrested, tortured, and jailed. At times, the PRI brought in "shock troops" from other states, or poor peasants from other areas, such as members of Antorcha Campesina from Puebla, who were used to attack the PRD protestors.[10] Some states became ungovernable and the Mexican Army was called out to remove protestors and restore order, in the course of which there was more violence.

The early elections of 1989 and 1990 set the pattern for the Salinas administration's strategy. To win elections, the PRI was prepared to use its political machine, the state's economic resources, the domination of the media, the presence of the military, police violence and massive fraud. The impact of the PRI's use of violence against the PRD can hardly be overstated. Between 1988 and 1994, the PRD documented 254 political assassinations, while another 32 were under investigation. The PRI party officials, police, or hired gangsters were directly responsible for many of these 286 murders. The PRI violence not only won elections, but also terrorized the opposition and created a climate of violence which harmed the PRD's organizing efforts.[11]

When dealing with opposition victories, the PRI treated the PRD entirely differently than the PAN. When the PAN exhibited overwhelming strength, as in Baja California, the PRI recognized its victories. But the government refused to recognize the PRD's victories, as in Michoacán, because Salinas had determined that the PRD would not become a substantial force anywhere in Mexico.

By the time of the August 18, 1991 national mid-term elections, the PRI had completely recuperated from its 1988 defeat, at least in terms of its showing in the National Chamber of Deputies. The PRI used all of its political and economic resources, but in particular, it relied on Salinas' National Solidarity Program or PRONASOL. PRONASOL distributed welfare programs in the districts which Salinas lost in 1988, creating a new and stronger patronage machine.[12] Just before the election and even on election day itself, the PRI distributed milk and tortillas to women in the slums, and beer to the men in the city. In the end, in 1991, the PRI received 14 million votes, 4.8 million more than in 1988.

But the PRI's shameless use of patronage, fraud and violence to win elections also caused indignation among many Mexican citizens, and gradually led to a revival of the civil society movement that expressed itself in the governors' elections of 1991. Recovering from the 1988 debacle, citizens reorganized poll watching organizations and human rights groups, and joined again in massive protests.

From a national point of view, perhaps the most important of the 1991 gubernatorial elections occurred in San Luis Potosí where civil society and politics fused in the career and campaign of Salvador Nava Martínez. Although he was not a member of any national political party, Nava created a powerful political organization, ran successfully for mayor of San Luis Potosí twice, built the broadest coalition for governor ever constructed, and finally founded the most important organization of Mexico's new civil society movement.

Salvador Nava Martínez was born April 17, 1914 in San Luis Potosí, the capital of the state of the same name in central Mexico. Nava's father was a professor who eventually became the rector of the University of San Luis. Nava himself studied medicine and became an ophthamologist. He dedicated a good part of his time to working among the less fortunate and became known as the "doctor of the poor." At the same time, Nava taught at the university in the Department of Medicine.

It was sometime in the late 1940s, as Mexico's ruling party was turning toward the right, that Nava began to get into political fights with the PRI bosses. Discouraged about the country's direction, he decided to get involved in politics. In 1958, Nava ran for mayor of San Luis Potosí and won, supposedly becoming the first opposition politician to win a mayoral race in Mexico since the revolution. Thereafter for almost 40 some years, dressed in a conservative suit, wearing a necktie, and always speaking in a civil and polite manner, even to his opponents, Dr. Nava became the symbol of the opposition in San Luis Potosí.

Nava won a following in the state capital and decided to run for governor in 1961. He first sought the nomination of the PRI, but when that was denied, he ran as an independent, creating his own political organization, the Potosino Civic Front. When the PRI's candidate won, Nava claimed there had been fraud, and organized protest demonstrations of his supporters. Violence broke out and President Adolfo López Mateos sent in the Mexican Army which occupied the state for three months. The authorities arrested Nava and his closest associates, accused them of plotting against the government, and put them in jail in Mexico City, where the police beat and tortured them. After being freed from jail, Nava returned to his teaching and doctoring in San Luis. Though he did not run for office again for more than twenty years, he remained active in his community, a widely respected figure.

In the depths of Mexico's economic crisis in 1982, Nava came out of political retirement and ran again for mayor as the candidate of the Potosino Civic Front. He had the backing of both the National Action Party and the Unified Socialist Party of Mexico (PSUM—the former communists), as well as other parties of the Left. Nava and his unlikely allies won the 1982 mayoral race in San Luis and became a model for such broad coalition races in several other states.

In 1991 Salvador Nava, in his late 70s, and suffering from bladder cancer, decided to run again for governor on the ticket of his Potosino Civic Front. By then he had become a kind of local legend and many believed he could defeat the PRI and win the governorship with a broad coalition. Not only did the PAN and the PRD put Nava at the head of their tickets, but even the neo-fascist Mexican Democratic Party (PDM) ran him as their candidate, as well. Here was a broad coalition indeed. In the 1930s, Lázaro Cárdenas' communist followers had fought the PDM's political forebearers, the fascist Sinarquistas. But now, almost 50 years later, they were all in the same party struggling together to bring down the state that Cárdenas had built.[13] Nava had the support too of Indian communities from the Huasteca region as well as that of local industrialists. If there was ever a candidacy of civil society at large, Nava's was it.

The PRI's candidate, Fausto Zapata, had been a congressman, a senator and a foreign ambassador. As is required in the PRI's political system, Salinas himself had approved Zapata's candidacy and put the resources of the state-party behind him. The Mexican Academy of Human Rights and the San Luis Potosí Center for Human Rights acted as election observers, and on election day produced 330 poll watchers who did their best to cover the state's 744 polling places. As might have been expected, on election day, August 18, 1991, the state election authorities and the PRI engaged in every conceivable form of fraud. Polling places were moved at the last minute, names were removed from the registration lists, some PRI party workers voted more than once, ballot boxes were stolen or stuffed. Poll watchers reported grave violations of voters' rights at over half of the polling places, and, as always, particularly in the countryside.

To protest the election fraud, Nava decided on a 265 mile "March for Dignity" to the Zócalo in Mexico City to demand that the president remove the "usurper" from the governor's palace. Women supporters of Nava meanwhile occupied the Governor's Palace and declared they would not let Fausto Zapata take office. Violent conflicts broke out between the PRI and the Nava forces and several people were injured. All the while, Nava and his supporters marched on over the mountains toward Mexico City.

Seeing Nava's dust rising in the distance, Salinas summoned Fausto Zapata to the presidential residence at Los Pinos. After a brief interview with Salinas on October 9, and after serving as governor for 13 days, Zapata resigned. Nava, interviewed *en route* to Mexico, declared that "orderly and peaceful protests have been recognized by the competent authories, by the president himself, and that this had opened the way for a transition to democracy."[14] Nava turned the march around, but he had not yet heard all the news. Salinas named Gonzálo Martínez Córbala, a rather popular old politician in the left wing of the PRI, to replace Fausto Zapata. Later Salinas rewarded Zapata for serving as the scapegoat by naming him consul general for Mexico in Los Angeles.

The interim governor, Martínez Córbala, was both amiable and liberal, and succeeded in getting all parties to agree to hold new elections in April 1993. Moreover, the government conceded that those elections would be run by citizens' councils without interference from the PRI. Martínez Córbala also announced that he himself would not seek election as governor, which would in any case have violated Mexico's no re-election tradition.

The March for Dignity made Nava a national hero, the man who had stood up to the PRI. The opposition press, left and right, now referred to Nava as Mexico's Gandhi. In some quarters his name was mentioned as the possible presidential candidate of a unified opposition in 1994. Nava used his new stature, to create a national citizens movement.

In February of 1992, Nava issued a call for the founding of the Citizens Movement for Democracy (MCD). On March 1, the MCD held its founding convention which was attended by over 60 indigenous, community, labor, citizens, and human rights organizations. The MCD called for the defense of human rights, including political rights, as defined by the United Nations Universal Declaration of Human Rights and the Mexican Constitution. The reformers urged the Mexican people to participate in elections and defend their vote. The MCD also called for "reconciliation, dialogue, and civil struggle to bring about the installation of a transition government in Mexico dedicated...to rebuilding the civil structure of the country."

To bring about "political reconstruction," the MCD detailed a number of specific political reforms: end the state monopoly of the administration of elections; dismantle the concentrated power of the presidency and create checks and balances; reform the judicial system and create an independent supreme court; give the state congresses and the federal congress the power of legislative initiative, authorization of the budget and expenditures; reduce the centralism in the Mexican political system; give autonomy to municipal governments; end communications monopolies in television and radio, insure freedom of the press; and finally, democratize labor unions, trade associations, political parties and educational institutions. The MCD's program represented both a thorough-going critique of the abuses of the PRI system, and a plan for the creation of a genuine political democracy.

Meanwhile, the April 1993 San Luis Potosí governor's election was drawing near. Nava was not going to make it to April, because his cancer of the bladder had advanced, and he was dying. On May 8, Nava spoke at his last public meeting. Wearing his customary conservative suit and necktie, the old doctor told the silent crowd to keep up the fight for electoral reform and political democracy. While many Potosinos stood sobbing, Nava said his last good-bye to his fellow citizens and political supporters, adding, "Perhaps we shall meet again."

The next day, Cuauhtémoc Cárdenas, the leader of the Party of the Democratic Revolution, stopped by to pay his respects to Nava. More surprisingly, in a demonstration of the most profound cynicism, President Salinas de Gortari, also visited Nava, chatted with the PRI's long-time opponent for an hour and a half, and then praised him to the media as a peaceful fighter for democracy. From his deathbed, Nava issued his last political statement, titled "A Call for The Foundation of a Citizens Movement for Democracy." In it, he urged the Mexican people to build "a citizens movement for democracy" and to bring about "international awareness of the violation of human rights and political liberties of the Mexican people."

Having said his good-byes and issued his last statement, on May 18, 1992, Nava died at the age of 78 from an infection and a heart attack resulting from his bladder cancer. His funeral was attended by Luis H. Alvarez, president of the PAN, Cuauhtémoc Cárdenas, president of the PRD, Fernando Gutiérrez Barrios, the PRI's Minister of the Interior as well as interim governor Martínez Córbala. No doubt with Nava's death, the PRI leaders could breathe a little more easily.[15]

Martínez Córbala had promised not to run for governor in the April elections, but he soon reneged on his promise and announced his candidacy. With Nava out of the way, Martínez Córbala must have believed he could win. In running for office, however, Martínez Córbala broke the Mexican tradition which prohibits re-election. True, he had been an appointed governor, but his candidacy was seen as re-election, and opposition arose not only from the citizenry at large, but also from within his own party. Martínez Córbala also violated the law which forbids an interim governor from resigning for anything short of the most dire circumstances. He did, however, and Salinas appointed another interim governor, Torres Corzo, to take his place.

Though Nava was dead, he lived on. Nava's widow, Mara Concepción Calvillo de Nava, came out of mourning to organize the National Anti-Re-election Front (FAN) made up of the Potosino Civic Front, PAN, PRD, MCD, Women for Democracy, the Democratic Assembly for Effective Suffrage and the Sinaloa-based Army for Democracy. She and her mostly women followers blockaded the governor's palace and attempted to keep Governor Torres Corzo from entering. A struggle ensued and 30 people were injured.

Because of the widespread opposition, both inside and outside the PRI, Martínez Córbala was forced to resign from the race, and the elections were wide open once again. Salinas, having paid his respects to Nava, now undertook to confound and destroy the movement that Nava had built. Salinas did so brilliantly. The PRI shrewdly chose as its candidate, Horacio Sánchez Unzueta, Nava's son-in-law, thereby claiming the mantel of the deceased reformer. The PAN also laid claim to the legacy of Nava, running as its candidate a former leader of Nava's movement, Jorge Lozáno Armengol. Finally, Manuel Nava, the son of the deceased doctor, helped organize the Nava Political Party (NPP), which chose as its candidate Concepción Calvillo de Nava, the widow. Cárdenas and the PRD also backed her campaign.

With Nava dead and his movement now divided, the PRI easily won the victory. On April 18, 1993 Horacio Sánchez Unzueta, PRI candidate, was declared the winner with 64.9 percent of the vote; Jorge Lozano Armengol of the PAN won 19.38; and Concepción Calvillo de Nava of the NPP received 11.02. Many voters stayed home: only 38.8 percent of those registered voted. The PRI also swept the state legislative election, getting all 13 of the regular seats, while PAN got five proportional representation seats, the NPP two seats, and the PRD one. The PAN, NPP and PRD claimed that there had been many irregularities and refused to recognize victory.

Even though Nava's movement in San Luis had collapsed, his campaign for political reform had not ended in failure, for it had served to help revitalize the civil society movement. The Citizens Movement for Democracy, which Nava had founded, became the center of the civil society movement in the 1990s. Many of those who had participated in local poll watching groups, and who had joined in Nava's protests, would become part of the Civic Alliance, the national poll watching group in the 1994 elections.

At the same time, Nava's campaign shows us all of the contradictions and confusions of the civil society movement. The struggle against the 60-odd-year rule of Mexico's bureaucratic and authoritarian ruling state-party led in San Luis Potosí to a coalition that stretched from communists on the left to fascists on the right, and contained all the nationalists, social democrats, liberals, and conservatives in the middle. On economic and social issues, these parties had wildly different views. But perhaps even more importantly, it is not clear that they had the same commitment to democracy. How could a coalition for democracy include the political opportunists in the PAN, who were busy negotiating deals with the PRI, and the creepy fascists of the Mexican Democratic Party, who dreamed of one day goose-stepping to power? Civil society contained some rather uncivil elements which called into question the movement's real coherence.

8

WORKERS PLOT REBELLION ON THE NORTHERN BORDER

While the spectacular uprising in Chiapas captured headlines around the world, another more modest rebellion was quietly and secretly being organized on Mexico's northern border in the *maquiladoras*, or border manufacturing plants of Chihuahua, Juárez, and Tijuana. Like the rebels in Chiapas, these workers were responding to an economic program foisted on the country by Salinas and the technocrats.

Since 1982, the hundreds of thousands of workers in the *maquiladora* plants had seen their wages fall by half, so that by 1994 most worked for US$4.50 per day. Their working conditions in the multinational electronic and auto plants remain intense, often dangerous, and environmental hazards, like chemical spills, threaten to engulf their communities. Neither the Mexican nor the U.S. government have any interest in seeing these workers organize, and both countries placed obstacles in their path. Faced with huge international corporations like General Motors and General Electric, Mexican workers have now joined with their Canadian and U.S. counterparts to organize a workers' insurrection in the border factories.

In November of 1993 Ofelia Medrano, a production worker at the Honeywell Mexican Export Factory in Chihuahua, Mexico, was called into her bosses' offices. Two Honeywell officials, Personnel Director César Martínez and Superintendent Gabriel Vargas reportedly kept Medrano in the office for several hours, intermittently threatening and bribing her. On the one hand, she was told she was going to be laid off or fired, on the other hand, she was told the company was going to give her financial assistance. All she had to do to get the money was give the company the names of other Honeywell MEF employees who were involved in a union organizing effort in the plant.

Medrano was one of a dozen workers who had attended a private meeting with the independent Metal Workers Union (STIMAHCS-FAT) a week before. One way or another, Honeywell got the names of 21 production workers and, two days after the ratification of the North American Free Trade Agreement (NAFTA), fired them. The women, who were called into the bosses' offices one after another, were told that in order to collect the severance pay due to them under Mexican law, they must sign a waiver of all claims against Honeywell. Most of the women, factory workers living in the poor *colonias* or working-class neighborhoods of Chihuahua, felt they could not afford to give up their severance money, and signed the waiver. Even members of the union's organizing committee signed, intimidated by their employers and fearful of losing their money.

Ofelia Medrano was one of 480 production workers at Honeywell MEF who produced thermostats, parts for circuit boards, heating and air purifier switches. Honeywell, headquartered in Minneapolis, Minnesota, is one of the giants of American business, and a leading firm in the electronics industry. In Minneapolis, Honeywell had a contract with Teamsters Local 1145 and paid wages ranging from $10 to $20 an hour. But in 1993 in Mexico, Honeywell paid its production workers at its MEF plant in Chihuahua about 15 pesos or US$5.00 per day, or about $45 per week. Mexico's "official" labor unions controled by the PRI, such as the CTM, CROC or CROM, sometimes organize unions in plants like MEF. But the unions generally cooperate with management to prevent strikes, identify troublemakers, and in general, keep wages low.

In 1993, workers at MEF began to take an interest in the possibility of affiliating with the Metal Workers Union (STIMAHCS), part of the independent Authentic Labor Front (FAT). FAT has long had a reputation for both internal democracy and firmness in dealing with employers. After learning of the November organizing meeting, Honeywell decided that the independent union had to be broken. Taking advantage of Mexican labor law, which allows companies to fire an employee and pay them severance pay in return, the company rounded up the suspects and fired the ringleaders. With the workers' waivers of their rights in the bosses' hands, the company had a strong case before the Mexican Labor Board. Back in Minneapolis, Honeywell Chairman Michael Bonsignore told the press that the workers in Chihuahua had been laid off as a result of "downsizing" and the transfer of work.[1]

Ofelia Medrano's case was no aberration of Mexican industrial relations, no miscarriage of justice. Rather it was standard practice in Mexico's *maquiladoras*. Take, for example, the case of Fernando Castro Hernández, a chemical substances technician at General Electric's Compañía Armadora, S.A. (CASA) in Juárez, Mexico. Castro was called into his boss' office on November 25, 1993, and fired supposedly for distributing union leaflets in the plant during working hours. Castro was one of a number of workers involved in a union organizing campaign with FAT's Metal Workers Union (STIMAHCS). Eventually, General Electric's CASA plant not only fired Castro, but either fired or pressured over 100 workers into resigning. Workers accepted the statutory severance pay, based on length of service, thus giving up their right to challenge their firing before the Mexican Labor Board. GE CASA later offered to reinstate some of the workers, but not Castro.

To say that the contest between General Electric and Fernando Castro is an unequal one would be a tremendous understatement. General Electric, according to *Forbes* magazine, is one of the most powerful corporations in the United States. Its 1993 gross sales exceeded US$60 billion, and its net profits were US$5.18 billion. Like other U.S. corporations, GE has been transferring work to Mexico: it moved 15 plants there by 1993. In 1989, for example, GE closed its small motors plant in Decatur, Indiana, and threw hundreds of long-time employees out of work. Many of those workers made over US$10 an hour, while most of the workers at GE's CASA are lucky to make a little more than US$5 per day. Low wages and poor working conditions, including health and safety problems, drove Fernando Castro to organize and continue his fight. Castro refused for months to accept his severance pay, and took his fight to the Mexican Labor Board.[2]

The cases of Ofelia Medrano and Fernando Castro are common enough, but what makes them different is that they are part of a growing group of Mexican labor union activists who are fighting on an international level. The Mexican labor union, the Authentic Labor Front (FAT), with which they were involved, decided that it was time to stop trying to fight the multinational corporations all alone. FAT joined forces with the United Electrical Workers (UE) and the International Brotherhood of Teamsters (IBT) to try to organize the growing number of factories near Mexico's northern border.

The workers involved in organizing efforts, like those of the FAT at Honeywell and General Electric plants in Mexico, have found that the struggle for democracy and social justice in Mexico leads them to join with workers in Canada and the United States who are fighting for those same goals in their countries. The new international organizing efforts have grown out of the special conditions that exist in the Mexican border industrialization zone.

Mexico established the border industrialization zone in 1965, granting special tax breaks and other incentives to foreign corporations to set up business in Mexico. The zone boomed in the 1970s and today, along the northern border, half a million workers labor in 2,000 manufacturing and assembly plants known as *maquiladoras*. Two-thirds of the *maquiladora* workers are women, mostly young women between 14 and 30 years of age, who earn about US$4.50 per day and work 45-48 hours per week. Many of these women, are the single heads of households and live in the *colonias*, some in little, two or three room adobe or brick houses, many in shacks made of scrap lumber and tar paper.

Multinational corporations such as General Motors, Zenith, and Sony own the majority of these plants. In some cases the *maquiladoras* are runaway shops which fled the United States or Canada to seek lower wages in Mexico. In other cases the plants were constructed in Mexico to avoid the more stringent enforcement of environmental or occupational health and safety laws in the United States.

Most of the *maquiladora* plants produce electrical or electronic products or auto-parts, and many use hazardous materials in the process. In *maquiladora* centers such as Tijuana (near San Diego) and Ciudad Juárez (near El Paso) there are reports of clusters of anencephalic births (babies born without brains), which some investigators believe may be due to the dumping of toxic xylene or other chemicals.

Most of the *maquiladora* workers have no union. Where unions do exist they are often "official" ones affiliated with the ruling Institutional Revolution Party. In a few cases, the official unions do get somewhat better wages, benefits and working conditions for their members. But in most cases, these are "low profile" unions with no visible presence in the plant, which are referred to as "phantom" unions because no worker has ever seen or heard them. In addition, some unions offer "protection" contracts, that is, contracts that protect the employers' interests.

Since the 1970s the Mexican government, state governors, multinational corporations and the unions have had an agreement that union organizing drives, independent unions, strikes or other disruptions of production simply would not be permitted. Union organizers were regularly fired, and when workers struck, the police broke their strikes. The PRI-controled government, the PRI labor unions and both Mexican and foreign multinationals in Mexico typically collude to deny independent unions official recognition, to deny legal status to strikes, and to fire union activists and remove them from the plants.[3]

Mexican labor unionists have been frustrated for decades by their inability to create genuine unions to fight for higher wages and better conditions. At the same time, U.S. and Canadian unionists have felt threatened that their employers would move plants and jobs to Mexico where unions were weak and wages low. The positive result has been that in the last few years, after the passage of NAFTA by the U.S., Canada and Mexico, some labor unionists from all three countries have looked for ways to coordinate their organizing activities in order to take on the multinational companies.[4]

Driven by developments such as NAFTA, labor union activists from Canada and the U.S. are developing a variety of strategies for working with their sisters and brothers in Mexico. After more than two decades of experience, several different strategies have emerged, four of which are discussed here. First, some groups are trying a community-based approach that attempts to organize the two-thirds female workforce of the *maquiladoras* primarily as women workers, often basing its work in the communities where the women workers live. Second, is a company-based or industry-wide organizing strategy that targets specific companies or industries and works through the cooperation of Canadian, Mexican, or U.S. workers and unions. Third, is a strategy of cross-border support committees, coalitions, some transnational in scope and others regional or local, who try to support workers and union organizing in Mexico (as well as workers in the United States and Canada). Finally, there is the strategy of building clandestine cells, which organize workers into unions, but try to avoid the Mexican labor boards' official recognition process. Each of these strategies is based on one or another aspect of the difficult reality of building cooperation between U.S. and Mexican workers, as well as, the problems of organizing in Mexico.

ꗃ

"We have a grassroots, community-based, largely women *maquiladora* worker organizing model," explained Phoebe McKinney, director of the Maquiladora Project of the American Friends Service Committee (AFSC), headquartered in Philadelphia. The AFSC project has been in existence for about 15 years and is involved in work in several cities along the eastern end of the U.S.-Mexico border.[5] The women involved in this project have organized the Comité Fronterizo de Obreras (CFO-the Border Committee of Working Women).

The CFO hires former women *maquiladora* workers as organizers, usually 12 or 15 women who organize in the working-class *colonias,* which surround the *maquiladoras* along the border.

"They hold meetings of other women workers in the neighborhoods where the women live," explains McKinney. "Obviously you can't really have a meeting at work. So, they meet on the weekends where the women feel comfortable: in their homes. In each *colonia* there's a weekly or bi-weekly meeting. The women in one meeting may come from five or six different factories in that town. The purpose of these meetings," says McKinney," is to help the women overcome their sense of isolation."

McKinney explains: "We recognize the reality that a lot of these people are 17, 18, and 19-year-old girls. They're young women. They're shy. Nobody's ever bothered to care about what it's like for them in the factories. Our organizing is a real confidence builder."

"We try to do an organizing model that in some sense makes it fun to learn about their rights," says McKinney. "We do role playing, we do sociodramas, we have the meetings in the workers' homes where they're relaxed and they have some time."

The CFO organizes consciousness-raising groups, often using Mexico's Federal Labor Law as its text. "It's a big thick book that's largely unenforced, and—believe it or not—we've found it to be a very, very successful organizing tool. Women become conscious about their rights, and they go back into the factories with a strategy about how to assert those rights." For example, women are taught that they should not be pressured into resigning their jobs, or they may lose their right to compensation.

"When they learn about their rights, their self-esteem goes up. When they start to assert their rights in the plant, their self-esteem goes up even more," says McKinney.

One of the crucial questions in labor union organizing in Mexico is how to deal with the official labor unions controlled by the PRI, such as the Confederation of Mexican Workers (CTM). Should Mexican workers attempt to reform the government-controlled unions? Or should they build independent unions? Historically, Mexican union reformers have tried both strategies in different places and at different times. Those doing cross-border organizing have different views, sometimes based on different experiences.

The AFSC Maquiladora Project does much of its work in the state of Tamaulipas, Mexico. The Tamaulipas Confederation of Mexican Workers (CTM), headed by Agapito González Cavazos, represents about 85 percent of the state's *maquiladora* workers, and is more independent and militant than most CTM organizations. *Maquiladora* workers in Tamaulipas work a 40-hour work week, instead of the usual 45 or 48, and earn somewhat higher wages.

"The CTM union in Matamoros is basically okay," says McKinney. Women involved in the Maquiladora Project, she says, "try to reform the union leadership. At this point, they are not interested in aligning themselves with an independent union movement. But they're very interested in reforming their local union leadership if they can and when they can." McKinney says, "I would credit the women involved in our project to a large degree with getting Agapito to be a more responsive labor leader."

McKinney concludes, "From the American Friends Service Committee's perspective, we're committed to a long-term organizing process that takes into account:the dynamics of the local union, the political context in Mexico, and the fact that these are young women who work 40-hour weeks."

"The workers are basically developing their own strategies for change, and they are developing their own leadership," says McKinney. "As the occasion arises, where workers are involved in trying to reform unions or trying to get new unions, we'll certainly support them in those efforts. But we also feel that this long-term community-based organizing model is a way to help workers regardless of any one particular organizing campaign."

ꟍ◻◻

Two years ago the United Electrical Workers (UE) and the Authentic Labor Front (Frente Aútentico del Trabajo-FAT), the former a U.S. and Canadian union and the latter a Mexican union, formally joined together in a "Strategic Organizing Alliance." So far, they have been concentrating their joint effort on organizing the G.E. and Honeywell plants in Mexico. Why and how did such an alliance come about?

Dave Johnson, international representative for the United Electrical Workers (UE) explains, "In General Electric alone, we've lost over 10,000 jobs in the last few years. They've moved to the South of the United States and around the world—but the biggest chunk of workers have moved to Mexico. G.E. currently has upwards of 20,000 workers in Mexico. A number of those jobs were formerly held by our membership."[6]

Because of regional economic integration and developments like NAFTA, says Johnson, "The wages and conditions of Mexican workers are the new floor of our economy. To put it a little simplistically, either our wages and conditions are going to go down to the level of Mexico's, or we're going to figure out ways to help Mexicans raise their wages and conditions up to our levels."

"So it's in our interest," says Johnson, "to help Mexican workers in GE figure out ways to raise their wages and conditions so that we can hold onto what we have. And given the strength of the forces that are arrayed against Mexican workers trying to organize democratic unions, we believe that there's a real necessity for international solidarity."

"Most of the plants in our industries in Mexico are non-union," says Johnson. "The few organized shops are in 'official' unions that don't have as their principal goal an aggressive fight to raise standards of living, but rather to continue the political control of the ruling party of Mexico, of which the official trade unions form a part."

So based on that analysis, says Johnson, UE has decided to join with the FAT to help Mexican workers organize democratic "independent unions," that is, unions not affiliated with the PRI-dominated CTM, CROM or CROC. In the case of the GE motor plant in Juárez, Mexico, the Compañía Armadora, S.A. (CASA), the UE is helping to organize workers into the Metal Workers Union (STIMAHCS) which is affiliated with FAT.

"What we're trying to do in the short-term," says Johnson, "that is, in the next couple of years, is to bring union organization and win collective bargaining agreements at some plants in the *maquiladora* sector in Mexico, principally right now at General Electric and Honeywell." Today there are virtually no independent labor unions in the *maquiladora* sector. Their organization would be a tremendous achievement.

"In the longer term," says Johnson, "what we see is a struggle coordinated between Mexican and U.S. workers of the same employers." Johnson suggests the creation of something like the Coordinated Bargaining Committee of GE workers, in which several U.S. and Canadian unions now participate, but on an even larger international scale.

Both the UE and the FAT bring important contributions to the organizing effort, says Johnson. "We provide financial assistance to allow the FAT to conduct some of the organizing work. We provide research help, and some staff assistance, both in terms of organizing work and mobilizing support in the United States. The FAT brings to the alliance a 35-year history of struggle in Mexico. FAT hires and directs the organizing staff in Mexico and decides the campaign strategy and tactics."

Johnson feels that the last point is particularly important. He believes that the Strategic Organizing Alliance "had to be based on mutual respect for the self-determination of the organizations involved." He emphasizes that "the organizing strategy and the decisions about what happens in Mexico is the responsibility of the Mexican organization, not our reponsibility. Likewise, what happens within our organization in the United States, and strategy and tactics in the United States, is our responsibility."

A good part of the effort is the organizing done in the United States. Because organizing in Mexico will not bring new members and new dues into the UE, says Johnson, international solidarity requires a higher level of understanding among the union's American rank and file. The UE leadership has taken the issue of international labor solidarity with Mexican workers to its membership.

"We've had a whole series of tours, plant gate meetings, lunch time cafeteria meetings, local meetings, a national convention attended by brothers and sisters from Mexico, both ranks and file members and union leaders," says Johnson.

To fight misunderstandings, myths, and illusions about Mexico, the UE has brought Mexican worker activists to its union's halls. This has been done, says Johnson, "to get people to understand that there are workers in Mexico who want to fight to raise their living standards." He emphasizes that "face to face contact with our rank and file has been key." Johnson believes that, over the last two years, a majority of UE locals have had some kind of direct contact with Mexican workers.

U.S. and Canadian workers have also been directly involved in the struggle. The UE has circulated petitions in its shops in support of Mexican workers, the workers then turning the petitions in to local plant management. In addition, there have been plant-gate collections soliciting voluntary contributions from workers to help organize in Mexico. Delegations of UE workers have also visited GE workers in Juárez and gone to their *colonias* to see how workers live. "That actually was a really rich experience for the brothers and sisters who came down," says Johnson, "to see how a worker's family lives on five dollars a day."

Similar problems of possible job loss in an altogether different industry, have led another U.S. labor union, the Farm Labor Organizing Committee (FLOC), to join with "official" Mexican unions to create another international alliance. The FLOC has joined with the CTM affiliate SNTOAC, the Sinaloa farm workers union, to create a U.S.-Mexico Commission to coordinate efforts among farm workers in the United States and Mexico.

"When we negotiated our first contract with Campbell's Soup in 1986," remembers FLOC leader Báldemar Velázquez, "they told us at the bargaining table, 'If you guys make tomatoes too expensive here in Ohio, we'll just make more paste in Mexico.' Right at that meeting I had a caucus with the other negotiators, and I told Fernando Cuevas, one of the strikers from Campbell's Soup who is now a vice president, "Fernando, we have to go to Mexico and talk to the people down there."'[7]

At first, Báldemar Velázquez and FLOC had some difficulty making contact with Mexico's official labor unions because FLOC was not part of the AFL-CIO. For years the AFL-CIO, in the United States, and the CTM, in Mexico, had strong fraternal ties and tended to deal with each other, often to the exclusion of other labor unions outside of those federations. Anxious to establish ties with Mexican unions, FLOC got support from the AFL-CIO, and later became affiliated with it. With AFL-CIO support, things in Mexico went more smoothly. Fidel Velázquez, the head of the CTM, called a conference of Mexican agricultural workers' unions to which FLOC was invited. At that conference, Báldemar Velázquez and FLOC were able to find out that the CTM's National Union of Farm Workers in the western Mexican state of Sinaloa (SNTOAC) represented workers in Mexico producing for Campbell's.

What did FLOC and farm workers in the United States have to say to SNTOAC and the farm workers in Mexico? Just this, says Báldemar Velázquez: "I want the Mexican tomato workers to get the best contract they can possibly get from Campbell's Soup, because that puts us in a better negotiating position with Campbell's Soup in the United States." Báldemar Velázquez adds, "Now we're not talking about dollar parity in terms of wages. Those workers are getting $4 or $5 a day in the tomatoes, and when we got our first contract we went from $3.35 to $4.60 an hour. So there is no parity in wages. But we can begin to neutralize some of the economic differences."

On the basis of their common interest in dealing with Campbell's Soup, FLOC and SNTOAC formed a U.S.-Mexico Commission. When SNTOAC began negotiating its contract with Campbell's, FLOC mobilized the forces that had supported FLOC's Campbell's Soup boycott, unions, churches and others, only now in support of the Mexican workers. "It allowed those guys to negotiate one of the best contracts they had ever negotiated," Báldemar Velázquez explained.

FLOC is now helping to organize farm workers in the pickle industry in both the United States and Mexico. The reason is the structure of the pickle industry. Aunt Jane Pickles, which is part of the Dean Foods conglomerate, grows and buys pickles in four states, one in the United States and three in Mexico: Texas, Querétaro, Michoacán and Guanajuato. "So," says Báldemar Velázquez, "there has to be a joint organizing campaign in those three states in Mexico. Because it makes no sense for workers to do a campaign in Texas when the company can just tell them to get lost and just bring in the pickles from Mexico. And vice versa. It would do no good to organize those workers in Mexico, when that effort could be broken by producing pickles in Texas."

"What I'm talking about is not revolutionary, it's not radical," says Báldemar Velázquez. It's just what unions have always done, that is, collectivize workers around production. And where's the production? The production just happens to be in Mexico and the United States." Or to put it another way, he says, "Let's look at it that we are becoming less citizens of the nations in which we are born, and look upon ourselves as citizens of the companies that we work for. So what we're dealing with is the development of an international worker community."

Many U.S. unions are expressing interest in the FLOC-SNTOAC experiment, says Báldemar Velázquez. He hopes that it may contribute to other cross-border organizing, and eventually change the character of the AFL-CIO. "So little by little we have to get this big machine turned around, and instead of being so insular and so provincial in its economic, social and political outlook, it will start looking more at international issues and its unions will be the international organizations their names claim they are."

❏❏❏

The organization of genuine unions in the *maquiladoras* is exceptionally difficult because of the Mexican political and legal systems. The City of Juárez, for example, has about 200 *maquiladoras*, but only about 30 are organized. Where unions do exist, they are so-called "official unions" controlled by the Institutional Revolutionary Party (PRI). The official unions do little to represent the workers, and the Boards of Conciliation and Arbitration (the Mexican labor boards) generally refuse to recognize independent unions.

However, under the Mexican law, workers need not organize labor unions to negotiate with their employers. Under Article 355 of the Federal Labor Law, workers may organize temporary "coalitions" instead. But the "coalition" has proven equally ineffective in defending the workers' interests.

For example, in 1992, groups of workers organized in several plants of General Motors's Packard Electric Division (PED) in Juárez. The workers formed a coalition and demanded higher salaries and job protection. As was to be expected, PED declined to pay the higher wages, and instead got rid of the problem.

Under Mexican law, the company can terminate workers at any time if only it pays them an indemnity for doing so. Packard Electric decided to do just that. The company fired some 300 men and women who participated in these struggles, preferring to pay US$190,000 in indemnities rather than grant wage gains that would have cost much more.

"Consequently," says a man we shall call Juan Gómez, "there was no core group left to continue the struggle, but rather the experience left a sense of the impossibility of achieving improved conditions of work."[8]

There is another problem with organizing in the *maquiladoras* as well, Gómez explains. "When workers turn to attorneys, the attorneys take over political leadership of the movement and follow an invariable tactic: they form a coalition and give strike notification, turning over to the board a list of the coalition members." The board gives the list to management. "Management makes up its blacklist and begins to fire the activists. In the end, management waits until just before the outbreak of the strike and then fires all the workers involved."

"There's one more thing to take into consideration," says Gómez. "Some workers, tired of the exploitation and lacking opportunities to move into better paying positions, utilize the coalition as a way to get fired and be indemnified." Those workers take their money and then move on to another job. Some unscrupulous lawyers may collaborate in these schemes, taking as much as 40 percent of the workers' indemnification as their cut. Such cynicism, Gómez suggests, is communicated to the rest of the workers, demoralizing entire groups. So what is the alternative?

Gómez works with a group called El Alacrán, which publishes a newspaper by the same name. An *Alacrán* is a scorpion, yet the word is also used locally to mean an alarm clock. In this way, *El Alacrán* is a wake up call to the workers, a potential pain for the bosses.

What must be done, says Gómez, is to organize secret cells of five or six workers in each plant. These cells must reject the organization of either coalitions or official unions. The organization of independent unions is ruled out by the board's refusal to recognize them. Instead of those tactics, workers must gradually expand their influence until they are able to negotiate with the employers.

Through semi-clandestine organizing over issues of working conditions, wages and benefits, the cells of El Alacrán will gradually expand in each plant until one day they form a strong network through the most important *maquiladoras* in Ciudad Juárez. At that point the organization of independent unions will become a real possiblity.

Gómez says that the activities of the worker cells in each factory are coordinated by a workers' center, which can help to share information and generalize the experiences of each clandestine group. The creation of this entire network is the inspiration of a revolutionary socialist party, which has been organizing in the border plants for a dozen years.

El Alacrán's strategy results from both Leninist theory and the oppressive conditions in the *maquiladora* zones. Gómez, and other activists with El Alacrán, are prepared to work with independent unions like the FAT and with democratic activists in the official unions, but they feel that cells of committed activists are the the key to any future organizing successes.

ロロロ

Much cross-border organizing is done through support committees. Some of these committees, like the Support Committee for Maquiladora Workers in San Diego, have grown out of local issues and struggles. Others, like the Coalition for Justice in the Maquiladoras, have attempted to grapple with many of the biggest issues, such as environmental pollution along the entire border. Both play important roles in building the cross-border activist network.

In January of 1993, heavy rains and flash floods swept through the Tijuana canyons, carrying away many of the humble homes and few belongings of *maquiladora* workers. In response, a group of San Diego activists pitched in to help their sisters and brothers across the border, explains organizer Mary Tong, creating the Support Committee for Maquiladora Workers. Through the Support Committee, labor unionists from the United States and Canada, and soon other concerned people as well, offered food, clothing, and funds.

Working out of the independent Telephone Workers Union hall in Tijuana, the support committee was soon involved in attempts to help 450 workers at the Plásticos Bajacal coat hanger factor. Plásticos Bajacal, a subsidiary of Carlisle Industries, had changed names and moved from Santa Ana, California, to Tijuana to escape an organizing campaign by the United Food and Commercial Workers (UFCW). The Bajacal workers were attempting to organize an independent union affiliated with the Revolutionary Workers Confederation (COR). It was the first election for an independent union in Tijuana in 13 years, and it had the full support of many U.S. and Canadian unionists.

But workers faced opposition from the company, the official union and the government. The company brought in an official union, the Regional Confederation of Mexican Workers (CROM), which threatened and intimidated the workers, and, according to independent observers, orchestrated various irregularities. The Mexican government Board of Conciliation and Arbitration supported the Plásticos Bajacal and the CROM, so that the campaign for the independent union was defeated. But as Mary Tong says, "the mere fact that it occurred was a tribute to the great effort by organizers on both sides of the border."[9]

Mary Tong believes that she learned some lessons from the Support Committee experience. "One key lesson that I learned is that in all the work that you do, both with people from the United States and with people from Mexico, you constantly have to talk to people about the meaning of solidarity and the building of mutuality," says Tong. Because the committee began by distributing food and clothing and helping to provide some financial assistance, some people from the United States and some from Mexico, related to the work as charity, and that was a problem.

"There's a tendency on the part of many people in Mexico to think in certain stereotypes, that everyone from the United States has a lot of money. And at the same time, we had a lot of people coming on tours who had a certain stereotype of the Mexican worker needing aid and needing advice on what to do. And both of those stereotypes needed to be broken down. I see our work as really doing a lot of the educational activity to overcome those stereotypes."

The largest cross-border alliance is the Coalition for Justice in the Maquiladoras (CJM), headquartered in San Antonio, Texas. Founded four years ago, CJM is made up of over 60 environmental, religious, community, labor, women's and Latino organizations from Canada, Mexico, and the United States.

CJM has focussed much of its activity on worker and community health. It has launched a "Warning Labels in Spanish" campaign to protect workers from dangerous chemicals, and it has targeted multinational corporations on the "chemical row in Matamoros. And CJM has demanded investigations into the 386 anencephalic births in the state of Tamaulipas in the past five years."

CJM pressures multinational corporations to adopt its "Maquiladora Standards of Conduct" based on Mexican and U.S. labor law, on International Labor Organization, and on United Nations standards. CJM has also taken its demands for justice in the *maquiladoras* to corporate stockholders' meetings. For example, CJM has gone after the Zenith Corporation, whose 21,000 Mexican employees, such as those in Reynosa, earn only US$30.43 for a 45 hour week.

CJM also supports worker and community struggles for social, economic and environmental justice in the *maquiladora* industry. "We encourage union-to-union organizing, and contacts among workers in all three countries," says Susan Mika, O.S.B., CJM president. CJM has worked to create links between Stepan Chemical workers in Maywood, New Jersey, and Matamoros, Mexico, as well as backed the UE, IBT and FAT in attempts to organize Honeywell and GE.[10]

"We also help workers to document their conditions in the factories," says Mika. That information is used both in legal and legislative work, as well as in direct organizing. "We're trying to educate everybody, from management in the company to the public, about what they're actually doing in those factories. We're helping workers claim their own rights and be able to empower themselves toward better working conditions, higher salaries and better union representation for themselves."

Concerning some of the differences in emphasis among those doing cross-border organizing, Mika says, "We see those different types of strategies as complementary. Each of the groups will bring their own tool to the common work."

There are many models of cross-border organizing, from the broad coalitions like the CJM, to the union-to-union company and industry models such as the FAT-UE alliance, to the women's community-model of the AFSC's CFO. No doubt Susan Mika of CJM is right, that many of the strategies are complementary. What is most important is that there is a growing trend toward international labor solidarity, and toward alliances between Canadian, Mexican and U.S. workers. At the heart of these strategies, as Dave Johnson of the UE suggested, are direct worker-to-worker contacts and the strengthening of the rank and file movement among workers in all three countries.

The Canadian, Mexican and U.S. workers trying to organize the *maquiladoras* cannot expect any assistance from the National Administration Office (NAO) created by the NAFTA "side agreements." In theory, the NAO is supposed to determine whether or not workers' rights have been violated under the laws of the country in question, or under the NAFTA side agreements. In February 1994, the UE and the Teamsters filed the first complaints with the NAO, established by NAFTA labor side agreements. On September 12, 1994, the NAO heard the complaint on the firing of Fernando Castro and the 100 other workers fired by GE CASA in Juárez. UE and FAT presented witnesses and sworn affidavits from a number of workers testifying to the company's efforts to break the independent union's organizing efforts. Like the Mexican labor boards, however, the NAO concluded that because the vast majority of workers had accepted their severance pay, the NAO could not determine whether Mexico had failed to enforce the relevant labor laws. President Clinton's Labor Secretary Robert Reich stated that the charges against GE CASA were unfounded.[11] Neither Mexican nor U.S. officials have any interest in seeing the development of a more democratic and militant labor movement on the border.

Time alone will show whether or not the cross-border organizing efforts will be successful in organizing the Mexican border factories. Workers' right to organize independent unions are an important component of democratic rights. If the labor movement is to become a factor in Mexican political life, it will have to be able to organize the *maquiladora* zone.

But the efforts to organize the *maquiladora* zone are important for other reasons as well. A genuinely democratic movement in Mexico would have to find ways to control U.S. based multinational corporations, as well as to regulate and limit their role in Mexican affairs. These initial efforts at worker-to-worker, cross-border international solidarity represent some important first steps to curb the power of the multinationals and increase the power of working people in Canada, Mexico and the United States.

The creation of a genuinely international labor movement, based on mutual respect and solidarity, would also represent a significant contribution to attemping to democratize Mexican society. Wage workers represent the majority of the populations of Canada, Mexico and the United States; that which improves the organization and political strength of those groups could potentially represent a force for democracy throughout the continent.

9

MEXICAN WOMEN: BETWEEN REBELLION AND REFORM

On January 1, 1994, Chiapas became a war zone, as first the Zapatista Army of National Liberation, and then Mexican Army troops invaded several towns. While the truce on January 12 stopped most of the fighting between the two armies, Mexican Army troops continued to arrive and soon occupied much of the state. The Mexican Army blocked highways and roads, surrounded and cut off many villages, as well as collective farms or *ejidos*.

The Indian peasants, particularly young men and women, feared leaving their small towns and farms because they might be detained by the army and be accused of supporting the Zapatistas. Their fears were well founded. Some villagers were detained and even tortured. Because of the military encirclement, in many areas there were no government welfare checks for poor farmers, there was no food, and no medical service. While the Mexican Army established checkpoints, dug foxholes and built bunkers, terror, hunger and sickness stalked the villages.

Many Mexicans hesitated to become involved because the situation was so explosive. Two armies stood poised and apparently prepared for another outbreak of fighting. The wealthy cattle ranchers and plantation owners organized their own private armies of "white guards" who appeared to be prepared to massacre the rebels and every other Indian they could lay their hands on. In such a situation, any incident could easily escalate into a violent confrontation.

The situation was especially tense and most dangerous around the town of Altamirano which had become a virtual military garrison. Isolation, hunger, and sickness were the greatest problems in little villages around Altamirano, like the Ejido de Jalisco, and, as is often the case, those at greatest risk were the elderly, pregnant women and infants. Many Mexicans sympathized with the Indians in Chiapas and the conditions that led them to rebel, but most hesitated to become involved.

A group of women in Mexico City from various stations in life, professionals and housewives, working and union women, as well as the urban poor, decided that they must break the military blockade and the circle of hunger that was closing around the Indian peasants of Altamirano. Collecting money, gathering food and medicine from friends and neighbors, about a dozen of these women, who later took the name the "Rosario Castellanos" Group, put together a small caravan of cars and vans and drove hundreds of miles through the mountains of southern Mexico to Chiapas.

When the Mexican Army stopped them at its sandbagged checkpoints, the women stood up to the soldiers and argued with the officers. They insisted that they were going to take their food and medicine to the women and children of Altamirano. After several days of travel and negotiation, the women finally succeeded in breaking the military blockade and entering the beleaguered Ejido de Jalisco.

These women are part of a new wave of women activists who have been created by the Chiapas Rebellion and the new civil society movement. . While rushing to bring aid to the Indians in Altamirano, these women have changed themselves, changed the Mexican women's movement, and are changing the shape of Mexican society as well.[1]

Mexican feminism in the 1990's has shaped and been shaped by both the Chiapas Rebellion and by civil society's struggle for political reform. After the January 1 uprising in Chiapas, one of the first acts of the Zapatista Army of National Liberation (EZLN) was the promulgation of a "Women's Revolutionary Law." The law gave women equal rights, both in society and in the Zapatista Army, recognized women's right to choose their own partners, and determine how many children they would have.

The Women's Revolutionary Law was a response to the extremely difficult conditions that indigenous women face. Over half of Mexico's indigenous women are illiterate, compared with about one-third of Indian men. Only 8.2 percent of Indian women ever reach high school, while 44 percent of Indian men attend secondary schools. Nearly half the Indian women in Chiapas are malnourished.[2] Yet Indian women typically rise before 5:00 a.m. and work until 8 or 9 p.m., take care of children and animals, work in the *milpa* or corn field, gather firewood, and spend hours grinding corn for tortillas.

"We are not fighting just for ourselves but also against the injustice, exploitation and marginalization that afflicts most indigenous women," explained EZLN Comandante Ramona. "If we are soldiers today, perhaps tomorrow our daughters can be doctors and lawyers," added Zapatista leader Ana María.[3]

"A significant part of the untold story in the Chiapas Rebellion has been the high level of organizing carried out by women before, during, and after the rebellion," writes anthropologist Lynn Stephen. The Chiapas Women's Convention of 1994 brought together women from 25 non-governmental organizations, peasant and indigenous groups to voice the needs of women throughout the state. The Convention called for an end to violence against women, including rape. Women also demanded demilitarization of the state, respect for human rights, economic justice, and democratic practices that include women. "This is the first independent state-wide women's network in Mexico and also the first large-scale organization of indigenous women," writes Stephen.[4]

At the same time, in Mexico City and in other cities and towns throughout Mexico, urban women's groups and feminist organizations have reoriented their work to support their sisters in Chiapas. Many feminists and women's organizations, were moved into action by the Chiapas Rebellion and later participated in the National Democratic Convention (CND) of August 1994. Civil society's struggle for political reform has also influenced the women's movement. The struggles of civil society also led some Mexican women in the 1990s to become more involved in party politics.

The two women's groups discussed here, the "Rosario Castellanos" Group and Women in Struggle for Democracy show common features of the Mexican women's movement, but also reveal two divergent trends. On the one hand, the Chiapas Rebellion led some women, like those who formed the "Rosario Castellanos" Group, to decide to work with poor peasant and working women, thus reinforcing what has been the dominant trend of Mexican feminism as part of the social movements.

On the other hand, the fraud associated with the 1988 election led to the creation of an altogether different kind of woman's group. The group Women in Struggle for Democracy (WSD) oriented toward the middle class and prioritized electoral reform and parliamentary politics. Both of these trends have developed out of the Mexican feminist movement of the 1970s.

ㅁㅁㅁ

The origins of Mexican feminism leads us back to the stormy days of the Mexican Revolution. Mexican feminism began with the rise to power of the Socialist Party of the Southeast, in the state of Yucatán in 1916. Two radical socialist governors of the Yucatán, Salvador Alvarado and Felipe Carrillo Puerto, were also militant feminists who saw the liberation of women as essential to the creation of a socialist society. The two radical governors convened the First Feminist Congress in Mexico in 1916, created militant Feminist Leagues, reproduced Margaret Sanger's birth control pamphlets, which had been banned in the United States, and gave women the right to vote in state elections. The revolutionary Yucatán also elected the first women to public office in Mexican history.

Supporting divorce, contraception, abortion, women's right to vote, and decent wages for female domestic workers, the Yucatán socialist feminists were too radical for most men and women of their times. The socialist feminist movement collapsed in the mid-1920s with the assassination of governor Carrillo Puerto and with the federal government's successful suppression of the radical labor and peasant movements.[5] But revolutionary Yucatán set the long-term agenda of the Mexican women's movement, and many of its demands are still being fought for, eighty years later.

Led by feminists and communists, the second feminist wave came during the presidency of Lázaro Cárdenas in the 1930s and set about organizing peasants and working-class women. But the communists, then in their ultra-left "'Third Period,'" sabotaged all efforts to organize a national feminist organization, arguing that feminism was bourgeois and women should fight only through the Communist Party and the labor unions.

But in 1934, under the leadership of María del Refugio García, a group of feminists broke with the communists and established the Sole Front for Women's Rights to fight for women's suffrage, a unifying demand. When Lázaro Cárdenas became president in 1934 he encouraged the new Mexican women's suffrage movement, and even pushed a women's suffrage amendment to the Constitution, which passed the Mexican Senate, was ratified by all 28 states and had only to be approved by the Congress.

By 1939, however, the political situation had changed. The conservative General Juan Andreu Almazán had announced that he was running for president in 1940, and had organized the ultra-conservative Feminine Idealist Party to support his campaign. Cárdenas, and other leaders of the ruling National Revolutionary Party, feared that if Mexican women got the vote, many would vote for Almázan who might win what was expected to be a close election. While Cárdenas made a statement of support for passage of the suffrage amendment in his final address to the Chamber of Deputies on September 31, 1939, at that point neither he nor his party intended to press for women's suffrage. Congress let the amendment die. As Anna Macías wrote, Cárdenas and the PRN believed that "many Mexican women were, indeed, enemies of the revolution."[6]

Only in 1958 did women finally vote in a Mexican presidential election. The Mexican Revolution had begun in 1910 under the slogan, "Effective Suffrage and No Re-election," but women did not win suffrage until almost 50 years later, and then their suffrage was not very effective. For by 1958, Mexico's government had become a powerful one-party state which marched voters to the polls to vote for the ruling Institutional Revolutionary Party. Throughout the 1950s and 1960s, Mexican feminism remained a very small and isolated current in Mexican society.

But in 1968 in Mexico, as around the world, everything changed.[7] The Tlatelolco massacre in 1968 led to a new radicalism and a third wave of feminism, as well. The election of populist Luis Echeverría Alvarez to the presidency, and his proclamation of a new democratic opening in Mexico, encouraged many groups in the society to attempt to organize, including women.

The U.S. women's movement, which had become a mass movement by 1970, also began to have an impact in Mexico. In particular, Mexican women's attention was caught by the demonstrations accompanying the National Organization for "Women's Strike for Equality" on August 26, 1970. As a result, in 1971, a group of women in Mexico City formed Women in Solidarity Action (MAS), the first modern feminist group.

This independent feminist movement began with the formation of consciousness raising groups among women involved in left-wing political movements and parties. From the beginning some secretaries and housewives were also involved, but most feminists were women who had attended the university. Arising after the 1968 massacre, the new women's movement rejected participation in the organizations of the Institutional Revolutionary Party. But, since the political reform legalizing the Communist Party and other left parties was not passed until 1977, electoral opposition to the PRI was not yet an option for most of these women. Voting for the Catholic and conservative PAN would have been out of the question. With no electoral alternative available, women turned to the social movements.

These women attempted to link their new-born feminist movement to the new groups of worker activists emerging in the 1970s, offering support to women textile workers. However, the militant workers' first priority was the struggle for a labor movement independent of the state and feminist issues were not high on their list of demands. Some women played dual roles, as both feminists involved in consciousness raising groups and as activists in the new independent labor movement. Some were also members of the parties of the far Left: communists, Maoists and Trotskyists.

Again Echeverría provided the next opportunity for the women's movement to grow. The United Nations had proclaimed 1975 to be "Year of the Woman," with the slogan "Equality, Development, and Peace." Seeing an opportunity to enhance his administration, Echeverría invited the U.N. to hold the First International Conference of Women in Mexico City from June 19 to July 2, 1975. Nearly all feminists criticized Echeverría for attempting to coopt the feminist movement. Eventually, most Mexican feminists decided not to participate in the U.N. conference, but instead to organize a parallel event. Betty Friedan, author of the enormously influential *The Feminine Mystique*, spoke to a meeting of approximately 300 Mexican women who met outside the structure of the conference.

Throughout the mid-1970s, Mexico's workers, peasants, and the urban poor organized and fought to improve their situation. The center of this movement was the Democratic Tendency (TD) led by the electrical worker Rafael Galván. The formation of this radical coalition of workers, peasants and the poor carrying out massive political demonstrations inevitably affected the new feminist movement. Feminists, too, decided to unite and brought the proliferating small feminist organizations together, in 1978, in the National Front for the Liberation and Rights of Women (FNALIDM). By the late 1970s, the small feminist movement was demonstrating for free abortion on demand, and defending lesbianism.

The lesbian and gay movement first appeared in the 1970s, forming such groups as Lambda for Homosexual Liberation, Oikabeth, and the Homosexual Front of Revolutionary Action. The gay and lesbian groups held their first public demonstrations in 1979, and those demonstrations of a few thousand were immediately larger than those organized by the feminist movemen so far. Lesbian groups continued to organize through the 1970s and 1980s, forming a national network in 1987.

Meanwhile, the women's movement continued to fight for birth control and abortion rights. President José López Portillo's political reform led to the legalization of the Communist Party in 1978; the communists and other leftists then joined together in 1979 to form the Coalition of the Left. In 1980, the feminists succeeded in getting the Coalition of the Left to present to Congress a bill for Free and Voluntary Motherhood which would have given women the right to contraception and abortion. While the bill never became law, it represented a step both in the growth of feminism and in the unity of feminists with the Left.

Feminism suddenly achieved national visibility in 1982, when Rosario Ibarra de Piedra ran as Mexico's first woman candidate for president. Ibarra became a political activist after her son Jesús Ibarra disappeared, presumably kidnapped, tortured and murdered by the government, as had happened to 500 others in Mexico in the 1960s and 1970s. To search for her son and others like him, Ibarra and a number of other mothers of the disappeared organized the Committee in Defense of Prisoners, the Persecuted, the Disappeared, and Political Exiles. Later, after succeeding in finding out the fate of 148 such disappeared persons, the committee changed its name to Eureka, the Greek word meaning "I have found it."

Ibarra ran for president on the Revolutionary Workers Party (PRT) ticket, not only as a socialist, but also as a feminist candidate. She campaigned as the candidate of the working class, and particularly, of the common working woman and housewife. Ibarra advocated economic, social and political equality for women, defended the right to abortion, and supported gay and lesbian rights. The government said she got 500,000 votes representing less than 2 percent of the total, though she believes that she received more. Rosario Ibarra's campaign represented a high point for feminism and the Left.[8]

Women's struggles became more difficult in the 1980s. The deep economic crisis which began in 1982 was accompanied by plant closings, layoffs, rising unemployment and a 50 percent cut in purchasing power. In response, women's organizations directed their energies toward working women, peasants and the poor. Some feminists attempted to organize female domestic servants.[9] Others turned toward the organization of women in poor neighborhoods.

In Mexico, women of all social classes took up the struggle over community issues, water service, electricity, sewers, and schools. In Monterrey, for example, between 1978 and 1984, women led demonstrations for improved water service in 156 of 300 Monterrey neighborhoods. Mostly poor and working-class women, they held demonstrations, blocked streets, seized water service vehicles and sometimes kidnapped government officials. Women took mountains of dirty laundry and washed it in the public fountains in front of the governor's palace. Eventually, their protests led the state and federal governments to improve water service.[10] In the late 1980s, other women organized land seizures, and fought for water and electricity in Mazatlán.[11]

Eventually many of these movements coalesced. The First National Meeting of Women of the Urban Popular Movement was organized by the National Coordinating Movement of the Urban Popular Movement (CONAMUP) in 1983. After that meeting, the women of CONAMUP returned to the shanty towns and working-class neighborhoods and organized women's networks, centers and workshops for poor and working-class women.[12]

The Mexico City earthquake of 1985, which had such an enormous impact on all of Mexican society, had an especially important effect on the women's movement. The earthquake destroyed much of Mexico City's garment worker district, killing about 300 garment workers and severely injuring another 225, who were pulled from the rubble. The employers sent rescue workers not to save their female employees, but to rescue their sewing machines. The bosses moved the machines to other shops, and attempted to weasel out of paying wages owed to their employees, living or dead.

The garment employers' shocking behavior infuriated the seamstresses, who met among the ruins of their former workplaces, eventually forming the "19 of September" Garment Workers Union, named after the date of the earthquake which had killed their sisters. Led by white-haired, soft-spoken, Evangelina Corona, and a dozen other women workers, the organization immediately attracted both feminist and socialist supporters. Eventually the seamstresses, the socialists, and the radical feminists set aside their theoretical differences on abortion, lesbianism, and Marxism for the good of the union.

After months of marches and demonstrations, with support from the independent Authentic Workers Front (FAT), the "19 of September" Garment

Workers Union won the long political battle and was registered as a national independent labor union. Customarily, the Mexican government denied independent unions their legal registration, so the registration of the "19 of September" represented a particularly important victory. While the "19 of September" union encountered enormous obstacles in organizing shops and winning contracts, its very existence was an inspiration to both women and workers.[13]

After 1985, women began to appear as leaders in a variety of social movements. Student Rosalba Lomelí helped to lead the environmental movement against the Laguna Verde nuclear reactor, a movement in which women were particularly active.[14] Women also played a leading role in the struggle at the National University (UNAM) in 1986 when Rector Jorge Carpizo attempted to end open admissions and impose fees. Women helped to organize the Student University Council (CEU) in opposition to the reforms, and made up at least a quarter of the student demonstrators, who numbered into the hundreds of thousands. Unlike the student movement of 1968, which largely excluded women, in 1986 women such as Leyla Méndez, Andrea González and Guadalupe Carrasco played a leading role in the struggle.[15]

In 1988, feminists, working women and the rest of the social movement turned toward the new political movement led by Cuauhtémoc Cárdenas. When Cárdenas ran for president as the candidate of the National Democratic Front, most feminists and many women's organizations supported his campaign enthusiastically. Some peasant women from the countryside, poor women from the urban popular movement, teachers and women from the universities brought their grassroots organizations into the Cárdenas campaign. They organized meetings, handed out literature, and also put forward women candidates through the parties which had joined the National Democratic Front. (Rosario Ibarra was one of a handful of women on the Left who refused to back Cárdenas in 1988. She ran for president as the candidate of the PRT, but found little support and the Revolutionary Workers Party lost its legal recognition because it received so few votes.)

Cárdenas' defeat demoralized and disoriented the Left in general, and women as well, as the movement lost its overall objective. The result was that many women abandoned politics and returned to grassroots organizing.

By the 1990s, every political tendency understood the importance of making an appeal to women and nodding in the direction of feminism. For instance, in 1989 and 1990, when a democratic rank and file insurgency threatened to overturn the PRI's loyal bureaucracy in the teachers union, President

Salinas removed union boss Carlos Jongitud Barrios, and replaced him with a woman, Elba Esther Gordillo. Clearly, Salinas intended both to appeal to 60 percent of the women teachers in the union, and to the vaguely feminist sentiments in the country.

In 1990, some of the macho Maoists who had built community organizations throughout Mexico decided to make peace with the PRI. They negotiated a deal with Salinas, which got official recognition for their Labor Party (Partido de Trabajo - PT), in exchange for support for the PRI's policies. In order to do well in the 1994 elections and keep its legal party status, Alberto Anaya offered the PT's presidential nomination to the charismatic Cecilia Soto who had previously been a leader of neo-fascist Lyndon LaRouche's Mexican affiliate (the Partido Laborista or PL). Cecilia Soto reached out for the votes of women.

Despite token representation in political parties, women still faced many social and economic problems. While half of all elementary students were female, only one-third of those in vocational school were women, and only four out of ten university students were women. The illiteracy rate for adult women was 20 percent compared with 14 percent for men.

By 1990 women accounted for more than one-third of the work force. But women's wages remained far below those of men, and most women were lucky to earn US$5.00 per day. Abortions remained illegal, contraceptive devices expensive and elusive outside of large cities. As of 1990, 52 percent of all women living with male partners used birth control, yet sterilization was the most common form of birth control (36 percent). Feminism and the women's movement continued to struggle against widespread machismo. Divorce remained uncommon, and husband's abandonment of wives and children continued to be widespread. According to one study, 55 percent of Mexico's married women had been physically attacked by their husbands.[16]

In Mexico in the early 1990s, there were many women's and feminist groups, but there was no national women's or feminist organization, nothing equivalent to the National Organization for Women (NOW) in the United States. Many Mexican women felt uncomfortable being called feminists because that term had become identified with controversial issues such as abortion and lesbianism. But at the same time, feminist values of economic, social, and political equality for women had permeated much of Mexican society.

The outbreak of the Chiapas Rebellion in January of 1994 suddenly provided women with a new focus for activism. The urgency of the situation—the armies at war, the endangered civilian populations, the television coverage of the bombing of villages, photographs of the frightened faces of Indian peasant women—moved some women to act on behalf of their sisters.

One of the original organizers of the "Rosario Castellanos" Group was María Atilano Uriarte.[17] Atilano can usually be found in a small office in the headquarters of the Authentic Labor Front (FAT), one of Mexico's few independent labor unions. Using an office donated by FAT, she works for the "Mexican Action Network on Free Trade" (RMALC), a group that opposes NAFTA. While Atilano works during the day with Mexican labor unions and peasant organizations, she also volunteers her spare time as an organizer of the new women's movement.

"The 'Rosario Castellanos' Group, of which I am a member," says Atilano, "was formed as a result of the armed uprising in Chiapas in January of 1994, and has as its goal to fight for peace and democracy. The group is a pluralistic organization which has its origins in a first caravan to Chiapas. We came together as a group of women from various backgrounds, artists, intellectuals, social leaders, activists, neighborhood women.

"We organized a caravan to break the military encirclement in the Ejido de Jalisco, which is in the Municipio de Altamirano. When we arrived, people were completely without food. We found lactating mothers who were trying to nurse their babies, but they had dried up because of the shock they had suffered. But beyond that, the children didn't even have the bare minimum of food. We also brought along a team of medical women to give attention to the population there, principally for the women and children."

But perhaps as important as hunger, was the demoralization of the peasant community. "We organized an assembly of the people of the community who were very frightened," said Atilano. "We held a meeting with everyone to try to help them overcome the paralysis that they were suffering. We explained that they had support from people outside, and that they should not think that they were lost and alone."

Recognizing that the *ejidos* in Chiapas would continue to need help, Atilano and the women in the "Rosario Castellanos" Group made plans for on-going work with the community. "We adopted one of the *ejidos*, so we could follow up and continue giving support in the form of food and medicine. Afterwards, we also gave information to the people in Mexico City and other parts of Mexico about what we'd experienced.

"We explained that in this first incursion in Altamirano, the army had occupied all of the public institutions, schools, and oddly enough, even the offices of the IFE, the Federal Electoral Institute. On the roofs of the churches the Mexican Army had posted soldiers. We spoke out against the continuing aggression against the nuns, who ran a little hospital in the Municipio de Altamirano."

The "Rosario Castellanos" Group also intervened with the political authorities on behalf of the peasant communities. "We had a meeting with the then Commissioner for Peace, Manuel Camacho Solís, to protest the situation in those *ejidos,* in the Municipio de Altamirano, and the fact that the women could not come and go.

"We also pointed out, for example, that the army had set up a center for food for the population. But when the families arrived at the army offices, which had been set up to distribute the food, many men never came out of the office. They were held by the army, accused of being Zapatistas. We gave examples of women we had met who had been left alone because of that problem."

In addition to the army, there was also the problem with the ranchers and their "white guards," their hired thugs. "The rich ranchers of the area had begun a campaign of harassment against the population. So we also went and spoke to the Ranchers Association and protested their aggression against the community and against the nuns in the hospital."

After the women returned to Mexico City, they decided to form an ongoing organization. "We formed the Grupo 'Rosario Castellanos.' The name comes from a very important woman writer, a poet from Chiapas, who worked in the indigenous communities for many years. She was also a feminist who put forward very interesting ideas about feminism. Because she was a woman dedicated to the struggle of the indigenous people of Chiapas, and the struggles of women as well, we took her name.

"The Grupo 'Rosario Castellanos' has not yet declared itself to be a feminist group, rather we describe ourselves as a group of women. Our goal was to help the indigenous women of Chiapas, especially of these first *ejidos* we had visited."

The "Rosario Castellanos" Group also organized among the women of Mexico City. "When we organized as a group, we left open the possibility that more women might join. Every Friday afternoon we hold a semi-public forum in the Centro Cultural el Juglar, and all the women who want, and the men who want too, can come to these organizational meetings. This is a place where people have come freely.

"Our most important task is to try to put out truthful information to people in society. So we set up a public information table in the Plaza Coyoacán where we get together every Sunday to give weekly information to the people about what's happening in Chiapas. But we also talk about the relationship between the Chiapas situation and our national life."

It was through their work supporting the communities of Chiapas, that the "Rosario Castellanos" Group became one of the organizers of the National Democratic Convention (CND), held in August in San Cristóbal and in Aguascalientes, Chiapas. "We were involved with the very important 'Caravan of Caravans' in the spring of 1994, in which 360 people participated, giving support to the Zapatista communities which had not been receiving aid. The 'Caravan of Caravans' was the organization which, together with the EZLN and the Chiapas State Convention, issued the call for the National Democratic Convention, the CND."

Meanwhile, the national presidential campaigns were taking place, and the women of the "Rosario Castellanos" Group also thought it important to participate in the election. "Some like myself naturally worked in the training of women observers with the people from the Urban Popular Movement (MUP). Others worked through Civic Alliance, the coalition of poll watchers' groups. On election day, we participated as representatives or observers through the Civic Alliance."

The overwhelming victory of Zedillo and the PRI came as a shock to many Mexicans, including the women of the "Rosario Castellanos" Group. But immediately after the election, they set up their usual Sunday public information table, and had a large sheet of paper where people could express their opinions about the election and about the National Democratic Convention.

"People reacted very favorably to us. The people were anxious to express themselves, and to express their opposition to this whole process. They wrote down very interesting phrases, such as, 'Change can't take place if there is fear. We have to break with fear,' and 'To have real democracy you have to break with the state-party.'"

For women like those in the "Rosario Castellanos" Group, the Chiapas Rebellion reinforced the dominant historic tendency of the Mexican feminist movement, which has been an orientation toward peasants, workers and the urban poor. Because of the Chiapas Rebellion, women like María Atilano and the others in the "Rosario Castellanos" Group once again found that path.

While the Chiapas Rebellion has been the principal influence on one group of women, electoral politics has also been a major force shaping another branch of the women's movement. Patricia Bracho is one of the principal organizers of Women in Struggle for Democracy (WSD), an organization which firmly rejects the "feminist" label, proudly asserts it middle-class character, and has focussed its energies on electoral reform and political power in the most traditional senses of those words.[18]

Patricia Bracho counts her closest friends among the PRI's elite, but she says her political sympathies often lie with the PRD opposition. For three years, Bracho lived in Cincinnati, Ohio while her husband studied medicine and she learned to speak English fluently. While she speaks Spanish in the characteristic accent of the "Chilangos" of Mexico City, and in the style of the university educated elite, Patricia Bracho spices her speech with English words and phrases, and her political ideas also seem influenced by U.S.-style politics.

"In 1988," Bracho explained, "I was part of a group of women who felt that the people's will hadn't been respected in the election. We were women from the middle classes, basically educated women who had been to the university, and we found ourselves facing this phenomenon of fraud which pained and disturbed us. We said to ourselves: 'What can we do in the face of this?'

"So we decided to found this organization and that's why we called ourselves 'Women in Struggle for Democracy.' This might seem like a feminist observation, but the men said, 'Women in struggle for democracy? What's going on?' But today there is not a single organization which is not called such and such 'for democracy.' Today everyone is for democracy—but we were for democracy in 1988."

Bracho asserts emphatically, "Women in Struggle is not a feminist organization. We were women who had come together to discuss the question of what was happening in this country. Many of the women who signed the founding statement of the organization were renowned women, such as author Elena Poniatowska; human rights activist Mariclaire Acosta; Paulina La Vista, the photographer, and many others. There were women scientists, women from all areas."

So in 1988, these rather distinguished women formed Women in Struggle for Democracy. "Our natural clientele was the middle class. Those of us who make up the board of directors of the organization are women from the middle class who are fortunate in that we don't have to worry about how we're going to get the next day's food, and this has made it possible for us to organize our work."

Bracho defines WSD by counterpoising it to the Mexican feminist groups which, she says, focussed their struggles on issues like abortion. "We think that as a women's movement the feminists are a step behind," said Bracho. "In 1988 the fight was for democracy, for respect for the vote as the beginning of democracy. The feminists continued with their very specific demands: the legalization of abortion or the problems of domestic violence. Now I don't minimize those issues and they must be dealt with. But it seemed to us that there was a much broader issue: the transition to a democratic life.

"The feminists said, your interest in politics is no guarantee for us that you will take up the issues of gender. And they had a point, because we can see from history that this has happened in some cases. But it just seemed that history has passed them by. And today"—we were talking on August 20, 1994—"at five minutes before midnight before the elections, all the feminist groups suddenly woke up to the need to have political consciousness and saw the need to have a more open political role. It seems to me that the feminists instead of joining together into a broad common front to give battle, continue breaking up into little groups with apparently different interests."

While Bracho rejects the label feminist, she makes a feminist critique of politics. "We believe in raising the consciousness of women so that they can participate more actively in the political life of Mexico," she explained. "We found that women do all the organizing work in the communities, and yet, when it comes to naming people to important posts and to changing political policies, women aren't there.

"The rank and file of the unions and of the political parties, are in their majority women, but when those organizations appear in the media, the women have disappeared. We have a statistic that of 1,500 public functionaries there are 34 women at the national level. That is, their representation is minimal."

Bracho and WSD decided to focus their activities on getting women to run for office, and getting women to vote. In 1991 they helped to organize the Women's National Convention for Democracy. "We created this convention," said Bracho, "with the goal of bringing together talented women and offering them to the PT, to PARM, to PRD, to PRI, to whatever party they wanted. The idea was to put forward a number of potential women candidates and to go to the political parties and say, 'Here, we are a group of women and we want to participate.'"

Bracho complains that the feminists wrecked the convention. "The convention was based on five points, but particularly this idea of running women as candidates. The feminists understood that this convention was important, and they came. The PAN women were also involved and so were the PRI women. And what happened? In the middle of the convention, when we had a previous agreement, the feminists said, 'What about abortion? Are you prepared to support abortion?' The PAN women, said, 'Goodbye.' Then the PRI women left too because they couldn't support the electoral reform we proposed. So who was left? Ourselves! This is the kind of action I don't understand, and it bothers me. It bothers me because far from increasing our forces, it reduces them."

In the end, despite the internal disputes and the walkout by the PAN and PRI, the Women's Convention for Democracy did select 20 women candidates from various women's groups, including poor peoples' neighborhoods, working women, prostitutes and lesbians. These candidates developed a women's platform on sexuality, reproductive rights, domestic violence, and rights to land and housing.

"We were the only organization, an organization of women, which carried a bill on electoral reform to the Chamber of Deputies," said Bracho. As the 1994 election approached, Women in Struggle for Democracy made voter education their top priority. Bracho said the group wanted to fight the growing tendency of Mexican voters to stay away from the polls, presumably because they are cynical about the candidates and the process.

WSD sought foundation funding and received money from Novib of Holland and from the U.S. government's National Endowment for Democracy (NED) to carry out voter education among women. "We dedicated ourselves primarily to producing training manuals so that women would know their obligations and their rights as citizens," Bracho explained.

"Our idea was to inform the citizens about the political alternatives which were at hand, so as to be able to make more rational choices." During the 1994 campaign period, Women in Struggle for Democracy also held forums with candidates Cuauhtémoc Cárdenas and Luis Donaldo Colosio, and spokespersons from the PRI, PRD, and PAN. The forums were well attended, and widely reported in the press and on television.

Like other women activists, Patricia Bracho is also concerned about the economic situation of Mexican women. "I think that economic independence is fundamental for freedom in all senses," said Bracho. "The problem is that women's work is not considered as productive work. But it should be accounted for as productive work within the home, taking care of home and the children. This is a contribution by women which should be considered as part of the gross national product.

"We need women's banks which would offer easy credit for women, which don't require all the bureaucratic paperwork and collateral. Women don't have collateral anyway, because very often a woman is single, or divorced, or has a miserable income. A woman's bank would allow her to open a little shop, or business and would allow them to grow. In the United States there is the Good Faith Fund, which Hilary Clinton helped to create. This kind of thing has been done in Africa. The bank loans money to women who are basically artisans, or have manual skills, and they create cooperatives."

I interviewed Patricia Bracho just before the election. She was meeting with members of the Civic Alliance to discuss what should be done in the event of a PRI victory. "We are part of the Civic Alliance, and we are for civil resistance if the vote is not respected. But," added Bracho, "I don't doubt that the PRI will win." As it turned out, Patricia Bracho was right.

Women in Struggle for Democracy represents an important trend within the Mexican women's movement. Throughout the period from the 1920s to the 1980s, the feminist movement was a leftist movement, oriented toward workers and peasants. Today, under the impact of the political reform movement and the influence of U.S. political models, some Mexican women are more interested in developing a middle-class movement.

But Patricia Bracho's analysis fails to recognize that as long as the PRI dominates the Mexican state, a bloc of women voters is only a sham. As long as the PRI controls Mexico's one-party state, women's political power remains an illusion, at least for the vast majority of Mexico's women, and probably even for most of the middle class. While Mexican capitalists continue to concentrate economic power at the top, women's banks could at best only create small islands of economic independence for a few women.

The "Rosario Castellanos" Group and Women in Struggle for Democracy represent two tendencies within the contemporary Mexican feminist movement, one oriented toward the social struggle of peasants, workers and the urban poor, and the other oriented toward electoral politics. Throug lout the last several years, there have been many times when María Atilano, Patricia Bracho, and Rosario Ibarra might all have been present in the same demonstration demanding a fair election or justice for some group of women who had been trampled on by the system. But two tendencies are pulling at the women's movement, one pulls from above, offering opportunities for political participation, narrowly conceived. The other pushes from below, driving the women's movement to join the oppressed in struggle against the one-party state.

If the PRI and a small economic elite continue to take the initiative, they may be able to shape a women's movement subordinate to the technocrats political program. But if the lower orders of society, and in particular, the working class organize independently, Mexican feminism might be drawn back to its socialist roots.

10

THE SECOND AGUASCALIENTES: THE NATIONAL DEMOCRATIC CONVENTION

Hundreds of vehicles moved slowly through the mountains, heading into the jungle. Every hour or so, one of the buses broke down or went into the ditch, and the whole caravan came to a halt as repairs were made or buses were abandoned. The trip from San Cristóbal de las Casas to the Lacandón rainforest took over 24 hours, and most of the 6,000 delegates were unable to sleep. Many could not sleep from worry, after all, they were entering rebel territory. If only briefly, they were joining the rebellion.

In June of 1994, Subcomandante Marcos and the CCRI had announced that the EZLN and its supporters would convene in August a National Democratic Convention (CND) to find a peaceful solution to Mexico's problems. The convention would be held in a new town—Aguascalientes, Chiapas—which the EZLN soldiers would carve out of the Lacandón rainforest. This new Aguascalientes took its name from the town in central Mexico where Emiliano Zapata and Pancho Villa had held their Convention in October of 1914. At that first convention, Villa and the other delegates pledged to support Zapata's Plan of Ayala, calling for the distribution of land to the peasant communities.

The EZLN's call for a National Democratic Convention (CND) grew out of the impasse faced by the EZLN after the January uprising. By April, the Zapatista Army of National Liberation found itself surrounded by the Mexican Army and dangerously isolated politically. The EZLN called the CND to break out of its isolation.

At the time, Mexico was rapidly approaching the national presidential elections scheduled for August 21. The PRI had mobilized its massive political machine on behalf of its new candidate Ernesto Zedillo. The state-party was spending millions on television advertising, while the government social welfare programs distributed food and building supplies, in the city, and land certificates and PROCAMPO checks, in the countryside. If Zedillo and the PRI were elected—even if elected as usual, through fear, favors, and fraud— the government could interpret that as a mandate to crush the Chiapas rebels. If the left of center Party of the Democratic Revolution won, the EZLN would at the very least have a respite, and at best might become part of a new democratic government in Mexico. By calling this peoples' convention on the eve of the election, the EZLN hoped to shift Mexican politics to the left, and to influence the final outcome of the election.

The EZLN's convention call had a historic character. For the first time in Mexico's history, the Indians had summoned the people of Mexico to discuss the fate of the nation on the Indian's terms and on native soil. Nothing quite like this had happened since Columbus, Cortez and the *conquistadores* had broken the power of the Indians in the sixteenth century. There had been many Indian rebellions, but never before in Mexico's history had a group of indigenous rebels attempted to put themselves at the head of the nation.

The convention was organized by three groups: the EZLN, the local Democratic Convention of Chiapas, and the Caravan of Caravans, made up of those who had been bringing aid to the Indian communities from Mexico City. The EZLN's convention call invited all those who supported a peaceful transition to democracy and who vowed to participate in the coming elections. Those who advocated the armed overthrow of the government, or who called upon voters to abstain from the election were explicitly excluded. Only those approved by the organizers would be admitted to the convention. Those who came would have to leave all weapons behind and put themselves under the protection of the EZLN.

The EZLN's convention call was marvelously ambivalent. On the one hand, the convention could be seen as a guerrilla army's call for a peaceful alternative. On the other hand, the convention could be interpreted as the convening of a kind of national assembly to proclaim a national democratic revolution. Strategically, it appeared that the Chiapas rebels intended the CND to link the EZLN with the Party of the Democratic Revolution, and with the civil society movement as represented by the Civic Alliance. The EZLN must have believed that if the PRD made a strong enough showing in the election, say, one third of the vote, then it would be possible for the combined forces of the EZLN, the CND, the PRD, and the Civic Alliance to launch a national resistance movement to turn the PRI out of office. In any case, the convention would break the Mexican Army's military and political stranglehold on the EZLN. Eventually, summoned by Marcos' personal invitation or sent by local organizations, 6,000 delegates, observers and 600 reporters assembled. Thousands more had to be turned away.

Because the world's attention had remained riveted on Mexico ever since the January 1 uprising, the government dared not attempt to stop the convention. The PRI governor of Chiapas even provided the organizers with some 200 buses. Mexican Army officers waved the convention delegates and observers past the sand-bagged checkpoints. Mexican Army soldiers boarded the buses, tipped their caps, welcomed the delegates to the Lacandón rainforest, wished them good luck in the convention deliberations and in finding a democratic and peaceful solution to Mexico's problems!

The first day of the convention, held in San Cristóbal, saw a moving convocation of humble people from poor villages and urban slums. Many of those delegates embodied Mexico's vital communitarian traditions with their roots in the peasant village and the *ejido*. They represented cooperative movements in a life and death struggle with a privatizing, free marketeering government. [1]

Juan Hernández Morales, dressed in a plaid shirt and blue jeans, came from the "Baghdad" Transportation Cooperative in Buena Vista, Tobasco. "I am here," he said, "because we must show how the government attacks indigenous people." Hernández Morales explained that he and other indigenous Chontal people from Buena Vista had pooled their resources to create a local bus company. "We made sacrifices, investing our money so we could buy the vehicles and set to work. We had a social objective: to provide a public transportation service for passengers." But the government, said Hernández Morales, was destroying their cooperative. "When the state government became aware that we were working some route, they put eight or nine vehicles in competition, parallel to ours.

"How is a small cooperative society to compete with the government with all of its resources? With this act of deregulating transportation, they've taken away our right to work. So then, how are we going to survive?

"We tried all of the legal means," said Hernández Morales, "then we got in touch with Comandante Marcos and he invited us to come. So, I'm here."

A group of women had come from the town of Tulantzingo, Hidalgo. Too shy to speak to a foreign investigator, they pointed to their legal advisor Irma Moreno Ruíz and asked her to speak for them. Moreno Ruíz, one would guess, had worked in their community as a leftist organizer, for she was clearly not one of the village women. She wore a black beret, carried a large purse under her arm, and spoke with the accent of an educated person. She appeared to have the complete confidence of the women who were with her. "I am a delegate from Resplandez El Sol Azteca, S.C., an organization of colonos," Moreno Ruíz explained. "We want to show the government that civil society is mobilized, in struggle, wants peace and transparent elections. People want change. They want a government that really responds to the people."

The women had more specific local concerns, Moreno Ruíz explained to me. "The government is incapable of solving the housing problem. We are a group of people who had no housing. So we came together, and through our own efforts, and with our own money, we succeeded in buying some land in order to construct some houses. But the government has made things difficult for us. They won't let us build, they don't let us bring in utilities," said Moreno Ruíz. "Look, the problem of public services is that the government gets rich off of them. They are expensive and of poor quality. But they won't let people individually and privately solve their own problems."

Just as in other communities throughout Mexico, the people organized collectively to deal with the issues themselves. "We bought 14 hectares of land on which there are now more than 200 houses and 200 families living. The government tried to keep us from bringing in the utilities. They tried to stop us from putting in water. But, nevertheless, against their will, we've been doing it. One year after the founding of this *colonia*, we put in a tank and water pipes, and in that way we distribute the water. We are now excavating to put in some sewers.

"We now have streets and we're in the process of building a school. The people with their own labor and their own money are creating the public service, and the government—far from helping us—tries to stop us.

"We have had all kinds of threats, of course, and our leaders have been thrown in prison two or three times. They accuse us of robbery, they invent a thousand crimes in order to throw us in jail. But of course this doesn't just happen to us. This happens to all kinds of organizations all over the country. There is repression against all of those people who desire a real change and who want a solution to their problems."

Some of those who came to the CND were venerable old-timers and veterans of other movements like Esteban Salgado of Iguala, Guerrero. Salgado, a striking little man with a long beard and flowing white hair, a peasant sombrero, white tunic and trousers, carried a guitar and sang to all who would listen songs of the peoples' struggles past and present. His life was typical of the last generation of a peasant majority in Mexico. "I was born in 1924," Salgado told me, "I'm 70-years old. Until 1962 I was a peasant, and I worked the land on an *ejido*. But I saw that it was impossible to make a living there. The corn provided little, and I had a large number of children at that time, and they were small—now they're all grown and independent of me.

"In 1959, I went to the United States and I worked in Stockton, California. I went to pick asparagus. I was one of the so-called braceros who were contracted by the growers. At that time they paid US$1.00 an hour, and if we worked eight hours they paid us US$8.00.

"It was impossible to make a living on the land in Mexico. There was a lot of arid land. One year we worked it, and one year we let it lie fallow. So you can see we only worked every other year, and we had to look for other ways to make a living. The schools hardly gave any education to the children. Three years and that was it. They were 18 years old and they were still in the third grade."

Salgado had seen all the hopes and all the disappointments of Mexico since the Revolution ended in 1920. "I came for the same reason as you," he said to me, "to see the *compañeros*, the Zapatistas, to see what they're doing, and to ask them what they're thinking." Speaking slowly and thoughtfully Salgado added, "They've got some good ideas. We've been reading the articles in the newspapers. We agree with them, because they want to change the system. The system here in Mexico doesn't work. It's a system for the rich, a system which has harmed those of us who are poor. We don't have work, and if there is work they pay us poorly. Sometimes we only work one or two days a week. And that isn't enough to live on—not even in Iguala."

Slightly raising the guitar in his hand, Salgado added with a smile, "Now I sing. But I don't do it for money—I do it for the cause, for the cause of the people. Sometimes in my songs I say something to the rich. I tell them to pay attention to the people who've been screwed. I suggest that they give something to the people, so that the poor people don't get angry with them. But they don't understand words. They only understand when weapons speak, that's all they understand."

Most of the convention's delegates were indigenous people, peasants and the urban poor, yet all of civil society was present. The non-governmental organizations all attended: delegates had come, for example, from the "Rosario Castellanos" women's group, the Citizens Movement for Democracy and the Civic Alliance.

Intellectuals, writers and artists played an important part in the convention. The middle-class intellectuals' very presence provided a certain degree of protection for the convention. The Mexican Army could not attack a gathering of intellectuals the way it might assault a group of peasants. The famous artists' reputations also gave the convention legitimacy in the eyes of better-educated people. In most cases, these were intellectuals who had long been identified either with the indigenous peoples' struggles in Chiapas, or with the social movements and civil society in Mexico.

Elba Macías, for example, came to the convention with a group of her friends. "We came together," she said, gesturing toward a group of men nibbling candy bought from stalls set up for the "Annual Candy Festival" under the colonnade of the San Cristóbal plaza and added: "Heraclo Cepeda, short story writer; Carlos Olmos, dramatist; Carlos Jurado, painter; Oscar Oliva, poet; and Juan Manuelos, poet. We came as invited guests to participate in the National Democratic Convention."

Macías explained, "I was born in Chiapas and though I now live in Mexico City, I continue to participate in the cultural and political events in Chiapas. This little group of friends has been involved since we first demonstrated on the third day of the war. We wrote an analysis of the movement as an indigenous uprising, which was published in the press and reproduced in many papers. And we approved of the demands of the EZLN movement, but we wanted to find a democratic and peaceful solution. Since we have been intimately involved, and since we have published our opinions, we are invited guests of this convention."

Many of the famous Mexican intellectuals of the left came to the convention. There was Pablo Gonzáles Casanova, former rector of the National University (UNAM). Ofelia Medina, the actress who played the painter Frida Kahlo in the movie "Frida," also attended. At one point during the convention, she wore a long white dress and danced with a peasant to the music of a rural band. Carlos Monsiváis, who announced the birth of civil society after the earthquake of 1985, came to the convention as a journalist. Monsiváis obstinately refused to be an official CND delegate, because, he said, he did not want to give up his political independence.

On the other hand, Elena Poniatowska, one of Mexico's most famous and popular essayists, was delighted to be a delegate. "The intellectual's role has been to support, to solidarize themselves," she said. "After all," she asked me, "when have we ever seen a guerrilla movement whose first act was to create a library, and beyond that to convene a National Democratic Convention dedicated to peace? Never, right?"

"I think that here in Chiapas, and in the Selva Lacandóna, we are representatives of the people, of all of the people in the widest sense of the term," said the retired philosophy professor Enrique Gonzáles Rojo. "And, philosophers are also part of the people, even though that may seem impossible," he added laughing at the paradox.

Some of the university professors came not only as intellectuals, but also as union members and fighters. Professor Pilar Martínez of the Science Department of the National University (UNAM) put the university intellectuals' role in historic perspective. "We came here because the university professors have generally participated in all of the struggles of the workers and peasants, together with the Mexican people. We consider ourselves part of the people, because we are equally oppressed and exploited.

"Those of us who are professors often have salaries which are lower than the secretaries, for example. I am a full-time professor, I have a master's degree and twenty years of seniority at the National University (UNAM) and my salary is $2,500 new pesos each month. (US$830 dollars per month or about US$10,000 per year). We have minimal living conditions. True, we have an automobile and a small apartment, but, for example, we need to keep up with the scientific literature, but it's expensive, and we can't afford to do it. We should be studying all the time. But we don't have the economic resources."

Students also came to the convention because of their concerns about the university's economic situation. Ernesto Gonzáles of the National University explained that he had come as the delegate of a newly formed youth group. "We came both to make some proposals, and also to inform ourselves," said the young Gonzáles. "In education we need a bigger budget and more support. We think there should be more public rather than private universities, so that the majority of the population can have access to higher education."

Some of the university employees, especially those who teach at the National University's preparatory schools came to the Zapatistas' convention as much out of economic desperation as out of political conviction. "We are the *'pobresoras'* of CCH-Sur at UNAM, the high school," explained Rosamaría Villavicencia Huerta. Her pun, "Pobresora" is composed of the Spanish words for poor and teacher, *pobre* and *profesora*. "Our salaries are very low," said Villavicencia. "We call ourselves 'pobresoras' because since 1982 there has been a terrible deterioration of the purchasing power of our salaries. We are among those who have been worst hit and we have lost 70 percent of our purchasing power. It's not just the wages, but also the working conditions and the living conditions; both our students'and our own that have deteriorated."

Having attended many other radical events in Mexico, I was not surprised to find militant peasants and radical intellectuals. One of the really surprising things about the CND was the presence of a number of small businessmen, farmers, merchants and manufacturers, including some whose political experience had been in the right-wing National Action Party.

I found one group of businessmen standing in the shade near the front of the amphitheater in Aguascalientes. Among them were several officers of the militant farmers' organization, El Barzón. El Barzón refers to the piece of leather used in olden times to attach an oxen's yoke to a plow.[2] *El Barzón* is better known as the title of a folk song from the beginning of the century that tells of the *hacienda* owners who provided the *peones* with just enough land, and just enough food, to be able to continue working and paying their debts to the *hacendado*, the plantation owner. "Since we are in eternal debt to the banks, we took the name El Barzón," explained José Quirino Salas, national secretary of El Barzón. "Our situation is exactly the same as those *peones*, we never finish paying off the banks."

El Barzón began in 1993 when farmers demanded debt relief, Quirino Salas explained. "The farmers had the banks on their backs, seizing their goods, selling them off, or taking them to court. So we began to struggle. We carried out demonstrations, sometimes with our tractors. We took over banks.

We took over the state capital buildings. We demonstrated in the Federal District, and in every one of the state capitals. This has been our way of demanding a solution to our problems: mobilization and pressure."

The only thing the group had achieved, said Quirino Salas, was a very limited and inadequate restructuring of the farmers' debts, worked out by the Mexican Bankers Association and the Mexican government. "So the problem remains and we are still waiting for a solution to this serious problem in the countryside."

Though the farmers had not solved their own problem, their movement had grown by attracting other businessmen, explained Quirino Salas. "We've said that the second chapter of our struggle should be titled, 'The Rich Also Cry,' because it happens that not only small businesses, but also the medium-sized businesses, and even some big ones are being hurt by the debts.

"The profit levels of the firms are so low that there is no possibility of paying the high interest rates. The interest rates in Mexico are 2.7 times higher than those in the United States. But the three big Mexican banks, Banamex, Bancomer, and Serfin, annually obtain the same profits as the three biggest banks of the United States. That is, we have real speculators on top of the producers."

Quirino Salas went on to explain that El Barzón had grown so rapidly that it had come to represent hundreds of small businessmen all over the country. "Small- and medium-sized businesses whether agricultural, services, or manufacturing have suffered a tremendous blow during the last four years, as a result of the neo-liberal economic policy of Carlos Salinas. In particular, they have suffered because of the indiscriminate importation of products that enter through dumping, that come in with subsidized prices, and that compete in an unrealistic way with Mexican products. This has led to crises in the toy, lumber, furniture, and textile industries. So now we are all united as brothers in the same struggle, both farmers and entrepeneurs."

Another El Barzón member, Ignacio Campos Avila, an older farmer wearing a big sombrero, interrupted Quirino Salas, and spoke up in a voice filled with emotion. "It's not enough just to deal with the overdue accounts. One has to get to the bottom of the matter. What is the bottom of the matter? We must change Mexican society.

"The U.S. is a great influence here," said Campos Avila, "in political, economic and social matters. We are completely invaded by them. They absolutely don't allow us to organize ourselves."

Campos Avila spoke of his personal situation. "I have an avocado orchard, a small one, 15 hectares [37 acres], but with a debt of 800 million pesos owed to the bank. They loaned me 300 million, and now I owe 800 million. (Presumably these are old pesos or an originial debt of US$100,000.) If the price of avocados had stayed the same, I would have been able to pay it, right? But the price collapsed. The United States plays a rough game with us, they bring in avocados from other areas, or they buy from us, and sell them along the border, and they won't let us sell ours. And what has happened with avocados has happened with all the other produce. The United States has strangled us."

The old farmer went on, "We have to get rid of this government which has signed agreements with the most powerful countries in the world without thinking about the harm it has done to the Mexican people.

"You can see for yourself," he said to me, "from the trip that you've made through this state of Chiapas. This is one of the richest states in the country, yet the people live in poverty. It's sad, it's unjust, it's wrong. And we have to take this message not just to our government, but also to the government of the United States."

Another businessman at the CND, Ramón García Arias, is the vice-rector of the university in Puebla and owns a small lumber business that employs five people. García Arias has been talking with the leaders of El Barzón and thinks that he will join them in their struggle against the National Bank. "The National Bank is one of the curses of Mexico," says García Arias. "It's the best legal business on the planet, almost as good as the cocaine trade. There is no Mexican who doesn't owe the bank—credit cards, mortgage, automobile, or business—and ninety percent of those debts are now overdue and the people are in danger of having their credit cut off. And in spite of that, the bank is favored by the government.

"So El Barzón is carrying out a kind of civil resistance, a strike against the bank. None of them are paying the bank, and they are threatening that if the bank penalizes them in any way, they are going to take up arms. This is a very interesting example of civil resistance," says García Arias, and adds something else, but under his breath.

The business presence at the CND even included larger entrepreneurs involved in manufacturing. Rubén Barrios Graff is the former president of the National Association of Transformation Industries (ANIT), an "unofficial" association of small manufacturing companies founded in 1941. Barrios Graff also serves as the Secretary of Technological Studies of Foro Democrático, a split from the conservative National Action Party—which cooperated with the PRD in the elections—and had also come to participate in the peoples' congress in the jungle.

Business, said Barrios Graff, suffers from four principal problems: high interest rates, a confiscatory tax law, a corrupt government which practices extorsion. "And the fourth important problem is that in the last two decades, the purchasing power of salaries in Mexico has fallen 50 percent, which represents a serious fall in the market. It also means that workers are very poorly paid with little desire to work. This leads to baʒ production and low productivity."

"Finally," says Graff, "as if all this were not enough, the Mexican government has entered into a free trade agreement which makes it completely impossible for us to compete. So the imported products of the U.S. and Canada are displacing Mexican businesses. This is only the economic aspect, but there are so many unemployed workers that the situation puts Mexican stability at risk.

"We haven't come in order to get anything out of this for ourselves," said Graff. "Rather we're here to protest the systematic violation of democratic and human rights in this country. Article 20 of the Universal Declaration of Human Rights, for example, forbids entrepreneurs, or any person, from being forced to join an organization. But in Mexico, because of the Law of Chambers of Commerce and Industries, we are forced to join the government-controlled chambers of commerce and industry. So this violates a human right of business people."

Graff, Quirino Salas and most of the other entrepreneurs present at the convention want the government to raise wages and agricultural prices to expand the internal market, as well as protection from foreign imports.

These businessmen reject the importation of the American economic models. "We are more inclined to the European experience, the experience of the Socialist parties, in the sense that the best protection for capitalists is to have happy workers," said García Arias the lumber merchant. "In Mexico, there is no protection for capital, because the workers are upset. This is an explosive situation which isn't good for anyone."

As the discussion broke up, Ramón García Arias, remarked to me, "I am surprised at the absence of the labor movement here in this convention. But the reason is very obvious: the labor movement is completely controlled by the official unions." Moving among the convention delegates, I approached various union leaders and activists to ask them about the striking absence from the convention of unions and workers.

Alfredo David Díaz Castañeda, works at the National Institute of Neurology and Neurosurgery. He is the general secretary or top officer of Section 55 of the National Union of Health Workers (SNTSA). His union had sent him to respond to the Zapatistas' call for improved health care. "While this is a movement of peasants and the indigenous," he explained to me, "they have demanded solutions to the problems of all working people of Mexico. We feel that many of their demands are our own demands."

Díaz Castañeda adds, "But really there are very few unionists here. The unions have participated very little in this movement because of the concrete situation in this country. There is great government control over the unions. The corporativism [state control], to my way of thinking, is the strongest that exists in all of Latin America, and in many parts of the world."

In addition to health workers, there were also some delegates from the Independent Union of the Metropolitan Autonomous University (SITUAM) which represents both faculty and staff. David Villaruel Velasco, a SITUAM delegate to the CND, explained that his union had been on strike from the end of January to March 15, for 45 days. The strike over economic and political issues had been prompted in part by the Chiapas Rebellion. "We are here," he said, "because, for the workers, the movement towards democracy is fundamental."

Villaruel Velasco also noticed the absence of the unions at the convention. "In the 1970s," he explained, "there was an insurgent union movement. But, unfortunately, in the 1980s the unions were beaten down. The democratic leaderships in the unions were battered and the state exercised stronger control over the unions and the working class in general, and they tried to prevent any opposition movements." Villaruel Velasco, good organizer that he is, tried to put the best face on recent developments, pointing out that there were 64 labor groups of one sort or another at the convention. "This convention has," he said, "served as a space to try to regroup ourselves."

The truth is that at the National Democratic Convention, as in the Mexican presidential elections which followed, the working class was the absent factor that might have made all the difference. There were no contingents of oil workers, autoworkers or miners at the CND. Even the traditional independent and left-wing unions such as telephone workers and electrical workers were largely absent. Perhaps the absence of militant and independent working-class organizations helps to explain the convention's nationalist rather than labor or socialist program. The CND brought together the most remarkable assembly of the Left in decades, but it also embodied all of the Left's weaknesses and defeats, most importantly, the defeat of labor in the 1980s.

The working sessions of the National Democratic Convention took place on two days, August 6 in San Cristóbal de las Casas and August 9 in Aguascalientes. The August 6 working sessions were divided into five separate meetings. Meeting number one, dealing with "The Transition to Democracy and the end of the State Party," met in the Hotel Maya Quetzal and was attended by 950 delegates or observers. The second meeting, dealing with "Peaceful ways of Transition to Democracy, Elections, Civil Resistance and Defence of the Popular Will," was attended by 1,185 delegates and met in the Carmen Convention Center. The third meeting, "The Project of the Nation and the 11 Points of the Declaration of the Lacandón Jungle" met in City Theater with 1,427 participating delegates. Meeting number four dealt with the "Charter and Make-Up of a Transition Government," and for that session some 1,389 delegates met in the San Francisco Recreation Center. Finally, meeting number 5, dealing with a "Constituent Congress and a New Constitution," was attended by 1,170 delegates and met in the Palenque de Gallos, or cock fighting ring.

Altogether 6,121 delegates and observers participated in the sessions.[3] Somewhere between two-thirds and three-quarters of the participants in the sessions were men, though women generally made up perhaps two-fifths of the speakers. A majority of the delegates appeared to be Indians, peasants, and the urban poor. Mexico City university students served as ushers and performed security functions.

The five different working sessions followed similar formats. The Zapatistas had not only chosen the chairpersons and secretaries and established the agenda for each session, but also presented their own proposals. The EZLN called for a peaceful struggle involving participation in the coming election in order to bring about a transitional government, which would convene a constituent convention and write a new Mexican constitution.

In each session, the chairpersons attempted to select a speakers' list which represented the various geographical locations, classes, (peasant, workers, university, etc.), ethnic group (Indians, *mestizos*), and both men and women. Virtually all points of view were allowed a hearing, including the abstentionists who had infiltrated the meeting. Only those who advocated the violent overthrow of the government were prohibited from speaking, such as the Party of the Poor (PROCUP-PDLP), and even they distributed their literature outside of the meetings. In most sessions, more than 50 speakers presented their views, repeatedly attacking the Mexican government and the PRI as representing a corporativist one-party state that made democracy impossible.

As often happens in political conventions, the real debate at the CND took place in small meetings between the EZLN leadership, the leaders of the Party of the Democratic Revolution, and the convention's organizers. At one point, Marcos reportedly expressed the hope that the CND would not only call for participation in the election, but would also endorse Cuauhtémoc Cárdenas for president. However, not only was the PRD reluctant to receive the endorsement of a convention called by armed revolutionaries, many of the leftists at the convention hesitated to endorse Cárdenas and the PRD. The CND convention organizers, even those who wished to help the Cárdenas campaign, also feared that an endorsement would make the convention appear to be no more than a PRD event. In the end, the EZLN and the CND organizers decided against endorsing Cárdenas outright, but called for a vote against the PRI and the PAN, which was tantamount to a Cárdenas endorsement. In the event of a stolen election, the CND resolved to call for a national campaign of civil resistance.

The EZLN naturally enjoyed enormous prestige among the delegates, and in the end, most sessions adopted resolutions which closely followed the EZLN's initial call for participation in the election, peaceful struggle, transitional government, constituent Congress, new constitution, and the "eleven points of the Second Declaration of the Lacandón Jungle." Those eleven points—work, land, housing, food, health, education, independence, freedom, democracy, justice and peace—represented the essence of the EZLN's program and politics, a list of radical reforms to humanize Mexican society.

In political terms, the thrust of the CND resolutions was nationalist, democratic, and social—in a word, social democratic. This was in no way a revolutionary socialist convention. The CND saw no special role for the working class in leading the struggle for democracy. The CND resolutions neither called for the overthrow of the Mexican government, nor for the collectivization of the Mexican economy. Finally, the CND resolutions consistently called upon the Mexican "citizens" and its "civil society" to take leadership and transform Mexico into a democracy.

At one level, the CND represented the Mexican Jacobin tradition, the traditional petty bourgeois radicalism that had animated the Mexican Revolution of 1910. Mysteriously, at the end of the twentieth century in the La-candón jungle we could still hear the echos of the debates at the Convention of Aguascalientes of 1914, before the Russian Revolution and the rise of the modern communist movement. We had traveled south into the jungle and back into the past.

After the working session in San Cristóbal on August 6, the convention reconvened in Aguascalientes, Chiapas on August 8. Hundreds of buses carried the delegates to the convention site and the marvelous amphitheater carved out of the jungle. The Zapatistas had built an enormous stage out of logs and earth. Two huge Mexican flags had been set up behind the stage, rising to a peak in the middle, like a mountain or perhaps a pyramid.

On the afternoon of August 8, the 6,000 delegates sat waiting patiently on the hard wooden benches. High up in the back of the amphitheater, a brass band called "Chile Frito" (Fried Pepper) periodically let out a blast on a trumpet and broke into a traditional song, immediately eliciting a dozen sympathetic "Ays!" from the crowd. When the band played a particularly popular tune, whole sections of the massive crowd broke into song.

Every few minutes a shout went up from a fellow down in the front of the amphitheater, "¡Zapata Vive!" (Zapata Lives), and then someone up in the back responded, "¡Y la lucha sigue!" (And the struggle goes on.)

Then a chant began, coming from the MPI, "Lucha, lucha, lucha, no dejes de luchar, por un gobierno obrero, campesino y popular." (Fight, fight, fight, don't stop fighting for a government of workers, peasants and the people.)

At about five o'clock, Major Tacho and Subcomandante Marcos marched in at the head of the EZLN troops. The crowd fell into an awed silence, all but "Chile Frito," which intermittently blasted away irreverently on the trumpet and the trombone like a band at a bull fight. The crowd whistled and shouted until even the musicians finally fell quiet.

Major Tacho and Subcomandante Marcos introduced themselves, and the crowd began to chant, "Ramona, Ramona, Ramona..." demanding that the woman comandante Ramona also appear. But Ramona did not appear, and it was later explained that she was sick. The crowd was delighted that the famous Marcos had appeared—Ramona's absence was soon forgiven.

The sun was setting behind the mountain as Marcos and Tacho commanded their army and its civilian supporters to pass in review before the convention. Hundreds of Indian civilians marched by, many of them bare-foot, clad in ragged clothing, and carrying crude clubs instead of guns. The EZLN troops marched past, the tips of their rifles tied with white flags to symbolize the peaceful nature of the convention.

Moved by the procession of the courageous Indian soldiers and civilians, who had risen up against the Mexican government in January, some in the crowd began to sing "Venceremos," the anthem of socialist revolution in Latin America in the 1970s. "We know how to break the chains," they sang. "We know how to conquer poverty."

At 6:30 P.M. Marcos named the convention's 100 presidents, two respected movement leaders from each of the 31 states and the Federal District, totalling 64, and then 36 other distinguished human rights activists and intellectuals. Rosario Ibarra de Piedra, the human rights activist and first woman candidate for president in 1982, and at the time a PRD candidate to represent the gulf states including Chiapas, was named the first president. One sole voice went up protesting that the convention had not nominated or voted on the presidents, but applause overwhelmed the voice of protest. The presidents were approved with acclamation if not with a democratic vote.

Marcos addressed the convention. "We ask respectfully," he said, "that you go forward with your ideals, your principles, your history. We ask you to stand up for what you believe in, to say 'Enough!' to the lie that governs our history today." The EZLN, Marcos explained, would have only 20 delegates participating in the convention. "This is a convention in search of a peaceful change," he said, "and in no way should it be presided over by armed people. We thank you for giving us a place, one more among all of you in order to say our piece."

Having finished his remarks, Marcos held up a beautiful, silk Mexican flag and walked up to the presidium to present it to Rosario Ibarra. Ibarra, one of Mexico's greatest orators, was almost too moved to speak. She held the flag in her hands and told the crowd, "We must make this convention the beginning of a new road in our history, a glorious, luminous, beautiful road to democracy, liberty and justice. And then we will know how to live in peace, because we will have earned it." The crowd came to its feet and broke into the Mexican national anthem. Many stood singing and sobbing as a light mist began to fall.

No sooner had Marcos and the EZLN troops marched out of the amphitheater than a tremendous tropical thunderstorm broke out. The wind roared and the water fell in torrents. The rain shorted out the electric lights that had illuminated the stage, and the gale blew down the enormous canopy that covered the entire amphitheater. As the huge cloth slowly settled over the crowd, hundreds of flashlights came on and shined like distant stars through the white tarp. The storm turned the amphitheater into a river of mud. The delegates, drenched to their bones, shouted, screamed and ran for cover they could not find in the dark on the edge of the jungle. From time to time a shout went up: "¡Zapata Vive!" (Zapata lives!), and then came the response, "¡*Pero la lluvia sigue!*" (But the rain goes on.)

Wandering through the mud, looking for shelter, one man stopped, almost crying and said, "This is so wonderful, finally, because of the storm, all of us on the Left are sharing the same experience. Finally we are united!" Smiling he walked off into the rain, the mud, and the dark.

In Aguascalientes the next morning, the convention opened with a brief session adopted the resolutions from the five working groups held in San Cristóbal a few days before.

The 97-year-old revolutionary, Francisco Espinoza Zárate of Michoacán, sat in the front row of the auditorium in Aguascalientes, his eyes shaded by his sombrero. He was one of a few veterans of the Mexican Revolution of 1910-1920 who were among the honored guests of the convention. Ancient and emaciated, with sunken cheeks, deep-set eyes and skin that looked like the gullies and ravines of Chihuahua, Espinoza Zárate told me in his scratchy voice, "I was a Villista, and I knew Zapata. I could relate to Zapata. It was the same fight then. We were fighting for the same thing then that they are fighting for here today. We wanted a government with real justice for all citizens.

"Since I have been in this fight," he said, thinking back over the meaning of his life, "I have never done so for my own benefit. Until the last moments of my life that remain, I will continue, without changing. Now I have grandchildren, great-grandchildren, and great-great-grandchildren, and if I don't fight for them—and for all our citizens—what are they going to do with this corrupt government? We can no longer continue living like this."

Raising his voice, lifting his arm and pointing his finger, the old man said, "Today at my age I say with even more conviction, if the government gives us no other out, then let's take up arms."

11

CAROUSELS, RACOONS, AND CRAZY MICE: THE FIGHT FOR ELECTION REFORM

Over the years, Mexicans developed a colorful language to describe the events on election day. In Mexico the *mapaches,* or racoons, were the official party's professional election thieves. The *mapaches* won the election by riding the *carrusel*, the merry-go-round that carried them around from one polling place to another, voting repeatedly. Or they produced *urnas embarazadas*, pregnant ballot boxes, already filled with votes before being brought to the polling place. When that tactic did not work, the *mapaches* turned to the *taco*. A *mapache* would instruct loyal voters to take one ballot, fold it in half, and stuff it with half a dozen others—thus making a taco—before depositing it in the ballot box. To confound the ordinary citizens, at the last minute, ideally on the morning of the election, the *mapaches* moved the polling place to an unknown location, producing what the *mapaches* considered the amusing effect known as *los ratones locos*, or the crazy mice, as the citizens ran about looking for their voting booths.

The *mapaches'* most reliable techniques, however, were *caciquismo* and *acarreo*. The *caciques* or political bosses could be relied upon to *acar-*

rear or haul the peasants to the polling place, mark the peasants' ballots and deposit them in the boxes for them. The Party, in return, often generously distributed *pulque* to the men and promises to the women before returning them to their villages. Peasants who declined the *caciques'* proposition to exchange their votes for a bottle of *pulque* might find themselves evicted from their land, fired from their job, or beaten and left for dead. Between the creativity of the *mapaches* and the ruthlessness of the *caciques*, there was never any doubt about who would win the election.

However, after the scandal surrounding the PRI's stealing of the 1988 election, there was constant pressure for electoral reforms, both from citizens within Mexico as well as from the United States government.[1] "The democratic movement developed throughout the country as we began to become aware of the cost of political fraud for Mexico, and the cost of authoritarianism as a permanent form of government," explained Luz Rosales, executive secretary of the Citizens Movement for Democracy (MCD). "The proposal was that we would struggle together in a broad movement of the citizens—young people, intellectuals, academics, peasants, indigenous people, all kinds of people—all those who wanted democracy in the country."

The MCD was founded in March of 1992 by Salvador Nava Martínez, the gubernatorial candidate of the broad opposition movement in the state of San Luis Potosí. "Many of the people that make up our movement are people who don't have a party," said Rosales. "They find in our movement a way of working which is freer, more autonomous, more a citizens' movement. Here they can express their views, they can talk, they can fight for the objectives of the movement, without being in the structure of a party."[2]

As the 1994 presidential election approached, the MCD and other such citizens' groups felt they needed a much larger organization with a national scope. On April 28, 1994, the MCD and six other reform groups established the Civic Alliance/Observation 94 (AC), a broad citizens' organization of over 400 groups to oversee the 1994 elections.[3] Civic Alliance adopted the slogan "*Juego Limpio*" or "Fair Play," and launched a great public education program toward that end.

The question of whether or not Mexico should permit international poll watchers gradually developed into one of the most important issues of the election. The PRI, and even some opposition party leaders, argued that, given the history of foreign, and especially United States intervention in Mexico, foreign observers would be a threat to the sovereignty and an insult to the dignity of Mexico. Mexico, they argued, could look after its own affairs.

The MCD advocated the presence of international observers, and argued that they strengthened the Mexican struggle for democracy. "We didn't think they violated our sovereignty," said Rosales. "On the contrary, they came to affirm us, to accompany us as we worked to achieve our real sovereignty, which comes with democracy." Moreover, said Rosales, when they returned to their own countries, the observers became witnesses to the Mexican people's struggle for democracy and gave it an international dimension.[4]

While Mexicans like Luz Rosales were organizing this new citizens' movement, the United States was also pressuring Mexico to clean up its notorious elections. The U.S. government, under both Bush and Clinton, supported the PRI and Salinas, and preferred to see the ruling party stay in power. U.S. business interests by and large felt the same way. At the same time, however, the U.S. State Department and its embassy in Mexico put pressure on Salinas to carry out electoral reforms to preserve political stability in Mexico. During the debate over the North American Free Trade Agreement, the U.S. government wanted Mexico to present at least the semblance of political democracy. The U.S. may have hoped to eventually create a U.S.-style two party system—the PRI and the PAN—but in any case, the United States wanted reforms that would stabilize Mexico and protect U.S. investments.

After the assassination of the PRI's presidential candidate Luis Donaldo Colosio in March, U.S. political figures began to express grave concerns about political instability in Mexico. For example, on April 21, Bernard Aronson, the former undersecretary for Hemispheric Affairs at the U.S. State Department during the Republican administration, in a *New York Times* opinion piece called for international supervision of the Mexican election.

Meanwhile, Mexican non-governmental organizations (NGOs) hoping to get foreign observers turned to the U.S. government. In December of 1993, the MCD and 12 other Mexican NGOs met the U.S. State Department to discuss the question of foreign observer participation in the Mexican election. Four months later, in April of 1994, a group of half a dozen Mexican NGOs met with the U.S. government's National Endowment for Democracy (NED) to arrange for financial help in bringing foreign observers to Mexico.[5]

The NED, which had already been giving small amounts of money to Mexican NGOs, increased its contributions as the election approached. In 1993 and 1994, the NED put nearly one million dollars in the hands of Mexican organizations involved in electoral reform.[6] In addition to the NED, the National Democratic Institute (NDI) and the National Republic Institute (IRI) also gave funds to Mexican groups. These three U.S. government groups gave $1.42 million altogether in 1994.[7] While this was not a large amount of money by U.S. standards, it went a long way in the hands of organizations in Mexico. Among the organizations chosen by the NED to receive funding were the Citizens Movement for Democracy (MCD) and the Citizens Alliance (AC), two of the groups most representative of the new civil society movement.

The leaders and activists in groups like the MCD and the AC were genuine patriots and sincere democrats who wanted civil rights and political freedom in Mexico. They were often progressives who stood on the left of Mexican political life and fought for significant social change in Mexican society. Yet the NGO's turn to the U.S. State Department, the NED, and U.S. political party organizations for assistance, raised several serious questions. First, from a Mexican point of view, did their discussions with the U.S. State Department compromise Mexican sovereignty by inviting the U.S. government to meddle in internal Mexican affairs?

Second, from the point of view of civil society, what happens when civil society, in the struggle against its own state, turns to another state? Civil society might argue that this was a turn from an authoritarian to a democratic state. But this was also a turn to the government which had been the most important external prop of Mexico's authoritarian regime. Moreover, since the fall of the Soviet Union, the United States was the only superpower, the dominant imperial power. In its own terms, how would Mexican civil society expect to fulfill its own lofty ideals by turning to the United States?

However one answers those questions, the result was that the NGOs—whether they intended to or not—provided yet another vehicle for U.S. political influence in Mexico. The U.S. government's National Endowment for Democracy believed that the NGOs electoral activities would, while democratizing the electoral process, also help to stabilize Mexico and protect U.S. political and economic interests there. From the U.S. government's point of view, electoral reforms were not radical or destabilizing reforms. In fact, such reforms might even legitimize a victory by the PRI. Or in the event that Salinas and the PRI lost, the U.S. would have connections to the Mexican reformers who could claim credit for its defeat. By supporting the electoral reform movement and by influencing civil society, the U.S. government could help shape future developments in Mexico.

Mexican business organizations also began to speak in the language of civil society, which they had learned after the 1982 nationalization of the banks. They, too, called for election reform. COPARMEX, the Mexican Employers Association, announced that, at the invitation of the Southwest Business Federation, it was supporting the presence of observers from the U.S. Congress Foundation for Human Rights and Democracy, the Arias Foundation for Peace and Development, and the Carter Foundation.

Under the pressure of its own citizens' movement, business groups, and the U.S. government, the Mexican government gradually changed its position on foreign election observers. Victor Flores Olea, Mexican ambassador to the Organization of American States (OAS) declared in mid-March 1994 that foreign observers were no threat to Mexico. "There is nothing to hide and the Mexican electoral process can be freely observed."[8] Cuauhtémoc Cárdenas, speaking before a businessmen's group in Los Angeles, demanded that the Mexican government formally invite a delegation from the United Nations to be present as observers on August 21.

Two months later in mid-May, the United Nations officials Tanto Horacio Boneo and Dong Nguyen met with Mexican NGOs to discuss United Nations assistance to the Mexican election watching effort. The UN eventually arranged to work with 15 Mexican NGOs.[9] Some, like the Civic Center of Solidarity had been formed in the midst of the 1985 earthquake, and epitomized the new movement of civil society. But others were traditional, conservative associations like the Grand Lodge of the Valley of Mexico, a Masonic organization founded in the 19th century, which promised to field 33,000 observers and the Mexico City Rotarians Club, which said it would sponsor 24,000 election watchers.[10] (Both claims were vastly exaggerated.) Civic Alliance remained the most important group, and the one with the most moral authority. Its 400 member organizations would put some 15,000 Mexican observers in the field. The UN eventually provided $1,500,790 in financial support for the Civic Alliance's operations.[11] On election day, the presence of some 50,000 Mexican election watchers, as well as 950 foreign visitors would make the 1994 election the most scrutinized Mexican election in history.[12]

The debate over democracy and reform had fundamentally shifted from the terms of the 1988 contest. In 1988, Cárdenas and the National Democratic Front (FDN) had demanded democracy and social justice. The FDN opposition, while demanding democratic rights, had focussed the debate largely on the PRI's economic policies, the privatization of the nationalized industries, the loss of jobs, and the workers' and peasants' standard of living. The 1988, the FDN campaign had been a massive, amorphous movement not only for political democracy, but also for fundamental social change. In 1994, civil society's struggle for democracy tended to focus attention on political democracy to the exclusion of social democracy. At the same time, civic activism became an alternative to political activism. Many of those who might have been building an opposition party, found themselves poll watching.

Both the pressures of Mexican reformers, and the influence of the United States, helped bring about electoral reform in Mexico. First, there were reforms in government structure supposedly to increase the role of minority parties. The Congress doubled the Senate's size from 64 to 128, and gave the largest minority party in any state one seat. Second, no party was permitted to hold more than 63 percent of the seats in the Chamber of Deputies, in order to prevent any single party from changing the Constitution. Third, the famous governability law, which gave the largest party an automatic majority, was repealed, so that any party with less than a majority would have to make coalitions.

In 1990 the PRI, with the support of the PAN, passed through Congress a new electoral code (COFIPE). These reforms dealt with everything from the actual voting, to the tabulation of the results, and the final adjudication of decisions. The new Mexican Electoral Institute (IFE) was to administer the new reformed system. Theoretically, the state and district citizen councilors—the IFE advisors—were independent, though in practice they were often PRI sympathizers.

COFIPE established new bodies to administer the election process. At the top, the new law created a General Council with "citizen councilors," approved by the Chamber of Deputies, who were neither government officials nor party activists, and who had the controlling votes. The new law also created similar citizen-controled councils for the 32 states and the 300 electoral districts. The IFE citizen councilors were given responsibility for validating the election.

Below the General Council was the Federal Electoral Institute or IFE, established as a permanent, autonomous and professional administration, with officials who were supposedly non-partisan and independent of the government. Because most IFE officials came out of other government service, however, the new IFE also tended to resemble the PRI establishment. The IFE remained under the control of the Ministry of the Interior, which had for decades served the official party as political enforcer.

The new COFIPE permitted each party to have two representatives at each polling place to observe the process and report irregularities. However, the PRI was the only party which, at least initially, could take advantage of such an opportunity. With 95,000 polling places, a party would require 190,000 party representatives.

In addition to the party representatives, COFIPE also permitted the presence of Mexican non-governmental observers and foreign "visitors" at all polling places. But again, it turned out that the PRI with its historic domination of so many institutions and organizations in Mexico, was best placed to take advantage of the changes. The PRI's "official" teachers' union, the SNTE, headed by Salinas's hand-picked leader Elba Esther Gordillo, created the National Organization of Teacher Election Watchers (ONOEM) which had observers in 9,718 polling places. Not surprisingly, ONOEM reported a "legal and transparent" process in 90 percent of the election polling places.[13] COPARMEX, the Mexican Employers Association, which was close to the PAN, also created an election observation group.

There were reforms of the electoral process at the local level as well. To insure that the polls were impartially administered, the IFE selected local precinct officials and alternates by lottery. Those selected were trained to run the polling place on election day.

The IFE spent millions of pesos to conduct a public education campaign. Television public service announcements, newspaper advertisements, billboards, and posters told voters to participate in the election and to vote their conscience. The education campaign often involved cartoons, no doubt because comic books are one of the favorite forms of working-class literature in Mexico.

Campaign funding reform in Mexico was extremely complicated. Parties and candidates raised their own funds, but the government also provided funds for all parties, some equally and some proportionally, depending on the number of electoral contests in which they were engaged. Proportional distribution of most funds favored the PRI establishment. The General Council decided in January that total public financing for the 1994 election would be set at US$67 million, of which approximately US$33.1 million went to the PRI, US$9.7 million to the PAN, and US$6.9 million to the PRD. The rest went to the smaller opposition parties.[14]

President Salinas's attempt to raise US$25 million from each of several wealthy businessmen, created both a scandal and a debate about campaign funding limits. Salinas and the PRI resisted serious reforms, but under both foreign and public pressure, were forced to negotiate restrictions. The PRI finally agreed that presidential campaign expenditures should not exceed US$42,018,800. Conveniently, only the PRI was in a position to spend such an enormous amount on its presidential contest. In fact, the PRI spent close to the US$42 million limit, between ten and 20 times the size of its nearest competitors. The Washington Office on Latin America and the Mexican Academy of Human Rights concluded that "The PRI has enjoyed massive resource advantage over the opposition during this campaign."[15]

The parties were free to spend as much of their budget as they wanted on television, radio, and newspaper advertising, the PRI spending by far the most. Reforms were passed requiring the networks to give each participating party 15 minutes of free television and radio time each month. There were also restrictions on advertising for government social welfare programs such as PRONASOL and PROCAMPO. Finally, the PRI candidate agreed to a television debate with the two leading opposition parties.

A study by the Mexican Academy of Human Rights (AMDH) found that between January and April of 1994, the PRI received 43 percent of the total air time given to political parties, while the PAN received 14 percent and the PRD 13 percent. The results were similar for candidates: the PRI candidate received 41 percent (22 percent for Colosio before he was assassinated, and then 19 percent for his successor Zedillo), while Cuauhtémoc Cárdenas got 19 percent, and Diego Fernández received only 11 percent.[16] As the Washington Office on Latin America and the AMDH concluded in another study, "Television has unfairly favored the PRI and its presidential candidate Ernesto Zedillo."[17]

Polling place and ballot box fraud were seen as huge problems. To prevent them, the 1990 electoral code provided that polling places would be geographically dispersed. In 1994, 95,000 precincts were established throughout the country, and the authorities decided that most precints would have no more than 300 ballots. To prevent coercion, the law also established new restrictions on campaigning in or near polling places. In addition, the presidents of the polls were authorized to call on the police to preserve order.

Another problem in Mexico had been repeat voting or the *carrusel*. To prevent this practice, a new registration list and special voter identification cards were created. The new national voter registration list eventually contained the names of over 45 million Mexican citizens.

While there was general agreement about the need to create a new list, there were serious questions raised about its integrity. Less than a month before the election, the PRD's Samuel de Villar presented a number of objections to the General Council. First, de Villar pointed out that in the Federal District alone with 4.3 million registered voters, there were over one million homonyms or voters who had the same first and two last names. (In Mexico all citizens are registered by both their father's and mother's last names, for example in the case of Juan Gómez Sánchez: Juan is the first name; Gómez is the father's last name; and Sánchez is the mother's last name. A homonym occurred when all three names were identical.) De Villar argued that such a high rate of homonyms suggested either errors in the creation of the registration list, or cases of potentially fraudulent registrations.

De Villar also claimed that appoximately 17 percent of the potential voters had been eliminated from the voter registration list. In addition, a statistical analysis of the list had shown indications of large numbers of false registrations. In the end, the IFE either ignored or rejected all of de Villar's claims, and the list was approved. Nevertheless, going into the election there were still doubts about the registration list and voter identification cards.[18]

The Electoral Registry issued specially designed voter registration cards to all eligible citizens. These cards included several security devices: a photograph of the voter, a bar code, a thumbprint, watermarks, signatures, and molecular-fusion card construction. Also, because so many Mexicans have identical names, there were special homonym security codes. The IFE issued voter identification cards to 45,729,053 citizens before election day 1994.

In addition to the voter identification cards, the IFE also devised other methods to prevent multiple voting. Each voter registration card would be punched after its owner had voted, and each voter's thumb would be stained with a specially formulated indelible ink that would be clearly visible and impossible to remove with any solvent. Both of these methods depended on conscientious officials, party observers and poll watchers.

In past elections, *los mapaches*, the "racoons" or professional election thieves, stole elections for the PRI by destroying boxes or ballots, marking as many extra ballots as needed, and stuffing them into other ballot boxes. To prevent these practices, COFIPE decided that all ballots would now have numbered stubs corresponding to the precincts. In this way, the officials could insure that there were not more ballots than voters. The ballots were not numbered, IFE explained, to insure the secrecy of the vote. Theoretically, each polling place should have received just enough ballots for the number of registered voters at that precinct.

The ballot boxes were also redesigned. To prevent *urnas embarazadas* or ballot box stuffing, the boxes were made of transparent plastic. To prevent the use of *tacos*, the practice of one voter depositing one ballot folded in half and stuffed with several other ballots, the slot in the top of the ballot box was narrowed from 1 centimeter to 3 millimeters, or just enough space to allow the insertion of one ballot so that *tacos* would not fit.

There were also reforms to help prevent *caciquismo* and *acarreo*, bosses hauling dependent voters to the polls and telling them how to vote. COFIPE created new ballot booths, closed on three tall sides, and with a curtain that closed behind the voter to create privacy in the polling place. To make it possible for illiterate voters to vote without asking for assistance, the parties each had color coded logos or emblems.

Mexican elections had frequently been stolen after the polls closed and the famous "alchemists" arrived to cook up the right numbers. So COFIPE also created new rules for tabulating the election results. Party representatives, non-governmental Mexican observers, and foreign visitors were all permitted to witness the opening of the ballot boxes, and the counting of the vote. Once the vote was tallied, the precinct president was required to post an official, signed tally sheet on the door of the polling place. Mexico promised to avoid a fiasco like the alleged 1988 computer crash, and bought a new IBM-designed computer system for the 1994 elections. Three back-up computers were put on-line to prevent an election day disaster. As a check against the official tally, the IFE arranged for parallel vote tabulations by Mexican observer groups, as well as a "scientific" exit poll to be conducted on election day.

Finally, Congress established the Federal Electoral Tribunal with special jurisdiction over electoral issues and a carefully defined appeals process. An agreement by the various political parties also resulted in the appointment of a special federal prosecutor in charge of prosecuting electoral crimes. In the Federal Penal Code of 1994, Congress made the punishment for electoral crimes much more severe. Penalties ranged from fines to prison sentences of nine years without parole.

Mexican civil society nevertheless remained dubious about the reforms. "We struggled a good deal so that the electoral law would guarantee a free and transparent vote," Luz Rosales of the MCD explained just before the election. "We also fought so that the elections would not be in the hands of the government. We won little in the law, though we won the support of the people.

"The thing we really wanted was the autonomy of the electoral organizations," said Rosales. "At the national level, the citizen councilors were from our movement, but nevertheless they were not in control of the elections. They were a moral force, but they did not get control of the registration, of the results, of the procedures and methods. We have not gotten an electoral list controled by citizens. This is something we have to continue fighting for."

While Luz Rosales, the Citizens Movement for Democracy, and the Civic Alliance carried out the hard work of mobilizing the citizenry to pressure the government into granting reforms, other Mexican activists tried other strategies. Jorge G. Castañeda and the San Angel Group attempted to dazzle the PRI into submission.

Castañeda was born and raised in Mexico City, the son of a wealthy, politically connected family. His father, Jorge Castañeda Domínguez, served as Foreign Minister in the cabinet of José López Portillo, making the young Jorge a sophisticated world traveler. He got his B.A. at Princeton University in the United States and then studied at the University of Paris, where he received his Ph.D. In 1978, he became professor of economics and international affairs at the National University (UNAM).

The prolific Castañeda wrote half a dozen books, served as a columnist for the Mexican magazine *Proceso*, the *Los Angeles Times* and *Newsweek International*, and became the foremost interpreter of Mexican politics to the outside world. While pursuing a successful academic and literary career, Castañeda was also active in the Mexican Socialist Party (PMS). After 1988, Castañeda, a friend of Cuauhtémoc Cárdenas, was politically supportive of the PRD, though he played no leadership role in the new party.

At the age of 40, Castañeda became more ambitious and, in his 1993 book *Utopia Unarmed: The Latin American Left After the Cold War*, he assumed the role of prophet of the Left. Ironically, given developments in Mexico, Castañeda announced the end of armed revolutionary movements, and called upon the Latin American Left to abandon its traditional opposition to capitalism and to adopt a program of not-quite-social-democratic reform.[19] At the same time, in Mexico, Castañeda attempted to turn the 1994 Mexican election into a laboratory for his new reformist politics.

In *Utopia Unarmed*, Castañeda argued that the fall of communism in Eastern Europe and the Soviet Union was a watershed for the Latin American Left. Without the existence of the communist utopia, revolution in Latin America was dead. Castañeda insisted that the Left must face this reality. On the other hand, with communism out of the way, the Left was also liberated from its Stalinist past and free to chart a new course. Latin American leftists still had a vocation and a future, fighting for the continent's millions of desperately poor people. The free market economic systems being adopted throughout Latin America would in the end lead only to more poverty and inequality, and to social explosions like the Maoist guerrilla group Sendero Luminoso in Peru. The reformist left, Castañeda wrote, must point to the violent Sendero and say, "We are the lesser alternative."

In order to be able to put itself forth as the lesser evil, Castañeda argued, the Latin American Left would have to abandon its shibboleths and adopt an entirely new program. With the collapse of communism, the struggle for socialism may be off the agenda, said Castañeda, but the Left could fight for a more humane capitalism. Castañeda believed that the new program for a capitalism with a human face should be based largely on the models of Germany and Japan. From Germany, the Latin American Left should take the model of a comprehensive welfare state. And from Japan, the Left could borrow the example of a state-business alliance to capture new export markets. "Export sectors must adjust to market principles to be competitive, and they must compete in international markets to capture market shares," wrote Castañeda, sounding more like Milton Friedman than Karl Marx.

To these German and Japanese economic models, the Left would add a thorough-going program of democratization, reaching from parliament to the social movements in the streets. On the basis of the projected economic success of this admittedly eclectic model, it would be possible, Castañeda concluded, to create a more comprehensive social welfare system through progressive taxation. To put it another way, if Salinas had been a socialist, he would have been Jorge Castañeda, emphasizing the capture of export markets through competition in order to solve national social problems. The Left's new role then would be to help to bring about cooperation between the state, business and labor.

The Left had to give up not only the armed struggle for communism, but even the parliamentary struggle for socialism, and adopt a new and more sophisticated task as a pressure group within civil society, urging a more humane capitalism. The headline writer at *Business Week* titled that magazine's review of Castañeda's book, "Latin Revolutionaries Learn to Love the System." In essence, that was the message.[20]

The Mexican crisis of 1994 seemed like a laboratory that would allow Castañeda to test his ideas. Mexico's economic crisis had produced the millions of poor masses who certainly needed some form of political representation. The armed revolutionary movement in Chiapas, though not by any means the totalitarian and ferocious Sendero Luminoso, provided a threat to the Mexican government which allowed the moderate left to claim the role of lesser evil. Finally, the new civil society movement, which encompassed people from all walks of life, could serve as a pressure group on the government. Here was an ideal opportunity for Castañeda to try out his theories. His efforts proved to be both remarkably successful at one level and completely futile at another.

After the Chiapas Rebellion and the assassination of Colosio had raised the spector of violence and repression, Jorge Castañeda began to organize a group of dissident intellectuals, politicians and businessmen to push for democratic reforms. The group would take the form of dinner discussions or *tertulias*. After Castañeda held the first dinner party, in his home in the luxurious San Angel neighborhood, the press dubbed the reformers the San Angel Group. The name "San Angel Group" turned out to be a very unfortunate—if a fundamentally appropriate and accurate—epithet, conjuring up the sumptuous homes of Mexico's wealthy intellectual elite.

That first San Angel dinner, held June 9, 1994 in the home of Castañeda, included famous writers, prominent figures from the PRI, the PAN, the PRD, and a number of the leaders of the non-governmental organizations of civil society. The most notable guest that first evening was Manuel Camacho Solís, the former Mayor of Mexico City, the PRI's chief negotiator with the Zapatistas, and a man who only a few weeks before seemed to be promoting himself for president. Eventually, scores of influential members of the intelligentsia joined the San Angel Group, among them Carlos Monsiváis, the journalist who had first introduced the term 'civil society' in Mexican politics; conservative historian Enrique Krauze; and Sergio Aguayo Quezada of the Mexican Academy of Human Rights. Elba Esther Gordillo, whom Salinas had appointed to head the teachers' union (SNTE), was among the dozen or so women in the overwhelmingly male organization. Some journalists suggested that the real authority of the San Angel Group came from an absentee member, Carlos Fuentes, the world famous Mexican author who resided in London but lent his name to the San Angel reformers.

The reform group proved far more successful in lining up intellectuals than in rounding up business support. Julio Faesler, the former director of the defunct Mexican Institute for Foreign Trade, played a role in getting the group off the ground but proved unable to attract many of his fellow entrepreneurs. With the exception of Gordillo, of the teachers' union, there were virtually no worker or peasant leaders involved in the San Angel group. A group of mostly wealthy, brilliant artists and intellectuals meeting for dinner, the San Angel Group's gathering took on the character of a film festival or a night at the opera. The stars would eat together and then come out and hold a press conference to discuss their latest foray into politics.

The Grupo San Angel at first defined itself as a pressure group which wanted to help bring about a transition to democracy in Mexico but Castañeda, and some of the others, had far greater ambitions for their coterie. One might say that Castañeda's strategy was to create "public opinion" in an authoritarian regime which had never quite had such a thing. By doing so, Castañeda hoped to play the key role in bringing about democratic reforms in Mexico by positioning the San Angel Group at the interface of civil society and the state. Castañeda saw his group as the catalyst of democratic change if it could only bring the pressure of the reformers to bear directly on those in power. Castañeda himself would provide the human conduit through which the current of popular power could pass into the batteries of the state.

The San Angel Group produced a document toward the end of June entitled "The Hour of Democracy," which proposed that all political parties and other groups sign a "Harmony Agreement" intended to guarantee a fair and free election, a plan of democratic modernization, and a program for a transition to a "government of national harmony."[21] The group also called upon both the Mexican Army and businessmen to respect the winner of the election. Castañeda and the San Angel Group proposed, much like Marcos and the Zapatistas, to set the future agenda of Mexico.

Unlike Marcos, Castañeda and the Mexico City intellectuals had no army and no liberated territory, outside of a few living rooms in the homes of the intelligentsia, but they did have connections. Castañeda and the San Angel Group succeeded in meeting and talking with all three presidential candidates of the three most important parties: Diego Fernández of the PAN, Cuauhtémoc Cárdenas candidate of the PRD, and Ernesto Zedillo the new candidate of the PRI. The San Angel Group also met with Jorge Carpizo McGregor, Minister of the Interior, to discuss with him the group's concerns about the elections. In these meetings, the San Angel Group emphasized electoral reform and the prevention of violence on election day and after.

During these weeks of activity between June and August, the San Angel Group recieved criticism from various quarters. Conservative journalists ridiculed the "Beautiful People" (*Los Exquisitos*) of San Angel, the rich and famous, who had condescended to involve themselves in the dirty business of politics. The pundits of the right derided Jorge Castañeda for his unabashed self-promotion. They also suggested that the San Angel intellectuals really represented no one other than themselves, a leadership with no followers. Most frequently the press suggested that the San Angel Group was really a front for the PRD and Cuauhtémoc Cárdenas. When Subcomandante Marcos invited the San Angel Group to the National Democratic Convention to be held in the Lacandón jungle in August, there were yet other accusations of the San Angel Group's links to the Left. At the same time, several of the six small parties, particularly those on the Left, criticized the San Angel Group for failing to meet with their presidential candidates.

Mexico's urban poor also served notice on Castañeda that San Angel's elite were not the only ones entitled to speak about democracy and reform. Super Barrio Gómez, the masked wrestler who acts as public spokesman for Mexico City's poorest districts, announced the formation of the Santa Julia Group, named after one of the metropolis's poorest neighborhoods. The Santa Julia Group issued a statement saying, "We don't want any more of the Pacts of Civility...." The new group also demanded to meet with Salinas, Minister of the Interior Jorge Carpizo, and the three presidential candidates. Super Barrio called upon the San Angel Group to create a democratic community movement involving all of Mexico's citizens, rather than just the elite cenacle over which Castañeda presided.

Whatever their critics might say, Castañeda and the San Angel Group proved remarkably single minded in their pursuit of publicity and influence. The San Angel Group was the only group from civil society to succeed in meeting with President Salinas, who praised the calibre of the group's members and the sincerity of their efforts. Minister of the Interior Carpizo adopted the San Angel Group's idea of a harmony agreement and put forward his own "Pact for Harmony, Civility, Justice and Democracy," which was signed by all the presidential candidates, with the exception of Cárdenas. The PRI's pact called upon all parties to respect the results of the election and avoid civil unrest.

The upshot of the San Angel Group's efforts at democratic reform turned out to be self-defeating. The PRI's Harmony Pact, modeled on Castañeda's, served to legitimatize the less than free and fair election of 1994. Because it primarily sought publicity, influence and dialogue, the San Angel Group constantly moved to the right, toward the system's center, which in Mexico is the president. The San Angel Group appropriated the credit of the real broad front of civil society, as represented by the Citizens Movement for

Democracy and the Civic Alliance, and squandered that political capital by gambling it away, betting on Carpizo or Salinas to carry out meaningful reforms. Finally, by meeting with the San Angel Group, President Salinas succeeded in strengthening the PRI's claim to openness and a willingness to dialogue with its critics. Perhaps it would not be going to far to say that Salinas successfully co-opted Castañeda and the San Angel Group, luring them into the ruling party's game.

The last great event, before election day 1994, was the nationally televised debate between PRD's Cuauhtémoc Cárdenas, the PRI's Ernesto Zedillo, and the PAN's candidate, Diego Fernández de Cevallos, the bearded battler, the man they called "The Boss."

They called Diego Fernández "The Boss" because he was arrogant, authoritarian, and domineering.[22] He acted the part of a biblical patriarch, or some said, a messiah. He was the *pater familias*, the pious Roman Catholic, the National Action Party stalwart, and sometimes the wild-eyed zealot. His long, graying beard looked like it had been styled after the conservative party leaders of the nineteenth century, and his manner was as imperious as theirs. His real political role remained obscure because he carried it out in secret meetings with the rival PRI.

Diego Fernández de Cevallos was born in Mexico City on March 16, 1941, the son of José Fernández de Cevallos and Beatriz Ramos. Like his rival Salinas, the boy spent his youth riding horses over the fields of his father's estate. Diego grew up on the San Germán Ranch in the state of Queretaro, where he received his education with his brothers and sisters from private tutors. When he got a little older, the adolescent Diego studied at a Jesuit preparatory school in Guadalajara.

After finishing his prep school education, Diego left Guadalajara for Mexico City, where he enrolled in the small Iberoamerican University. Unhappy with the Ibero, he transferred to the larger, busier, and more political National University (UNAM) where he took his law degree. Later Diego returned to the Ibero as a professor of criminal and business law.

Until his mid-30s, Diego remained single and a playboy, but in 1975 he began seeing a 14-year old girl, Claudia Gutiérrez Navarrete. Three years later, he proposed to her and they married, when she was 17 and he 37, in the church of Nuestra Señora del Rayo in Coyoacán. He and his wife raised four chlidren, three sons and a daughter.

Diego Fernández once said, "I was a PAN member while still in my mother's womb." His father, José Fernández de Cevallos was one of the founding members of the National Action Party and a long-time party activist. Diego Fernández remembered that he first spoke at a PAN meeting when he was only 11 years old. In 1968, during the debate over President Luis Echeverría's agrarian reform law, which so incensed the right, Diego participated in street demonstrations against the measure. When the disabled PRI legislator Octavio Hernández passed by, Diego shouted, "You're crippled— but in the brain!" Diego continued to shout down the agarian law and its supporters until he was reportedly pistol-whipped by the cane workers' leader José María Martínez. These sorts of incidents won Diego a reputation as something of a fanatic and a hot-head.

While studying at UNAM, Diego became National Youth Secretary of the PAN and worked on PAN campaigns. PAN President Luis H. Alvarez, made Diego his protégé and promoted him into the party's leadership. Diego subsequently served in a series of posts for the PAN: member of the National Executive Committee, member of the Political Commission, national counselor, and federal congressman. In 1988, Diego became a member of PAN presidential candidate Manuel Clouthier's shadow cabinet. Perhaps the most important step in Diego's career was his role as the coordinator of the PAN Parliamentary Group and representative of the PAN before the Federal Electoral Commission in 1988. As party leader, Diego became known as "*El Jefe*," the Boss, because of his heavy-handed control of the party. Other PAN leaders criticized him for his secret meetings with the PRI.

As parliamentary leader and representative before the commission, Diego acted as the PAN's principal interlocutor wth the PRI. Diego established a reputation for cooperation with the ruling party, rather than opposition to it. He worked with PRI leaders to pass key legislation, and then lined up the PAN votes. In September of 1990, PAN leader Diego voted in favor of the government's controversial election reform law (COFIPE), and urged other PAN members to do so as well. Both the PRI's leaders and the organizations of big business, which were so influential within the PAN, began to appreciate that Diego might be the leader who could negotiate the PAN's gradual inclusion into what might one day become a conservative two-party sytem. Or in any case, a PAN led by Diego would make the ideal junior partner of Salinas's technocratic PRI.

As the 1994 election drew closer, Diego decided to run for president, and won the backing of the *neo-panistas*, the PAN's conservative pro-business leadership. At the PAN convention on November 21, 1993, the Boss, got 65 percent of the delegates' votes. The Boss ran for president as "Diego," with the slogan "For a Mexico Without Lies." Diego's platform was as conservative economically as socially; he stood for free markets and against abortion. Diego, his patriarchal beard trimmed to more modest proportions, made an attractive candidate, but what really made him famous was the national television debate.

Before 1994, Mexican presidential candidates had never debated each other on national radio or television. With its domination of the media, the PRI had no desire to jeopardize its own chances or to enhance those of its opponents by engaging in a public debate. But civil society clamored for debate and discussion, and both the National Action Party and the National Democratic Front demanded debates in 1988. Before the 1988 election, Cárdenas had repeatedly demanded that Salinas debate him before the people, but Salinas, fearing he would lose, evaded the challenge. After the fraud of 1988, pressure for a public debate grew as part of the more general demand for electoral reforms.

On November 28, 1993, Salinas chose Luis Donaldo Colosio, the former president of the PRI who had orchestrated the party's election victories over the PRD, as the PRI's candidate for president. Perhaps as one of the PRI's most experienced and accomplished public speakers Colosio had no fear of the contest. "I will invite the candidates of the other parties to a full debate which contrasts our ideas and programs. Our votes will be those of conviction," said Colosio. "We will win the debate, we will win the vote."[23] Yet, at the time he was assassinated in March of 1994, Colosio had still not arranged the time and place of a national debate between the three candidates.

When Salinas chose Ernesto Zedillo Ponce de León to succeed Colosio, the PRI and Zedillo faced a different situation. The nation was in a crisis, the PRI was deeply divided over the choice of a successor, the fortunes of both opposition candidates had improved, while Zedillo was an unknown. In those circumstances, the PRI leadership felt that a debate could only rebound to the good of the ruling party. By putting Zedillo before the public, at the very least the PRI would enhance his face- and name-recognition, and, if he did well, the party would also prove his presidential stature. The debate would focus national and international attention on the elections rather than on assassinations, kidnappings or the Chiapas Rebellion. The debate would reinforce the channeling of the civil society movement into electoral activities rather than broader social movements. Zedillo decided to debate, limiting the encounter to the three major parties.[24]

On May 12, 1994 more than forty million Mexicans tuned in to watch the three rival candidates present and debate their programs. All three candidates' initial statements emphasized the need for democracy, economic development and concern for the poor. The three seemed to have converged at the middle of the political spectrum, presenting the public with little real political alternative. Hearing their statements, Mexicans found it difficult to explain why conflict among these parties had caused the deaths of hundreds of people in the last six years. Throughout the debate, Zedillo, sticking close to his prepared speech, gave a competent if uninspired performance. Cárdenas, who usually reads his text, and always has important things to say but is almost never a moving speaker, appeared wooden and dull.

After the rather listless initial presentations, Diego got his chance in the rebuttals to show his skill at skewering his opponents. Diego turned to Cárdenas and said, "You have gone around saying in different forums that the dividing line in Mexico is between the government position and the democratic position which you represent. I am going to demonstrate with the facts that you don't represent a democratic option and you are a man who has one face for the opposition and another for the government." Holding up some document, Diego told Cárdenas, "Look here, today you argue in the opposition with democratic intransigeance that the government should take its hand out of the electoral process. But you made this electoral law in Michoacán, where you had control of the elections, here it is."

Putting down the document, Diego went on. "Second, today you present yourself in the schools and universities as a man who is tolerant, pluralistic and repectful of youth, liberty of expression and academic freedom, but in your time [as governor] in 1985 in Michoacán, you imposed [the educational theories of] Marxism-Leninism. Here is the text if you want to look it over, it's at your disposal."

Turning next to Zedillo, Diego told him. "Look Dr. Zedillo, I want to tell you something that many millions of Mexicans want to say: according to the information that has been given us recently, we know that you have been a good boy with high grades, but we sincerely believe that you don't believe in democracy. I am going to tell you why. Permit me to make a comparison: I am here because thousands of free men and women from the National Action Party voted freely for my candidacy. And you, with all due respect, I want to tell you that you are here because of two tragedies: on the one hand, the death of Colosio, and on the other, the PRI's practice of presidential appointment."[25]

Neither Cárdenas nor Zedillo took off their gloves to strike back at Diego who came out of the match unscathed. While most Mexican and foreign commentators agreed that Fernández had won the debate, still Zedillo may have been the man who profited most from the exposure. Virtually unknown to the Mexican people the day before, the day after, Zedillo was a national figure. Cárdenas had fared the worst, proving unable to take his message before the Mexican people over television, the most influential medium in the country.

In the end, the debate that civil society had fought for helped to shift national politics to the right. Television tended to put the emphasis on style rather than substance, on presentation rather than program. The television debate format homogenized the candidates rather than brought out their political differences. The medium tended to become the message, and the message was modernization. Naturally, such a situation benefitted the ruthless modernizers, Zedillo and Diego. Cuauhtémoc, the nationalist from backward Michoacán, appeared to be a man out of time, a man from the past, and, moreover, a rather dull man from a too-troubled past.

Many Mexicans, of course, were not fooled. They realized that the PRI conceded to give the country 90 minutes of democracy on television, which fell far short of civil society's demands for a democratization of the country's political system. But millions of others, with few other sources of information, took away from the debate only the image of Diego, the strong, outspoken, daring critic of both the old nationalists and the new technocrats.

Surprisingly, after the debate, Diego disappeared from sight for several weeks, failing to capitalize on his successful national television debut. Many Mexicans speculated that the PRI and the PAN had reached an agreement that Diego would make himself scarce in exchange for the PRI granting a greater role for the PAN in national politics in the future. In any case, Diego's spectacular success in the national debate did not, in the end, produce a victory for his party.

There is no doubt that televised debates like that between Cárdenas, Diego Fernández and Zedillo are important elements of a democratic society. But the political context means everything. When Mexico's one-party state deigned to permit the broadcasting of a debate, it did so on its own terms. The Mexican state, and ultimately the Mexican president, set the rules of the game, and the odds were not very good. Indeed, the game was fixed.

12

THE ELECTION OF ZEDILLO:HOW FREE? HOW FAIR?

During the August 1994 elections, a Mexican poll watcher and an international observer came across a voter who was completely distraught. The woman was pleading with poll watchers to permit her to vote. The observers calmed her down long enough to get her to tell her story.

The woman had gone to vote at her regular polling place. There she was told by local officials that, though she had a voter's credential, her name was not on the voter registration list, and she would not be allowed to vote. The officials suggested, she could go to one of the special polling places for voters in transit, such as tourists or truck drivers, and she should be able to vote there.

So the woman went to the special polling place in the center of town. When she arrived there, late in the afternoon, she found that the special polling place had been issued only 300 ballots, and those ballots had been used up by soldiers and policemen who had showed up to vote early in the morning. No more ballots were left. So the woman, now on the verge of tears, was begging the election officials to let her vote. Or, if they would not let her vote, to at least stamp her voting card or stain her thumb with the indelible ink so she could claim she had voted.

"Why," asked the poll watchers, "are you so upset?"

"Because," said the woman, "I was told that if I did not vote for the PRI that my child could no longer go to school, and I would lose the milk program. So I have to prove that I voted." The woman returned to begging the officials to stamp her card or stain her thumb.

What is particularly important about this story, is that it is not just one story about one mother. While interviewing voters and observers, I heard this same story, with slight variations, told several times about different women in different towns all over Mexico.[1]

The Mexican government's Federal Electoral Institute (IFE) proclaimed the 1994 election the fairest in Mexican history. The Institutional Revolutionary Party (PRI) agreed, and took credit for the accomplishment. The Clinton administration congratulated the Mexican government on the success of its electoral reforms, and the *New York Times* called it, "the cleanest in living memory."

Perhaps, this was the fairest election in Mexico's history. Yet there are some rather disturbing stories that should make us ask, What is free? What is fair? How many such stories, like those about the women desperately pleading to vote, turn a free and fair election into something less?

□□□

Many Mexicans vote in school buildings, though in many rural areas they vote out of doors under a shady tree; luckily there was almost no rain on election day anywhere in Mexico. In most polling places or *casillas* there were two sets of polls, a *básica* and a *contigua*, each for part of the alphabet. Voters presented a credential, got a ballot from the polling place officials, voted in the *mámpara* or voting booth, and then placed their ballot in the *urna* or ballot box.

Carrying out an election in Mexico is by no means an easy task. Mexico City is the world's largest city with nearly 24 million people in the metropolitan area, many living in sprawling slums that pour out of the Federal District into nearby states. Much of Mexico is mountainous, and many small towns in rural areas have poor roads, which are difficult to reach. Mexico has over 50 Indian groups each of which speaks its own language or dialect. In some areas of the country there are on-going ethnic or religious conflicts, such as those among the Mixtec Indians of Oaxaca or among the Chamula Indians of Chiapas.

The 1994 Mexican election was the most closely watched in Mexican history. There were about 50,000 Mexican election observers from citizens groups, business organizations, and the PRI's "official" labor unions. The government also permitted approximately 950 officially credentialed international visitors to observe the election, about 700 from the United States, 50 from Canada, and others mostly from Europe and Latin America. Most of the international observers were professionals with careers in social work, education or law, though some were students. Most had some knowledge of Mexico and most spoke some Spanish, many spoke Spanish fluently. International observers who worked in several different states tell a story of manipulation, intimidation, and chicanery which many Mexicans are reluctant to detail, for fear of reprisals.[2]

Steve Baileys lives in Victoria, British Columbia, Canada, where he works with the British Columbia Council of Human Rights as an investigation mediation officer. Baileys also volunteers with the Oxfam Canada Association, through which he became part of the "Ad Hoc Canadian Delegation of Women's, Religious and Non-Governmental Organizations," which sent observers.

Like many other observers, Baileys had a long-term interest in Mexico, had Mexican friends and acquaintances, and spoke Spanish. Perhaps because of his formal training and work as an investigator of discrimination cases, Baileys was a particularly conscientious and thorough election observor.

"I was sent to Tepic, the capital of Nayarit, which is on the West Coast of Mexico just above Puerto Vallarta, Jalisco. Our hotel was in Tepic, where we underwent our orientation with the local Civic Alliance group. But we actually observed in rural, agricultural areas just outside of Tepic, such as Jesús María Corte and Atonalisco, two *ejidos*."

Bailey's host was Carlos Rodríguez, a former student activist of the 1960s and the director of a small private school, who worked with the Civic Alliance. "We started off in an impromptu way, just visiting the precinct in our host's neighborhood so he could vote before he took us out," Baileys explained. "No question that it was a very strong PRI neighborhood. When we got to the polling place it was in the process of being set up. Everybody there seemed very excited about the whole process. It seemed like nobody really knew what they were doing, and they had to await instructions from the president of the precinct. People were waiting in line maybe 20 deep in the hot sun; there was a lot of talking, a lot of joking.

"We then went into other precincts, and every precinct we went to seemed to be running smoothly. In every polling place I went to, the PRI observers and supporters milled around or hung around, and the PRI seemed to have a much stronger presence than anybody else.

"The impression I got was that this was an event in these small communities. This seemed to be where the action was. So you got a lot of people just kind of standing around, old men in groups talking, women in groups talking, children playing around. It was almost like a picnic without the food."

Baileys observed that there were irregularities in the staffing of the polling places. "In five or six of the ten polling places I visited, the functionaries did not correspond with the names I had on my list. So some kind of a change had happened within the last 48 hours, because the list had come out on the previous morning, on Saturday. A lot of these people then had not been chosen impartially through the lottery process and had not undergone the training. When I asked people why these functionaries weren't there I got a whole host of reasons: they had to stay home with the kids or they couldn't get a ride, or they just didn't show up. So that could lead to questions about who was present at the table, why they were there, what kind of influence did they have over the voters?"

Those who were working as officials, often identified themselves as PRI members by wearing party pins, said Baileys. "Within the actual voting area, the majority of people wore PRI pins. People who were working at the voting table had PRI pins on, and people who were sitting right in front of the voting boxes had PRI pins on. That just struck me as really odd.

"There were also big strong men who wore cowboy hats and had their T-shirts open to the middle of their chest wearing lots of jewelry. I was told by our Mexican guide that they were *caciques* [political bosses], and they seemed to be watching everybody as they went to the voting booth and as they went back out to put their ballot in the box.

"Not knowing much about each community that we visited, it would strike me as just another day. But as I talked with my guide it became clear that there were real power relationships that existed there. When you have somebody who's in charge of giving you work, or somebody who's in charge of collecting your rent or collecting your electrical bills at the municipal hall, and that person is standing there watching you vote, it can be a very intimidating situation."

Baileys observed that there were problems with the voter registration list. "Every polling place had at least two people who had shown up with their voting credential but weren't able to vote. They were not to be found on the registration list. In one polling place there were 14. Again, on the surface that might not seem like a lot, but when you multiply that by 96,000 polling places you can get up into some pretty significant numbers."

One might expect older people to be more experienced voters, but that was not the case, because many had probably never before been permitted to vote. "A lot of older people didn't know how to vote. They had to be instructed very clearly: 'This is a ballot, you go into that white booth over there behind the curtain, you mark it.' Even then when people were given their ballot, many of them would walk around, holding it out, going, 'Where do I mark it? What do I do with it?' At that point some of the PRI people yelled out, 'Vote for the colors of the flag,' which corresponded with the PRI logo on the ballot."[3]

Liz Tanner, a health educator in a teen health center, became an international visitor through the Interfaith Council for Peace and Justice in Ann Arbor, Michigan. She observed in a "very, very beautiful rural area" in Santiago de Ayuna in the state of Hidalgo. "There were mainly older people living there, because the younger people had gone elsewhere to find work," she explained.

She reported that, on several occasions, the voters' behavior was inappropriate. "At one point," explained Tanner, "a woman came in and said to the president, 'So I vote like this, right?' and she pointed to the PRI box on the ballot. The president sort of nodded and smiled." A blind man came also into the polling place led by a younger woman who seemed to be his daughter, said Tanner. "When he walked in he announced very loudly, 'I'm voting for the PRI,' and two of the PRI reps came up and patted him on the back."

Other international observers complained of intimidation. Bridget Gilhool recently graduated with a master's degree in labor and industrial relations from Rutgers University. Gilhool came to Mexico with Solidarity Summer, a coalition of groups including the Democratic Socialists of America, the Hospital Workers Union of New York 1199, and MECHA, a Chicano student group. She was assigned to the Tlaxiaco District of Oaxaca.

"Irregularities," said Gilhool, "were regular practices. I discovered there is nothing called a secret ballot here. Everyone was told how to vote in one way or another. There were a couple of carloads of folks who were brought from town by a guy who told them to, 'Vote for the PRI.'

"There were others right in the polling place who told people to, 'Vote for the PRI.' A lot of people didn't know what to do, so they would be told that the way to vote is to put an X over the PRI mark."

As one listens to the accounts of Baileys, Tanner, and Gilhool, a pattern begins to emerge. What might appear at first to be a cultural difference, like the crowds milling about the polling place or the blurring of lines between officials and voters, turn out to be essential parts of the mechanism of fraud. Over and over again, one hears about the blind man or the old woman who walks through the polling place announcing that they plan to vote for the PRI, until it becomes clear that such dependent people have been made part of the official party's political machine.

Some international observers served as poll watchers in areas where ethnic conflicts complicated political divisions. Liz O'Connor, an organizer for the Justice for Janitors campaign in Washington, went to Mexico as an international visitor with Solidarity Summer. She accompanied four national observers to an area called San Martín Ituyoso, also in the district of Tlaxiaco, in the state of Oaxaca. There had been repeated violent confrontations between different factions of the Mixtec Indians of that area. O'Connor and other international observers had been sent there as protection for the national observers. She observed the election at two polling places set up within 20 feet of each other under the eaves of a public building. Most of the voters were Mixtec Indians who spoke only their indigenous language, and many of the voters were illiterate.

Almost nothing went right in San Martín Ituyoso. "On the morning of the election day the presidents of the polling places didn't show up," says O'Connor. "People assumed, though no one knew for sure, that the reason was fear, because the situation was so tense. A couple of PRI leaders were assigned as presidents at the last moment, and the polling places opened very late."

While she was at her assigned polling place, a truck showed up loaded with people. They had gone to their regular polling place to vote, but were told that it had been moved to another location. There was no other transportation available, so they climbed aboard a passing truck. When O'Connor asked them why this had happened, they replied, "Because they don't want us to vote."

O'Connor also saw suggestions of intimidation. "There was a gang of guys who, according to our contact in Tlaxiaco, were known to be part of a band of PRI *asaltantes* or thugs. They had some little kids running into the polling places and telling the older women who didn't know how to read and write how to vote. Then the kids ran back and told the thugs. As far as I could tell," says O'Connor, "there was no secrecy to the vote."

O'Connor believed PRI officials were bribing or rewarding voters. "One of the PRI leaders was seen buying sodas and carrying them to the center of town which was not far away. He was giving sodas out to certain people. I assumed it was according to who they voted for. During the day a group of young people came up to us and, assuming we worked for the government said, 'Where's our T-shirts, where's our T-shirts? We voted for the PRI.'"

Some observers witnessed violent reactions as voters became frustrated with the authorities. Michael Rolland, a Catholic priest, and he adds, "an all around good guy," serves as the university chaplin at the University of Arizona in Tucson. Rolland works with Witness for Peace, and through that organization, became aware of the Humanitarian Law Project's intention to send watchers to Mexico under the auspices of the Civic Alliance.

Rolland was assigned to the area where southern Veracruz borders Tabasco, where opposition parties have been strong, and where there have been protests in the recent past over elections. "We were to focus on the towns of Cárdenas and Huimanguillo," said Rolland. "In Cárdenas, on the evening when we arrived, the special polling places had run out of votes, and people had stood there for hours, and there was a huge, long line of at least 150 people waiting in the heat to vote.

"People were complaining that soldiers, who had their own polling places, had come to vote in the special polling place, using up all the ballots. The people were frustrated," said Rolland, "so later that night during the count they burned the box of ballots that was to be sent to Mexico City." Citizens in Villahermosa also burned ballot boxes because they had not been permitted to vote at the special polling places.

Things were particularly tense on election day in Chiapas, especially near the military zones. Andrés Peñaloza Méndez, a Mexican citizen who works in Mexico City with a non-governmental organization, was a poll watcher under the auspices of the Civic Alliance in a militarized area in Chiapas.

"I was assigned to Altamirano," explained Peñaloza. "All around the city there were military pickets, and there was a landing strip for military planes. It's a city that had been converted into a garrison."

In addition to the military forces in the area, both the Mexican Army and the Zapatistas, there were also some of the ranchers' "white guards," resulting in several violent incidents. Peñaloza heard of harassment of nuns who run a local hospital, attacks on government representatives to the peace negotiations, and assaults on a university caravan bringing food to the beseiged areas.

Peñaloza was responsible for covering a couple of polling places located in a school. Many of the voters were indigenous and spoke only Tzeltal. In addition to Peñaloza, there were two international visitors assigned to the polling place.

The election in Altamirano was neither fair nor free, according to Peñaloza. "The overwhelming majority of the polling place functionaries were people linked to the PRI. After the poll opened, a group of *caciques* and ranchers arrived with a group of PRI militants who could be identified by their caps and shirts bearing the PRI logo. They remained there during the whole day in order to force a vote in favor of the PRI.

"We saw people in line who were pressuring people to vote for the PRI. We couldn't understand Tzeltal, but we could understand the word 'PRI.' The polling official in charge of giving voters the ballots insisted that they vote for the 'colors of the flag,' which is the PRI symbol on the ballot. When the voters entered the booths they were watched by two or three people while they voted. It was odd because in the booth there was a sign with the slogan, 'The vote is free and secret.' But there was no curtain or partition that might keep them from being observed."

Peñaloza explained that he and the two foreign observers did what they could to help protect the peoples' right to vote. "Within the limits of the law we exerted pressure and pointed out irregularities. We took photos, we made ourselves very visible at moments in which there were irregularities or voting rights violations. In some way, this helped give the voters more confidence." Perhaps because there were three observers at that polling place, the PRI lost and an opposition party, the PRD, won. "This was not the case of the other four polling places which were installed in town," said Peñaloza. "In the others, the majority vote was for the PRI, although in some polling places the PRD received a large vote."

Because he was a poll watcher, Peñaloza himself had to go to one of the special polling places to vote. There, as in other parts of Mexico, he found that military troops had been sent to vote at the special polling places. "I spent two hours in line with the soldiers, and I heard and saw everything. The soldiers arrived and asked their officer, 'Lieutenant, who are we supposed to vote for?' And he responded, 'For the PRI.' There were even cases where a few military officers collected the credentials of the voters, and voted for them. They took five or six credentials and then voted for those people."

There were also refugees from the fighting in Chiapas who had come to the special polling places to vote. PRI officials and soldiers instructed them on how to vote using sign language or showing them newspapers with pictures of the PRI symbol. "In the end," said Peñaloza, "I couldn't vote because they ran out of ballots."

Not all international visitors reported violations of election law. Joan Atlin, a member of the Canadian delegation, works as an organizer for the International Ladies Garment Workers Union in Toronto, dealing with plant closures and displaced workers. She also works with Mexican women workers through an international women's group called Mujer a Mujer (Woman to Woman).

"I was with one other Canadian and with one Alianza observer in Amatlán, Morelos," said Atlin. "Election day, at least where I was, was quite unique compared to everything else we've heard. The election was extremely well organized and well run. The poll officials were highly educated people who were quite comfortable with the process. Amatlán is historically an opposition town with a strong PRD presence, and there was a landslide victory for the PRD."

In Amatlán, the PRD took more initiative in the polling place, though Atlin did not observe any significant irregularities or fraud. "It was sort of the flip side of what happened in some other places. The PRD members were closer to the ballot box and the table. One of them was checking the voters list and looking at credentials as they came in, while the PRI representative was not checking lists, and stood farther off."

Some experienced poll watchers saw few real violations of election law. Philip Russell is the director of the Mexico Resource Center in Austin, Texas, and the author of *Mexico Under Salinas*. He acted as an election watcher in the Purepecha Indian area near Pátzcuaro, Michoacán in conjunction with the local Civic Alliance group.

"In general, I think the elections were much cleaner," said Russell. "We were very impressed. There were always a few lost souls wandering around trying to figure out where they're supposed to vote. But it didn't seem to be the deliberate shuffling up of names to discourage voting that was commonly known in Mexico as *ratón loco* (crazy mouse). I had been in

Michoacán in 1989, so I had a good point of reference for comparison," said Russell. "I thought just the mechanics of it were very well done."

Asked if there were irregularities, Russell explained, "Well, it comes down to how big you want to draw the circle of electoral process. As far as the mechanics of it, I was very impressed with how well it was carried out, and I didn't see anything other than a small bit of confusion. After all, this is a very poor area with a high rate of illiteracy. In general, I thought they just did an excellent job of just carrrying it out.

"Yet, if you draw the election process in a slightly larger circle," says Russell, "then you begin to become aware of a tremendous number of problems. When we were in Pátzcuaro a couple of days before the election, you could see lines of peasants standing outside the bank, because they had just received money from the government support program, PROCAMPO. This was a not very well disguised attempt to buy their vote.

"We heard lots of reports of money being offered and of pressure. We heard reports of officials saying, 'If you don't vote for the PRI, you've got to watch your job.' Many permits also depend on good behavior as defined by the PRI."

Most of the international observers with whom I talked, however, did report seeing irregularities. The explanation for the international observers complaints about voting irregularities is not to be found in a difference in cultural values, or in a failure of the U.S. and Canadian observers to understand or appreciate Latin customs. Election observers from Latin American countries had many similar complaints about the election process in Mexico.

Mr. Monterroso, a civil engineer from Guatemala, was an international observor in the muncipality of Temoac in the state of Morelos. According to Monterroso, PRI officials brought voters to the polling place in trucks, and in some cases, persuaded them to vote in certain ways. As he put it, "*El voto fué inducido*." That is, the vote was pressured.

"I saw a PRI representative helping people vote," says Monterros. "This was something I thought was really incredible. The person came up to him and they went in to vote together. Sometimes there were two people in the voting booth."

At one point, says Monterroso, a woman came up, and an official said to her, "Do you know how to vote?"

"No, I don't know how to vote," she replied.

"Well," said, the official, "then you're going to vote right now in front of everybody. For whom are you going to vote?"

"Well, then, for the PRI," she said.

"So everybody heard, the guy marked the ballot for the PRI, folded the ballot, and put it in the box," says Monterroso.

Professor Enrique Oteiza, a professor in the Social Sciences Department of Buenos Aires University in Argentina, also reported serious irregularities. Professor Oteiza served as an international observer in association with the Civic Alliance in Toluca, Mexico.

"Why is it so difficult in Mexico," asked Oteiza, "to make a list of the population of voters 18 years and older, when this is done in every country in Latin America without any difficulty? But in this country, the party has been in power for 65 years and they haven't had enough time to make a list which is not full of all kinds of problems."

Professor Oteiza was very disturbed by the arrangement, organization, and conduct of the election by officials. "In all the elections I have seen in Chile, in Uruguay, in Argentina, in England, and in Switzerland, the officials from the parties and the observers sit on one side of the table, and the box is on the same table. The voter goes to a room alone. The authorities do not interfere with the people when they go to deposit their vote in the box.

"But here the box was placed away from the table, and around the box you sometimes have a representative from the official party, the PRI. I identified several 'assistants' who were not registered as polling place officials. They were moving around 'helping' voters. I saw them with my own eyes, picking ballots from the hands of the people, looking at them and then themselves putting the ballots in the boxes. So it's not secret. I mean this is totally illegal, no? I saw it myself, but others also saw it in many parts of the country."

Other political scientists who had come to Mexico to observe the August 21 election were equally appalled. Pong Hyun Chun is a graduate student working on a doctorate in the political science department at the University of California at Santa Barbara. Her dissertation deals with "the process of democratization—or the lack thereof—in Brazil, Korea, and Mexico."

Chun served as an observer in the Isthmus of Tehuantepec. "This area was a 90 percent rural area, and I think at least 50 percent of the people are bilingual. I stayed with a teacher who was bilingual in an indigenous language and Spanish. The voting places were all outdoors."

According to Chun there were many violations of voters' rights. "On the morning of the day of the election, my partner and I were told that a new polling place had been created that had not been announced before. There were about 150 people from the Rancho Chocolate who were asked to go and vote in this central area of San Juan Guichicovi. I think that's a clear indication of the tampering with voting lists.

"Secondly, with my own eyes I saw many voters who were just being turned away. I checked their credentials. They had come to the right polling place, but somehow their names were not there. The women were just baffled, and, even though it was not their fault, they looked like they felt it was their fault.

"There was also a general absence of the secret ballot. There were no curtains on many voting booths. Rarely did the voters fold the ballot. They handed in their ballots to people some of whom were wearing police uniforms. I think that was a kind of intimidation.

"People sometimes got help with voting. The most common case was families helping each other. But some officials also helped—'Si, si, si,'—and then they marked the PRI. There was just a general lack of secrecy."

Chun reported one particularly striking irregularity. "In at least three polling places that I visited, all the voters' credentials were already collected. So there was no line. The entire village was surrounding the booths and officials and people were being called: 'Antonio González...María whatever...' One by one they were called to vote. These *ranchos* are quite remote, we couldn't get there first thing in the morning, so, who knows how the whole thing started? I don't know whether the officials collected the credentials or whether the voters were never given the credentials. Apparently this was rare, I haven't heard from other observers that this happened."

"My first impression was I wouldn't want to vote in Mexico, and I think it comes basically from having seen experiences in other countries," said Sofía N. Clark. Clark is a political scientist with a master's degree in public international law who has worked for 10 years in the Nicaraguan foreign service. "I am a Nicaraguan citizen," Clark explained, "and I have recently been doing graduate studies in law in Europe, and then I did an internship at a D.C. law firm. I was most recently on field assignment with the United Nations as an electoral observer in South Africa."

Clark came to Mexico with the Humanitarian Law Project and was assigned to the municipality of Minatitlán, in the state of Veracruz. Minatitlán had about 135 voting precincts, 23 of which were visited by Clark and her group.

Like other observers, Clark complained of "people milling around" the polling places, and about unidentified people around the registration lists and ballot boxes. "That seems very different than the experience I've had in two Nicarguan elections and the experience in South Africa. You usually have an entrance and an exit, a well defined area inside of a voting precinct, and people that go beyond the entrance are very well identified.

"In a comparative sense, I found it much more difficult here, say, than in South Africa where people have never voted and you made a big point of teaching people the rules. Or in Nicaragua, where you always went through an educational process. But here you have the weight of tradition, and people are used to these kinds of things."

The observations of these individual observers correspond to the reports of the organizations involved. Civic Alliance, the most independent of the Mexican organizations which sponsored poll watchers for election day, had about 15,000 Mexican observers in local polling places. On election day, Civic Alliance undertook a global observation, based on a stratified sample of 2,168 polling stations and a random sample of 500 polling stations.

Civic Alliance found that "the vote was not secret in 34 percent of the polling stations." In rural areas, the vote was not secret in 45 percent of the polling places. Civic Alliance also found that in 16.5 percent of all polling stations there were "pressures exerted against voters." Again, in rural areas, abuses were greater, with pressures exerted against voters in 23 percent of all rural stations. Perhaps not surprisingly, the vote for the PRI was generally higher in rural areas.

Equally serious, Civic Alliance found that, "In 65.15 percent of the polling stations, there were voters of that section and polling station that did not appear on the list." That is, eligible voters were not permitted to vote because their names did not appear on the final voter registration list. This phenomenon was more common in urban areas, particularly in cities with a population between 150,000 and 500,000.[4]

International observers supported the statistical study of the Civic Alliance. Tim Wise, reporting on behalf of U.S. observers working with Civic Alliance, reported a long list of serious violations of Mexican election law. Wise said, "There was widespread use of government programs and PRI-allied organizations and agencies to coerce voters in five states." Wise reported that, "In one glaring example, there were documented complaints filed on behalf of 1,123 small farmers in one municipality in Oaxaca that benefits from the government's PROCAMPO program were denied people who refused to support the PRI."

Wise also reported that U.S. observers found intimidation of voters, denial of the vote, violation of the right to a secret ballot; direct tampering with the vote count, people being told how to vote, violations of the measures to prevent duplicate voting, presence of election propaganda at the polling place, and tampering with ballot boxes.[5]

Likewise, Global Exchange, which brought 120 international visitors, who served in 100 polling places in 30 communities in five states, reported that, "While several observers witnessed an orderly, clean process, a large majority (approximately 85 percent) noted a number of voting irregularities and a sizeable number reported signs of fraud (appoximately 20 percent)."

Some violations were outrageous. "In Guerrero," said the Global Exchange report, "there was an incident where 50 people went by bus from polling place to polling place to vote in more than one place. In several polling places, particularly in Oaxaca and Chiapas, many peoples' ballots were opened before they were put in the boxes. In the town of Ensenal Colorado in the Isthmus of Tehuantepec, Oaxaca, ballots that were cast for the PRD were ripped up by voting officials and people were told to vote again." In many areas there were problems with the registration list. "In Nuevo Zirosto, Michoacán, 5 percent of the credentialed voters (455 people) were not allowed to vote because their names did not appear on the lists of the voting places they were assigned to."

Things were often worse in Chiapas. Global Exchange reported that "People displaced by the fighting and military occupation came to vote at the special polling places after being told that they would not receive food or other services from local officials unless they voted and the PRI won their areas. They were distressed to be turned away from the polling places after 300 ballots ran out."

Intimidation was a serious problem, according to the Global Exchange report. "In the State of Mexico a woman reported: 'Two weeks ago I went to get a job at the Lala milk factory. I was told by the union that in order to get the job I had to guarantee that I would vote for the PRI.' Another woman chimed in: 'To get my stall at the market, they told me I had to vote for the PRI.'"[6]

Most of the observers with whom I spoke were critical of the election process. Political scientist Pong Hyun Chun, told me, "I think there were some very conscientious people. I think there was some extra effort in making sure that the election should be free and fair. But there was only, I think, this kind of hope. The bottom line of my assessment is that the election was not free, was not democratic, was not fair. I think that the winners of this election, as in the elections in the past, were the PRI and the international business community, who only come to Mexico, I think, for cheap labor. And I think the losers are workers and peasants and urban slum-dwellers."

But Chun also sees some positive aspects. "There was also a lot of grassroots organization, a lot of mobilization among indigenous *campesinos*, students and workers. So I think the international community should reach out to those grassroots organizations. I think that the only way you can challenge the system is pressure from below."

In the end, the Federal Electoral Institute (IFE) certifed that Zedillo of the PRI had won the election with 50.18 percent of the vote, while Diego Fernández Cevallos of the PAN received 26.69 percent, and Cuauhtémoc Cárdenas of the PRD got only 17.08 percent. While there had been some irregularities, said a spokesman for the IFE, they did not call into question the legitimacy of the election. Once again, as every time since 1929, the PRI had won.

What happens when a one-party state that has ruled for 70 years says it will reform its own political and electoral system? Ultimately, the Ministry of the Interior, the PRI-government's enforcer, remained in control of the IFE and thus of the electoral process. COFIPE and the electoral reforms it established were complicated, bureaucratic and largely technical in character. Perhaps the election process was more "transparent," as the Mexicans put it, and perhaps fairer and freer. Yet what the reforms failed to address is what some commentators have been calling Mexico's "subculture of fraud,"[7] or what another describes better as, "a culture of authoritarian praxis."[8] When the PRI moved its enormous state-party apparatus, it came lumbering along like some gigantic tank on the twin tracks of fear and favors, and rolled over everything in its path.

EPILOGUE

Mexico's powerful one-party state is at the beginning of the end. The current crisis opens the possibility of a democratic transformation of Mexico. If such a democratic transformation fails, there is a growing likelihood of social disintegration or the coming to power of an even more authoritarian regime.

The fraudulent Mexican election of August 1994 failed to resolve the question of democracy in Mexico. Ernesto Zedillo's installation was followed by another political assassination, a severe economic crisis, and another military intervention against the Zapatista rebels in Chiapas. Mexico entered 1995 in the midst of the greatest social and political demoralization and depression since 1928.

A little more than a month after the presidential election, on September 28, 1994, José Francisco Ruíz Massieu, general secretary of the PRI, and a former brother-in-law of president Salinas, was assassinated in downtown Mexico City. Ruíz Massieu had advocated that the PRI reform its internal life by establishing a democratic candidate selection process and called for sharing power with the major opposition parties. Many suspected that the responsibility for Ruíz Massieu's murder would be found at the highest levels of the PRI.

Those suspicions were confirmed when on March 1, 1995 Mexican authorities arrested Raúl Salinas, brother of former president Carlos Salinas, and charged him with planning Ruíz Massieu's murder. Raúl Salinas had been his brother Carlos's right-hand man. He had worked closely with the president to create PRONASOL and to rebuild the power of the PRI in the late 1980s. The Mexican special prosecutor suggested that Carlos Salinas might have been involved in the cover up of the murders of both Luis Donaldo Colosio and Ruíz Massieu. Some suspected Carlos Salinas might actually have been responsible for the murders.

The arrest of Raúl Salinas failed to restore the confidence of the Mexican people in their government. In the public mind, the three political murders—Ruíz Massieu in September 1994, Luis Donaldo Colosio in March of

1994, and Cardinal Juan Jesús Posadas Ocampo in May of 1993—remained linked and remained unsolved. The assassinations in any case were symptomatic of a political regime in decay.

In late 1993, Carlos Salinas de Gortari had been extolled as the mastermind of the modernization of Mexico's economy. While the Zapatistas uprising of January 1994 took some of the luster from Salinas, he still appeared as a hero to the Mexican middle and upper classes, as well as to U.S. investors and the Clinton administration. Salinas had not only sold off the state industries and opened Mexico's economy to U.S. investment and products, he had also held down inflation, and, above all, kept the peso stable. In gratitude, Salinas was named to the board of Dow Jones & Co., publisher of *The Wall Street Journal*, and backed by President Clinton to become the first president of the new World Trade Organization.

Then in late December 1994, Salinas's "Mexican miracle," like most miracles, proved to be a hoax. President Zedillo had inherited an overvalued peso, a depressed stock market, and the beginnings of a depression. He was forced to devalue the peso by 12 percent. But almost at once, the peso plummeted to half its former value, the Mexican stock market crashed, and Mexico entered into a depression.[1]

The crisis of the Mexican economy and the arrest of Raúl Salinas destroyed Carlos Salinas's reputation. Salinas seemed to suffer a nervous breakdown. He called TV and radio shows, denouncing Zedillo for causing the nation's economic problems. Then Salinas proclaimed that he would fast until his reputation was restored, but gave up the hunger strike less than a day later. Finally, Salinas left Mexico City and traveled to Monterrey, to the home of Rosa Ofelia Coronado, a PRONASOL organizer in the poor neighborhood of San Bernabé in Monterrey. Pathetically, he asked to spend the night and slept in her children's room.

Zedillo, fearing that the former president might attempt to organize an opposition force, drove Salinas into exile in the United States. Many Mexicans demanded that Salinas be returned to Mexico to stand trial not only for covering up the assassinations, but for ruining the Mexican economy.

The Clinton administration arranged a $50 billion bailout package for Mexico, with $20 billion of it in the form of loans and guarantees from U.S. taxpayers. In exchange, Mexico agreed to deposit its oil revenues in the U.S. Federal Reserve Bank. The bailout deal represented a historic defeat for the people of Mexico. Mexico lost not only its oil wealth and economic autonomy, but also its sovereignty. In effect, the United States took control of the Mexican economy.

The bailout was designed to protect the interests of U.S. and Mexican capitalists, but its terms were predicated upon high interest rates, low wages, and an economic depression in Mexico. By March of 1995, ten of Mexico's 12 largest banks were on the verge of collapse. Many Mexican businesses—from small shops to conglomerates—faced bankruptcy. The annual interest rate in Mexico rose briefly to nearly 100 percent, making it impossible for Mexicans to borrow or to do business. Unemployment also rose rapidly among both workers and peasants. Over 800,000 Mexicans lost their jobs between January and June 1995. For those still working, real wages had been cut by about 40 percent.

About 35 million of Mexico's nearly 86 million people live in poverty and nearly 17 million in extreme poverty. Now there will be many more. Without unemployment insurance or welfare, the jobless swell the ranks of the street vendors, peddling chewing gum and washing windows. Where there was hunger there may now be starvation. Where there was want, there will be desperation.

If things are bad throughout Mexico, they are, as always, worse in Chiapas where militarism and fascism threaten to destroy the Indian peasant movement. After Zedillo's installation, Mexican and foreign investors pressured the new president to take action against the Zapatistas. On January 13, 1995, Chase Bank's Emerging Markets Group published a "Political Update on Mexico," written by Riordan Roett, which stated, "The government will have to eliminate the Zapatistas to demonstrate their effective control of the national territory and national security."[2]

Responding to such pressures, on February 9, 1995, President Zedillo ordered the Mexican Army and police to arrest Subcomandante Marcos and the other leaders of the Zapatista rebellion. The government's warrant identified Marcos as Rafaél Sebastián Guillén Vicente, a 37-year-old former sociology professor. Heavily armed Mexican troops moved into the Zapatista territory and seized the rebel base near Guadalupe Tepeyac, Chiapas, but failed to capture the EZLN leaders.[3]

Only five days later, Zedillo lost his nerve and called a halt to the offensive, Mexican Army troops, however, continued to move through villages in eastern Chiapas destroying homes, brutalizing the population, and creating another 5,000 refugees. Meanwhile, the ranchers and their "white guards" began a campaign of terror aimed at breaking the Indian movement.

Mexico does not simply need a few democratic reforms to achieve genuine democracy. While not precisely a dictatorship, Mexico's Institutional Revolutionary Party oversees a profoundly authoritarian state which has created a corrupt and perverse political system. If they are ever to escape the continued domination of the Institutional Revolutionary Party, the Mexican people will have to carry out a thorough-going political transformation.

Historically, the struggle for democracy has meant two things: political democracy and social justice. The rise of democracy in the eighteenth and nineteenth centuries was predicated upon a social class which could take power and expand both political participation and the material wealth of the nation, and thereby the well-being of the society as a whole. Political democracy and social welfare have always been two aspects of the same question. The business class and the laboring classes have both interpreted democracy and social justice by their own lights, and that has provided the central dynamic for the social struggles of the modern age.

Using that classical definition, we might ask: Who—that is, what social class, group, or political party—will bring democracy to Mexico, democracy in this broader sense of both greater political control by the people, and an expanding economy capable of meeting their needs and desires? Certainly not the Institutional Revolutionary Party. In political terms, the PRI has no desire to dismantle either the governing party-state bureaucracy nor the patronage systems and clientelistic relationships which form the base of the party. The existing authoritarian system provides the power and perquisites of Mexico's governing bureaucrats, and they are loath to give them up. Salinas stole the 1988 election outright. Zedillo's election also depended on the power of the party and widespread fraud. A one-party state is not likely to democratize itself.

There are those in the party leadership who understand that, if it is to survive and retain power, the PRI will have to give up the old forms of the one-party state. Some PRI officials have called for changing the party's name and organizational structure, while others call for more electoral reforms. Many of these technocratic reformers would like to see some sort of power-sharing arrangement with the PAN. They envision the institutionalization of a bi-partisan system like that in the United States where two fundamentally conservative parties alternate in power. So far, however, the attempt to carry out a conservative political reform from above has failed, a victim of various interests within the old PRI. The road to this version of modern Mexico has been lined with tombstones, like that of Ruíz Massieu.

At the same time, the PRI has proven unable to defend Mexico's national economic interests. The PRI's development programs have led the nation into economic disaster. In dealing with the crises of 1982 and 1995, the PRI mortgaged the nation and finally turned the country's oil over to the U.S. government as collateral. The question of the foreign debt is the test case for a political solution to the problems of Mexico. Serving the U.S. bankers, the PRI has placed the burden of the debt on the Mexican nation and ultimately on its poorest people, the workers and peasants. The PRI proves unable to expand either political democracy or the economic well being of the nation.

What about Mexican entrepreneurs, the business class, can they bring democracy to Mexico? Since the nationalization of the banks in 1982, the Mexican capitalist class has, for the first time in its history, succeeded in organizing itself independently of the state and the ruling party. During the 1980s, businessmen became more active in politics, both through the Business Coordinating Council (CCE) as well as through the PAN and even the PRI. Yet, ultimately, the business class has proven unwilling to tackle the problem of breaking the power of the PRI-state. On the contrary, with the rise of the technocrats within the PRI, the capitalist class once again moved closer to the one-party state. The Mexican capitalist class has no particular vocation for democracy.

Beyond that, Mexico's business class seems never to achieve the economic independence which would make possible a real capitalist democracy in Mexico. Mexican business, too, is deeply in debt to U.S. banks, while U.S. multinational corporations have drawn Mexican corporations into a thicket of loans and joint ventures which subordinate Mexican capital to U.S. interests. Mexican businessmen hope to find economic salvation from U.S. loans and find themselves turned into junior partners or local agents of U.S. capital.

Much like the Mexican PRI-government, the businessmen of CCE, or the PAN, also accept the onerous foreign debt. Mexican businesspeople, too, shift the burden of debt on to employees, their tenants and their customers. Unable to establish its economic independence, Mexican business is unlikely to lead a struggle for the political transformation of its government.

The small businesspeople, like those of El Barzón, who are being destroyed by foreign imports and foreign debt, are the advocates of a return to Mexican nationalism. The PRI's privatization and integration into the American economy which have driven them to ruin, have also driven them into opposition. These farmers and small businessmen demand political democracy and civil rights, but they have no economic program beyond protectionism and inflation. They call for a moratorium on their debts, but they have no program to change the economic system, they just wish it would work like it used to.

Cuauhtémoc Cárdenas and the Party of the Democratic Revolution have been the major left opposition to the PRI in Mexico. The base of the PRD is made up of the lower-middle classes, workers and peasants who desperately demand an improvement in their living standards and a voice in their society. The leadership of the PRD, particularly Cárdenas and Muñoz Ledo, are nationalists and social democrats who would like to re-regulate the capitalist economy on a continental basis. Cárdenas and the PRD opposed NAFTA and proposed instead a "Continental Development Treaty." The PRD called, as well, for a renegotiation of Mexico's relationship to the United States, including a renegotiation of the terms of the foreign debt.

When Cárdenas thought he would win the 1994 election, however, he attempted to ingratiate himself with both the New York bankers and the Mexican corporations. Cárdenas feared offending the bankers, and feared, perhaps even more, setting in motion the social base of his party against the Mexican and international order. Cárdenas feared the very social explosion which might have lifted him to power in 1988. The leaders and the masses of the PRD hold implicitly two different programs, head in two different directions, and, as a result, have paralyzed the PRD at crucial moments. More importantly, this tendency has politically paralyzed the workers and peasants.

Civil society is a multi-class democratic movement, and plays an important role as a progressive force calling for the end of the PRI regime. One might uncharitably call civil society a petty bourgeois movement, certainly many of its activists fit that category. But if so, civil society has often had a radical character, and has allied itself with the nation's underdogs.

The new social movements which form the base of civil society—the urban popular movement, the women's groups, the Indian organizations, the environmentalists—have proven to be a genuine force for progressive social change. The problem is that precisely because civil society is a heterogeneous movement of many classes, ideologies, and organizations, it is intrinsically incapable of reorganizing Mexican society. How would civil society bring about the expansion of social wealth necessary to resolve the problems of workers and peasants? Civil society puts forth no proposal for the reorganization of the Mexican economy.

The Chiapas Rebellion thrust Indians and peasants into the center of the Mexican political stage. The heroism and idealism of the Indian peasant rebels, and the political perspicacity of their leadership, transformed the Mexican political scene in 1994 and 1995. It is one thing to seize the initiative, however and another to seize power. While the indigenous people and the peasantry constitute many of the poorest and most oppressed, they are not necessarily those best positioned for leading the struggle for a political revolution to bring democracy to Mexico. The EZLN has led a valiant struggle in Chiapas, but so far it has not put forward a program to mobilize the Mexican people, most of whom are urban workers, not rural peasants.

Mexico is no longer primarily a rural and agricultural country. At the time of the Mexican Revolution, 80 percent of the population consisted of peasants. Today in Mexico, 80 percent of the population is urban and working class, whether or not the people have been able to find jobs. The crucial question for the struggle for democracy in Mexico is: what will the workers do?

The great problem is that Mexico's workers remain the captives of the ruling party and its official unions. Since 1914, or at least since 1936, Mexican workers have been unable to construct their own ideology, labor organizations or political party.

The current crisis could soon bring a revitalization of the Mexican labor movement. In 1995, the Mexican government banned the annual May Day parade for the first time since 1920. For 75 years, Medico's "official" labor unions marched their members, sometimes as many as half a million, through Mexico City to the Zocalo and then paraded them before the balcony of the National Palace where they were saluted by the president. But in the spring of 1995, the official unions announced they would not hold the annual May Day demonstration, supposedly because it was too expensive, and the government banned the event. In reality, the union leaders feared that because of the deep economic crisis, the workers might turn the usually perfunctory performance into a protest.

With the official march called off, for the first time since the Mexican Revolution, the working people of Mexico organized their own May Day demonstration. For decades, workers had been forced by the government, the employers, and the union bureaucrats to participate in the march under threat of losing pay or even losing their jobs. But on May Day 1995, the workers marched of their own free will, and they marched not to support the PRI, but to oppose the ruling party and its policies.

The May Day 1995 demonstration was a grassroots affair. Many small parades of workers and the urban poor began in neighborhoods throughout the city, at private homes, workplaces and union halls. As they stepped off, some workers raised their fists and sang the "Internationale", the socialist workers' anthem. The feeder marches proceeded up side streets, into broader avenues, and finally converged at the Zocalo. The workers carried placards and chanted slogans condemning Fidel Velazquez and the PRI's official union movement. They demanded jobs and wage increases, and they called for union democracy. Among the marchers were petroleum workers, telephone operators, and school teachers; there were independent unions such as the Authentic Labor Front (FAT) and the university unions with their banners.

Among the most vocal of the marchers were the 13,000 members of the bus drivers' union of route 100, a union closely linked to the radical Independent Proletarian Movement which was accused of giving financial support to the EZLN. The Zedillo government had fired the lot of them. With their families and friends, the route 100 members must have numbered as many as 50,000 people, and they were among the most militant, no doubt because they were fighting for their jobs.

But the huge march was more than simply a union demonstration. Many marchers came from the National Democratic Convention to support the Zapatistas. The urban poor of the Assembly of Barrios marched by the thousands, together with members of the hundreds of groups which form the Civic Alliance. All of the parties of the left participated from the Party of the Democratic Revolution to the Green Ecology Party of Mexico.[4]

The May Day march of 1995 symbolized the declaration of independence of the Mexican working class. A political vanguard of Mexico's working people organized their own May Day to assert their independence— but they have a long way to go to win it.

May Day 1995 also represented a convergence of civil society and the workers' movement, or at least the token of such an alliance. Workers as citizens, and citizens who are also workers, joined together in their common demands for political democracy and social justice. May Day 1995 pointed the direction toward the best hope for a democratic Mexico: an independent labor movement leading a coalition of democratic forces to restructure society around the needs of the majority.

If the broader movement for democracy succeeds in opening up space for the workers, they will fight to end their material privation and to improve their lives in all ways. The workers' struggle is likely to give rise to demands which cannot be met by the existing economic order. The workers' needs for a higher standard of living, for education and health care can only be met by a reorganization of Mexico's economic priorities. A workers' movement is likely to quickly produce a radical socialist wing with a program calling for the repudiation of the foreign debt. Neither the New York bankers nor the Mexican corporations will tolerate such a development. At that point, the Mexican struggle for democracy would also become a new international struggle for socialism.

A radical movement from below, fighting for socialism, is one possible future development for Mexico. Economic crisis, disintegration, or right-wing military coups represent other alternatives. Meanwhile, the PRI-government stumbles toward the end, from crisis to crisis.

As I finish this book in May 1995, more than a year after the Chiapas Rebellion, Mexico stands at a crossroads. There exist, today in Mexico two contrary forces, two antithetical principles. On the one side—supported by the United States government, U.S. banks, and corporations—stands Mexico's authoritarian state-party, the PRI with its powerful political apparatus, its patronage army, and its dependent masses. On the other side stand those several populist and democratic movements described here: the peasants struggling for land, the workers demanding decent wages and working conditions, the indigenous people and women demanding social equality, and the members of all social classes calling for political democracy. Today the Mexican state-party confronts a broad, multi-class movement, an elemental and inchoate force, a society in search of democracy and social justice, a people in quest of a new government. The Party remains in power, the people remain in struggle, and the future of Mexico will be decided by the contest.

NOTES

1. REBELLION OF THE FACELESS

1. The Zapatistas various *communiqués*, letters, and other writings have now been collected in several places. I am refering here to two anthologies: Ejército Zapatista de Liberación Nacional (EZLN), *La palabra de los armados de verdad y fuego* (Mexico: Editorial Fuenteovejuna, 1994) 7. (Hereafter *Palabra*.) See also: Ejercito Zapatista de Liberación Nacional, *Comunicados y correspondencia: De 1o de enero al 21 de abril de 1994* (N.p.: Unión Nacional de Trabajadores, miembro de la CONAC-LN, n.d.) Third, enlarged edition. The first four pages of this edition are unnumbered, and the passage cited is from the first unnumbered page. (Hereafter *Comunicados*.)

2. EZLN, *Comunicados*, unnumbered 2.

3. EZLN, *Comunicados*, unnumbered 3.

4. Pedro Reygadas, Ivan Gomezcesar, Esther Kravzov, *La Guerra de Año Nuevo: Crónicas de Chiapas y Mexico 1994* (Mexico, D.F.: Editorial Praxis, 1994) 56. (Hereafter Guerra.)

5. EZLN, *Comunicados*, 5.

6. Tim Golden, "Rebels Determined 'to Build Socialism' in Mexico," *New York Times*, January 4, 1994; S. Lynne Walker, "Rebels battle Mexico Army, hold 3 towns," *San Diego Union-Tribune*, January 4, 1994.

7. Tim Golden, "Mexican Rebels Are Retreating; Issues Are Not," *New York Times*, January 5, 1994. Reuters quoted in S. Lynne Walker, "Rebels battle Mexico Army, hold 3 towns," *San Diego Union-Tribune*, January 4, 1994.

8. EZLN, *Comunicados*, 3.

9. Tim Golden, "Mexican Army Is Said to Abuse Rebel Suspects," *New York Times*, January 24, 1994.

10. S. Lynne Walker, "Mexican army strafes village," *San Diego Union-Tribune*, January 6, 1994.

11. Tim Golden, "Abuses Are Feared in Mexican Revolt," *New York Times*, January 6, 1994.

12. Pedro Reygadas et al., *Guerra*, 66-70.

13. EZLN, *Comunicados*, 12.

14. Ibid., 4.

15. Deedee Halleck, "Zapatistas On-Line," *NACLA Report on the Amercas*, September/October, 1994, 30-32.

16. Philip Russell, *The Chiapas Rebellion* (Austin: Mexico Resource Center, 1995) 64-68.

17. Cited in, Luis Méndez Asensio and Antonio Cano Gimeno, *La guerra contra el tiempo: Viaje a la selva alzada* (Mexico: Editorial Temas de Hoy, 1994) 76.

18. Anthony DePalma, "Mexico's Indians Heed Rumble of Distant Guns," *New York Times*, February 16, 1994; Gregory Gross, "Chiapas revolt ignites Baja campaign," *San Diego Union-Tribune*, January 21, 1994; Gregory Gross, "Mass call-to-work limits size of Indian protest rally in Baja," *San Diego Union Tribune*, January 24, 1994.

19. Guillermo Correa, Salvador Corro, Julio Cesar López, "Con el puño en alto, en San Cristóbal, representantes de 500 organizaciones indígenas de todo el país reivindicaron su 'derecho a la rebelión'," *Proceso*, March 21, 1994, 36-40.

20. UPI, "Mexican strikers close campuses, cite Chiapas revolt," February 4, 1994.

21. Tracey Eaton, "Mass protests overrun Mexico City," *Dallas Morning News*, March 13, 1994, 21A.

22. Fernando Ortega Pizarro, "Tocaron a Salinas en un punto sensible: Harp Helu forma parte de sú elite de supermillionarios," *Proceso*, March 21, 1994, 18-19.

23. Arthur Golden, "Aburto was full of contradictions," *San Diego Union-Tribune*, April 1, 1994.

24. See the various reports of Amnesty International, Americas Watch, the Mexican government's Human Rights Commission, and the Centro de Derechos Humanos Miguel Agustín Pro Juárez, A.C. Also see: Joe Gandelman, "Rights advocate speaks out in Mexico," *San Diego Union*, October 26, 1987; Tim Golden, "Mexico, Admitting Torture, Charges 12 for Rights Abuses," *New York Times*, September 18, 1991; Tim Golden, "Mexico Rights Agency Asks Arrest of 13 Police Agents," *New York Times*, April 1, 1992.

25. Larry Rohter, "Former Mexican Soldier Describes Executions of Political Prisoners," *New York Times*, February 19, 1989.

26. Alberto Aguirre et al, *El Asesinato del Cardenal, ¿Un error?* (Mexico: Planeta, n.d. [1994?].)

27. *Latin American Newsletters*, "Zedillo's Bungle," September 23, 1993; *International Reports*, "Controversy Over a Revised History," October 7, 1992; Paul B. Carroll and Dianne Solis, "Mexico Ruling Party Picks Zedillo to Run for President," *Wall Street Journal*, March 30, 1994; Timothy Golden, "Mexican Leader Picks Successor to Slain Nominee," *New York Times*, March 30, 1994; S. Lynne Walker, "Zedillo named PRI candidate for president," *San Diego Union-Tribune*, March 30, 1994.

28. Juanita Darling and Tracy Wilkinson, "Mexico's PRI Picks Economist Zedillo To Succeed Colosio," *Los Angeles Times*, March 30, 1994.

2. PEASANT REBELS

1. EZLN, *La palabra de los armados de verdad y fuego* (Mexico: Editorial Fuenteovejuna, 1994) 21. (Hereafter *Palabra*.)

2. EZLN, *Palabra*, 22.

3. Ibid., 23.

4. INEGI, *XI Censo general de población y vivienda*, 1992 and Consejo Nacional de Población, *Perfil sociodemográfico del estado de Chiapas*, 1992, in Pedro Reygadas, Ivan Gomezcesar, Esther Kravzov, *La guerra de Año Nuevo: Crónicas de Chiapas y Mexico 1994* (Mexico: Editorial Praxis, 1994), 30. (Hereafter *Guerra*.) Also, Mexican Census of 1990 and President's report of 1993 in "The Mexican Rebels' Impoverished Home," *New York Times*, January 9, 1994.

5. Thomas Benjamin, *A Rich Land, A Poor People: Politics and Society in Modern Chiapas* (Albuquerque: University of New Mexico Press, 1989) 228. (Hereafter *Rich Land*.)

6. Guillermo Bonfil Batalla, *Mexico Profundo: Una civilización negada* (Mexico: Grijalbo, 1989) 49-51. (Hereafter *México Profundo*.)

7. Jesús Silva Herzog, *Breve historia de la revolución mexicana* (Mexico: Fondo de la Cultura Económica, 1973) II, 310-14, 322-30, has the text of the original Article 27.

8. James W. Wilkie, "The Six Ideological Phases of Mexico's 'Permanent Revolution' since 1910," *Society and Economy in Mexico* (Los Angeles: UCLA Latin American Center Publications, 1990) 7(Hereafter *Society and Economy*); Luisa Paré, "The Challenges to Rural Democratisation in Mexico," in Jonathon Fox, ed., *The Challenge of Rural Democratisation: Perspective from Latin America and the Philippines* (London: Frank Cass, 1990), 81. (Here after *Challenges*.)

9. Information here from Arturo Warman, "La reforma al artículo 27 constitucional," and Armando Bartra, "¿Zapata Vive?" both in "Perfil" section of *La Jornada*, April 8, 1994.

10. Neil Harvey, *Rebellion in Chiapas* (San Diego: Center for U.S.-Mexican Studies, UCSD, 1994) 7. (Hereafter *Rebellion*)

11. Rigoberta Menchú, *I, Rigoberta Menchú: An Indian Woman in Guatemala* (New York: Verso, 1991) 54.

12. The impact of capitalism on peasant rebellions has been discussed by Eric Wolf, *Peasant Wars of the Twentieth Century* (New York: Harper, 1969); Barrington Moore, *Social Origins of Dictatorship and Democracy: Lord and Peasant in the Making of the Modern World* (Boston: Beacon, 1966); and John Tutino, *From Insurrection to Revolution in Mexico: Social Bases of Agrarian Violence* (Princeton: Princeton University Press, 1986).

13. Antonio García de León, *Resistenca y utopia* (Mexico: Ediciones Era, 1993), I, 89. I rely heavily on this book. (Hereafter *Resistencia*.)

14. García de Leon, *Resistencia*, I, 89.

15. Ibid., II, 201.

16. George Collier, "Peasant Politics and the Mexican State: Indigenous Compliance in Highland Chiapas," *Mexican Studies/Estudios Mexicanos* (Winter 1987) 3 (1) 83.

17. García de Leon, *Resistencia*, II, 167.

18. Ibid., 201.

19. Dan La Botz, *The Crisis of Mexican Labor* (New York: Praeger, 1988), 85-98.

20. Benjamin, *Rich Land*, 226.

21. Ibid., 235.

22. Ibid., 226.

23. Ibid., 230.

24. Cárdenas gave very few, a total of 69 for ranchers amounting to 114,369 hectares; but he established a precedent. Gustavo Díaz Ordaz (1964-1970) gave out the most, 749 for ranchers amounting to 2,262,575 hectares. James W. Wilkie, *Society and Economy*, 8-9.

25. Benjamin, *Rich Land*, 223.

26. Ibid., 232.

27. Amnesty International, *Human Rights in Rural Areas: Exchange of Documents with the Mexican Government on Human Rights Violations in Oaxaca and Chiapas* (London: Amnesty International, 1986). Benjamin, *Rich Land*, 223-43.

28. George A. Collier, *Basta! Land and the Zapatista Rebellion in Chiapas* (Oakland, CA: The Institute for Food and Development Policy, 1994) 107. (Hereafter: *Basta!*)

29. Collier, *Basta!*, 89-119.

30. James D. Nations, "The Ecology of the Zapatista Revolt," *Cultural Survival Quarterly* (Spring 1994) 31.

31. George A. Collier, "Roots of the Rebellion in Chiapas," *Cultural Survival Quarterly* (Spring 1994) 15.

32. EZLN, *Palabra*, 56-57.

33. Collier, *Basta!*, 81.

34. John Ross, *Rebellion from the Roots: Indian Uprising in Chiapas* (Monroe, Maine: Common Courage, 1995) 274. (Hereafter *Roots*.)

35. Vivian Bennett, "The Evolution of Urban Popular Movements in Mexico Between 1968 and 1988," in Arturo Escobar and Sonia Alvarez, *The Making of Social Movements in Latin America: Identity, Strategy and Democracy* (Boulder: Westview Press, 1992), 240-59.

36. Harvey, *Rebellion,* 31; Ross, *Roots,* 227.

NOTES

37. Phillip L. Russell, *The Chiapas Rebellion* (Austin: Mexico Resource Center, 1995) 33, says Maoists arrived in late 1960s. Joe Foweraker, *Popular Mobilization in Mexico: The Teachers' Movement, 1977-87* (New York: Cambridge University Press, 1993) 88, gives 1974 date; Jonathan Fox, "The Challenge of Democracy: Rebellion as Catalyst," *Akwe:kon: A Journal of Indigenous Issues* (Summer 1994) XI(2), 15; Harvey, *Ibid.*

38. Ross, *Roots*, 227.

39. Foweraker, *Popular Mobilization in Mexico*, 88-100.

40. Penny Leroux, *Cry of the People: The Struggle for Human Rights in Latin America—The Catholic Church in Conflict with U.S. Policy* (New York: Penguin, 1982) 31. (Hereafter *Cry*.)

41. Leroux, *Cry*, 37.

42. Miguel Concha Malo et al, *La participación de los cristianos en el proceso popular de liberación en México* (Mexico: Siglo Veintiuno Editores, 1986).

43. Humberto Angel Torres, "Faith and Political Commitment of Christian Base Communities," *The Other Side of Mexico*, October-December 1988, 7.

44. Luis Suárez, *Lucio Cabañas: El guerrillero sin esperanza* (Mexico: Grijalbo, 1984). See also the marvelous historical novel about the Guerrero movement by Carlos Montemayor, *Guerra en el paraíso* (Mexico: Diana, 1994).

45. Neil Harvey, "Peasant Strategies and Corporatism in Chiapas," in Joe Foweraker and Ann L. Craig, eds., *Popular Movements and Political Change in Mexico* (Boulder: Lynne Rienner Publishers, 1990) 188.

46. Collier, *Basta!* 66-76.

47. Paré, *Challenges* , 85.

48. Susan Street, *Maestros en movimiento: Transformaciones en la burocracia estatal (1978-1982)* (Mexico: CIESAS, 1992) 147-85. See also: Foweraker, *Popular Mobilization*.

49. Russell, *Chiapas Rebellion*, 34; Ross, *Roots*, 273.

50. Collier, *Basta!*, 78.

51. Ross, *Roots*, 249.

52. EZLN, *Voice of Fire: Communiqués and Interviews from the Zapatista National Liberation Army*, ed. by Ben Clarke and Clifton Ross (Berkeley : New Earth Publications, 1994) 74. (Hereafter: *Voice*.)

53. Ross, *Roots*, 281.

54. *Ibid.*, 287.

55. Nancy M. Farriss, *Maya Society Under Colonial Rule: The Collective Enterprise of Survival* (Princeton, N.J.: Princeton University Press, 1984), 138-39. While Farriss writes about the Yucatán, her remarks would also hold true for Chiapas.

56. Evan Vogt, "On the Application of the Phylogenetic Model to the Maya," in Raymond J. DeMallie and Alfonso Ortiz, *North American Indian Anthropology* (Norman: University of Oklahoma Press, 1994) 395-96.

57. Collier, *Basta!*, 120.

58. Bennett, *Evolution*, 240-59

59. *Voice*, 110.

60. *Voice*, 42.

61. Ben Clarke, Introduction, *Voice*, 9.

62. Collier, *Basta!*, 64-5.

63. *Voice*, 39, 93-4.

64. *Voice*, 48.

65. *Voice*, 48-9.

66. *Voice*, 47.

67. Jorge Castañeda has called them "armed reformists." Cited in Ross, *Roots* 287.

68. The Zapatistas inevitably invite comparison with *Sendero Luminoso*, the Shining Path of Peru. Both groups appear to have Maoist origins, to have built a social base among indigenous people in rural areas, and to have launched rebellions calling for the overthrow of their respective governments. But while the Zapatistas adopted a "Popular Front" version of Maoism, the Senderistas pursued the lunacy of Stalin's "Third Period" to its extreme. Abimael Guzmán's *Sendero Luminoso* is a party-cult that has engaged in an orgy of violence not only against the Peruvian military but also against hundreds of other leftists, labor union leaders, activists, and peasants who refused to follow Chairman Guzmán's line. *Sendero Luminoso* more resembles Pol Pot's Khmer Rouge than the Mexican Zapatistas. See: Simon Strong, *Shining Path: Terror and Revolution in Peru* (New York: Times Books, Random House, 1992).

3. MEXICAN REVOLUTION TO ONE-PARTY STATE

1. John Womack, *Zapata and the Mexican Revolution* (New York: Vintage, 1968) 168. (Hereafter *Zapata*)

2. For a general discussion of Mexico's economic and political development, including the role of U.S. economic and political imperialism, see: James D. Cockroft, *Mexico: Class Formation, Capital Accumulation and the State* (New York: Monthly Review, 1983). For these statistics see 91.

3. Cockcroft, *Ibid.*, 87.

4. Dan La Botz, *Edward L. Doheny: Petroleum, Power and Politics in the United States and Mexico* (New York: Praeger, 1991).

5. Abraham Nuncio, *El Grupo Monterrey* (Mexico: Editorial Nueva Imagen, 1982).

6. José Luis Cecena, *México en la órbita imperial* (Mexico: El Caballito, 1991), 51-54.

7. Cecena, *Ibid.*, 75-78.

8. Cecena, *Ibid.*, 100.

9. James W.Wilkie, *Society and Economy in Economy in Mexico* (Los Angeles:UCLA Latin American Center Publications, 1990), 4.

10. Womack, *Zapata*, 192.

11. Alan Knight, *The Mexican Revolution* (Lincoln: University of Nebraska Press, 1986) II, 115-129.

12. Womack, *Zapata*, 127.

13. Womack, *Zapata*, 228.

14. Adolfo Gilly, *La Revolución interrumpida* (Mexico: El Caballito, 1971) 135; John Tutino, *From Insurrection to Revolution in Mexico* (Princeton: University of Princeton, 1986) 358; Barrington Moore, Jr., *The Social Origins of Dictatorship and Democracy: Lord and Peasant in the Making of the Modern World* (Boston: Beacon, 1967) 479.

15. Ramón Eduardo Ruíz, *The Great Rebellion: Mexico, 1905-1924* (New York: W.W. Norton, 1980). Mark Wasserman, *Persistent Oligarchs: Elites and Politics in Chiuahua, Mexico: 1910-1940* (Durham: Duke, 1993) draws similar conclusions.

16. Karl Marx writing about Louis Napoleon Bonaparte and Bismark, later Leon Trotsky writing about Hitler developed the theory of Bonapartism. For the Mexican state see: Manuel Aguilar Mora, *El Bonapartismo Mexicano* (Mexico: Juan Pablos Editor, 1982), 2 vols.

17. Nora Hamilton, *The Limit of State Autonomy: Post-Revolutionary Mexico* (Princeton: Princeton University, 1982) 84-90.

18. Hamilton, *Limits*, 79-84.

19. Miguel Angel Calderón, *El impacto de la crisis de 1929 en México* (Mexico: SEP, 1982).

20. *La Jira del General Lázaro Cárdenas*, 82, in William Cameron Townsend, *Lázaro Cárdenas: Mexican Democrat* (Ann Arbor, Michigan: George Wahr Publishing Co., 1952) 86-87.

21. Adolfo Gilly, *El cardenismo, una utopía mexicana* (Mexico: Cal y Arena, 1994) 405.

22. Townsend, *Lázaro Cárdenas*, 131.

23. Enrique Cárdenas, "The Great Depression and Industrialisation: The Case of Mexico," in Rosemary Thorp, *Latin America in the 1930s: The Role of the Periphery in World Crisis* (New York: St. Martin's Press, 1984) Chapter 9, 222-41.

24. Hamilton, *Limits*, 185-215.

25. Javier Aguilar García, *La política sindical en México: industria del automóvil* (Mexico: Ediciones Era, 1982) 18.

26. Enrique Cárdenas, "Great Depression," 223.

27. In the discussion of business organizations from 1930 to the 1980s, I rely principally on: Roderic A. Camp, *Entrepreneurs and Politics in Twentieth Century Mexico* (New York: Oxford University Press, 1989) and René Millan, *Los*

Empresarios ante el estado y la sociedad (Mexico: Siglo Veintiuno, 1988). (Hereafter *Empresarios.*)

28. Wilkie, *Society and Economy*, 15.

29. In my discussion of PAN, I rely on Abraham Nuncio, *El PAN: Alternativa de poder o instrumento de la oligarquia empresarial* (Mexico: Nueva Imagen, 1986) and Luis Méndez Asensio and Pedro Reygadas Robles Gil, *El Jefe Diego* (Mexico: Ediciones Temas de Hoy, 1994).

30. Darrell Delamaide, *Debt Shock: The Full Story of the World Credit Crisis* (New York: Anchor Books, 1985).

31. Millan, *Empresarios*, 167, 175.

32. Méndez Asensio and Robles Gil, *El Jefe*, 44.

33. Dan La Botz, *Crisis of Mexican Labor* (New York: Praeger, 1988) 132-43.

34. Barry Carr, *Marxism and Communism in Twentieth Century Mexico* (Lincoln: Univ. of Nebraska, 1992) 315 Table 14.

4. THE RISE OF CIVIL SOCIETY

1. It is true that neighborhood groups independent of the government had been organized, especially in northern Mexico since the early 1970s, but most of those organizations were led by Maoist parties and defined themselves as poor people's or working-class movements, not as citizens's movements.

2. The Mexican left *did* develop a critique of the PRI government. But even when it developed a critique of the PRI state, most of the Mexican left, because of the pervasive influence of Stalinism, Maoism, and Castroism, had no democratic alternative. See: Juan Felipe Leal, *La Burguesia y el estado mexicano* (Mexico: El Caballito, 1972); and *México: estado, burocracia y sindicatos* (México: El Caballito, 1980); Arnaldo Córdova, *La política de masas del cardenismo* (Mexico: Ediciones Era, 1974). The one important exception would be the Revolutionary Workers Party (PRT). Manuel Augilar Mora, *El Bonapartismo mexicano* (Mexico: Juan Pablos Editor, 1982) 2 vols. Arturo Anguiano, *El Estado y la politica obrera del cardenismo* (Mexico: Ediciones Era, 1975).

3. Vivienne Bennett, "The Evolution of Urban Popular Movements in Mexico Between 1968 and 1988," in Arturo Escobar and Sonia Alvarez, *The Making of Social Movements in Latin America: Identity, Strategy, and Democracy* (Boulder: Westview Press, 1992).

4. Carlos Monsiváis, *Entrada libre: Crónicas de la sociedad que se organiza* (Mexico: Ediciones Era, 1987) 20. Other influential accounts of the earthquake are Elena Poniatowska's *Nada, nadie: Las voces del Temblor* (Mexico: Era, 1988) and Humbeto Musacchio, *Ciudad quebrada* (Mexico: Ediciones Océano, 1986).

5. Monsiváis, *Ibid.*, 25, 33, 38, 79.

6. Jean L. Cohen and Andrew Arato, *Civil Society and Political Theory* (Cambridge, MA: MIT Press, 1992). See Chapter 1, "The Contemporary Revival of Civil Society." For a discussions of civil society in Latin America see: Jorge G.

Castañeda, *Utopia Unarmed: The Latin American Left After the Cold War* (New York: Knopf, 1993) 197-236, and Carlos M. Vilas, "The Hour of Civil Socety," *NACLA* (September/October 1993) 38-42. Also: Jürgen Habermas, *The Structural Transformation of the Public Sphere: An Inquiry into a Category of Bourgeois Society* (Cambridge, MA: MIT Press, 1994).

7. From an interview in *Temps Moderns* cited by: Andrew Arato, *From Neo-Marxism to Democratic Theory: Essays on the Critical Theory of Soviet-Type Societies* (Armonk, NY: M.E. Sharpe, 1993) 171. See also: Jan Jozef Lipski, *KOR: A History of the Workers' Defense Committee in Poland, 1976-1981*, translated by Olga Amsterdamska and Gene M. Moore (Berkeley: University of California Press, 1985) Chapter 4 "The Ethos of the Workers' Defense Committee." And, Z.A. Pelczynski, "Solidarity and 'The Rebirth of Civil Society' in Poland, 1976-1981," in John Keane, *Civil Society and the State: New European Perspectives* (New York: Verso, 1988) 361-380.

8. Norberto Bobbio, "Gramsci and the Concept of Civil Society," in John Keane, *Civil Society and the State: New European Perspectives* (New York: Verso, 1988) 73-100.

9. See: Barry Carr, *Marxism and Communism in Twentieth Century Mexico* (Lincoln: University of Nebraska, 1992), Chapter 10, 306-28, and Castañeda, *Utopia Unarmed*, Chapter 8, 237-266.

10. Bennett, "The Evolution of Urban Popular Movements in Mexico," 254.

11. On the CEU events see: Monsiváis, *Entrada Libre, 246-306. Jorge Castañeda, Ibid.*, 204-5.

12. Dimitris Stevis and Stephen Mumme, "Nuclear Power, Technological Autonomy, and the State in Mexico," *Latin American Research Review*, 26(3), 1991.

13. I rely here on a brief history of the Mexican anti-nuclear movement to be found in Hugo García Michel, *Mas Allá de Laguna Verde* (Mexico: Editorial Posada, 1988), Part 2, Chapter 2, "Algunos datos sobre la historia del movimiento antinuclear mexicano," 229-257.

14. *Ibid.*, 237.

15. Genaro Guevara Cortina, "De la sociedad anónima a la sociedad civil: el Movimiento Antinuclear y Ecologista Veracruzano," in José Árias and Luis Barquera, eds. *¿Laguna Verde? ¡No Gracias!* (Mexico: Claves Latinoamericanas, 1988) 258-59.

16. García Michel, *Mas Allá, 239.*

17. García Michel, *Ibid.*, 246.

5. THE SON OF THE GENERAL

1. Adolfo Gilly, ed., *Cartas a Cuauhtémoc Cárdenas* (Mexico: Ediciones Era, 1989) 55.

2. Adolfo Gilly, *El cardenismo, una utopía mexicana* (Mexico: Cal y Arena, 1994) passim.

3. Paco Ignacio Taibo II, *Cárdenas de cerca: Una entrevista biográfica* (Mexico: Grupo Editorial Planeta, 1994) 27.

4. Carlos B. Gil, ed., *Hope and Frustration: Interviews with Leaders of Mexico's Political Opposition* (Wilmington, Delaware: Scholarly Resources, 1992) 151. Hereafter *Hope*.

5. Taibo II, *Cárdenas de cerca, 44*.

6. Gil, *Hope*, 162.

7. Ibid., 197.

8. Ibid., 200. I have modified the translation.

9. Jorge Laso de la Vega, ed., *La Corriente Democrática: Hablan Los Protagonistas* (Mexico: Editorial Posada, 1987) Chapter 2, "¿Vamos hacia la dictadura?"

10. Gil, *Hope*, 202.

11. Jorge Castañeda, *Utopia Unarmed: The Latin American Left After the Cold War* (New York: Knopf, 1993), 156.

12. Equipo Pueblo [a collective author], *Crónica del Nuevo México* (Mexico City: Equipo Pueblo, 1989). Equipo Pueblo is a political collective and the book is a collection of essays. The selection here is from: Carlos Monsiváis, "Notas a Partir de Una Gran Concentración," 65.

13. *Ibid.*, 66.

14. *Ibid.*, "Notas Sobre la Campaña de 1988," 89.

15. *Ibid.*, 87.

16. Adolfo Gilly, "Solidaridades," in Adolfo Gilly, ed., *Cartas*, 41-43.

17. Dan La Botz, *Crisis of Mexican Labor* and *Mask of Democracy*.

6. THE TECHNOCRATIC COUNTER-REVOLUTION

1. I rely heavily in this section on: Miguel Angel Centeno *Democracy within Reason: Technocratic Revolution in Mexico* (University Park, PA: Pennsylvania State University Press, 1994).

2. Centeno writes, "The Salinas *sexenio* represented a revolution in Mexico comparable to that presided [over] by Lázaro Cárdenas in the 1930s." (*Ibid.*, 3) "The challenge, and the subsequent response by the Salinas administration, resulted in a transformation of the political system perhaps as radical as that managed by Cárdenas in his battle with Calles." (*Ibid.*, 59) Denise Dresser, *Neopopulist Solutions to Neoliberal Problems: Mexico's National Solidarity Program* (San Diego: Center for U.S.-Mexican Studies, 1991) writes, "If the 1930s were the period of corporatist construction, the 1980s were the period of corporatist dismantling." (*Ibid.*, 25)

3. Centeno, *Democracy, 107*.

4. Centeno, *Ibid.*, 220-211

5. Centeno, *Ibid.*, 92.

NOTES

6. I rely heavily in this section on the essays in: Wayne Cornelius, Ann L. Craig and Jonathan Fox, eds., *Transforming State-Society Relations in Mexico: The National Solidarity Program* (San Diego: Center for U.S.-Mexican Studies, UCSD, 1994) and on: Denise Dresser, *Neopopulist Solutions to Neoliberal Problems: Mexico's National Solidarity Program* (San Diego: Center for U.S.-Mexican Studies, 1991). The quotation here is from: Cornelius, *Transforming*, from the "Introduction," 9.

7. Carlos Salinas de Gortari, *Producción y Participación Política en el Campo* (Mexico: Universidad Nacional Autónoma de México, 1980), based on his dissertation: "Public Investment, Political Participation and System Support: Study of Three Rural Communities in Central Mexico," Ph.D. Diss., Harvard, 1978.

8. Cornelius, *Transforming*, 7, citing, PRONASOL, "La solidaridad en el desarrollo nacional." (Mexico: Coordinación del Programa Nacional de Solidaridad, SPP, September) and Carlos Salinas, "Second State of the Nation Report," November 1, 1991 (Mexico: Office of the Press Secretary to the President).

9. Dresser, "Bringing the Poor Back In," in Cornelius, *Transforming*, 147.

10. George A. Collier, *Basta! Land and the Zapatista Rebellion in Chiapas* (Oakland, CA: The Institute for Food and Development Policy), 81.

11. Dresser, "Bringing the Poor Back In," 153.

12. Moguel, "The Mexican Left and the Social Program of Solidarity," in Cornelius, *Transforming*, 174.

13. Dresser, *"Bringing the Poor Back In*, in Cornelius, *Transforming*, 156.

14. Alan Knight, "Solidarity: Historical Continuities and Contemporary Implications," in Cornelius, *Transforming*, 39.

15. The account here is based primarily on: Paul Haber, "Political Change in Durango: The Role of National Solidarity," in Cornelius, *Transforming*, 255-79. I use Haber's account, but my interpretation of events is different and more critical of the CDP. Also see: Julio Moguel, "The Mexican Left and the Social Program of Salinismo," also in Cornelius, *Transforming*, 167-76.

16. Cited in Dresser, "Bringing the Poor Back In," in Cornelius, *Transforming*, 158.

17. Raúl Trejo Delarbre and Ana L. Galván, eds., *Asi Cayó La Quina* (Mexico: El Nacional, 1989).

18. I rely heavily on: Won-Ho Kim, "The Mexican Regime's Political Strategy in Implementing Economic Reform in Comparative Perspective: A Case Study of the Privatization of the Telephone Industry," (Ph.D. Diss, University of Texas at Austin, December 1992).

19. Kim, *Ibid.*, 114, citing *El Financiero* October 15, 1987.

20. Rodolfo Rojas Zea, ed., *Tres huelgas de telefonistas* (Mexico, D.F.: Editorial Uno, S.A., 1980). See also: Dan La Botz, *Mask of Democracy: Labor Suppression in Mexico Today* (Boston: South End Press, 1992) 126-30.

21. Kim, *Ibid.*, 126.

22. Kim, *Ibid.*, 135, citing *Proceso*, September 25, 1989.

23. Kim, *Ibid.*, 158-163.

24. Francisco Hernández Juárez and Mara Xelhuantzi López, *El sindicalismo en la reforma del Estado* (Mexico: Fondo de la Cultura Económica, 1993) 121.

25. "CE Employs 30,00 in Mexico Border Zone," *Television Digest with Consumer Electronics* (July 23, 1990) 13.

26. "Mexico Sets Extension of Freeze," *New York Times*, August 16, 1988; "Mexico Extends Economic Curbs to March 1990," *Wall Street Journal*, June 20, 1989; "Mexico Renews PECE, Unifies Exchange Rate," *Business Latin America*, November 18, 1991, 369).

27. "US Investment in LA Shows Growth in 1990, But Returns Are Mixed," *Business Latin America*, October 28, 1991, 347.

28. Tim Golden, "Boom Shows Its Dark Side," *New York Times*, December 23, 1994.

29. Banco de México, *The Mexican Economy 1993*, 212.

30. "South of the Border," and other several other articles in same issue, *Automotive News*, April 1, 1991, 1; Gray Newman, "Business Outlook Mexico," *Business Latin America*, December 2, 1991, 390.

31. Banco de México, *The Mexican Economy 1993* (Mexico: Banco de México, June 1993.

32. "Mexico's Oil Industry Heads Towards the 21st Century," *Mexico on the Record* (Press and Public Affairs Office, the Embassy of Mexico), January 1992, 1(2), 2.

33. Carlos Morera Camacho, "Los grandes cambios en los grupos financieros en 1988-1992," *Coyuntura* (PRD's official magazine), September 1993, 11.

34. John Summa, "Mexico's New Super-Billionaires," *Multinational Monitor*, November 1994, 24-26.

7. PARTY OF THE DEMOCRATIC REVOLUTION

1. Philip L. Russell, *Mexico Under Salinas* (Austin, Texas: Mexico Resource Center, 1994) 96-98.

2. PRD, *Llamamiento al pueblo de México*, 1988, cited in: Tom Barry, *Mexico: A Country Guide* (Albuquerque: The Inter-Hemispheric Education Resource Center, 1992) 41.

3. Russell, *Mexico Under Salinas*, 96-123 for the account given here of the founding of the PRD. The quotation from Rodríguez Araujo comes from 104.

4. Jorge G. Castañeda, *Utopia Unarmed: The Latin American Left After the Cold War* (New York: Knopf, 1993) 159.

5. Dan La Botz, *The Crisis of Mexican Labor* (New York: Praeger, 1988), 128-32.

6. Jaime Tamayo, "Social Democracy and Populism in Mexico," in *Social Democracy in Latin America: Prospects for Change* (Boulder: Westview Press, 1993) 259-60.

7. Carlos B. Gil, ed., *Hope and Frustration: Interviews with Leaders of Mexico's Political Opposition* (Wilmington, DE: Scholarly Resources Inc., 1992) 185.

8. In the following discussion of the elections, I rely on Russell, *Mexico Under Salinas* and Silvia Gómez Tagle, *La Fragil democracia mexicana: partidos politicos y elecciones* (Mexico: GV Editores, Mujeres en Lucha for la Democracia, A.C., and Mediodía, 1993).

9. Russell, *Mexico Under Salinas*, 33.

10. Tagle, *La Fragil democracia*, 154.

11. PRD, "Desapariciones y asesinatos políticos de militantes del PRD," typescript, August 1994.

12. Wayne A. Cornelius, Ann L. Craig, Jonathan Fox, eds., *Transforming State-Society Relations in Mexico: The National Solidarity Program* (San Diego: Center for U.S.-Mexican Studies, 1994 and Denise Dresser, *Neopopulist Solutions to Neoliberal Problems: Mexico's National Solidarity Program* (San Diego: Center for U.S. Mexican Studies, 1991).

13. The PDM is the political arm of the Sinarquista National Union, a quasi-fascist movement. See: Jorge Alonso, *El PDM: Movimiento regional* (Guadalajara: University of Guadalajara, 1989) and Jean Meyer, *El siniarquismo ¿un fascismo mexicano? 1937-1947* (Mexico: Editoral Joaquín Mortiz, 1979).

14. Tagle, *La Fragil democracia*, 173.

15. Tim Golden, "Salvador Nava," *New York Times*, May 29, 1992.

8. WORKERS PLOT REBELLION

1. Judith Scott, General Counsel and Earl V. Brown, Jr., Associate General Counsel, International Brotherhood of Teamsters, Complaint Before the United States National Administrative Office Bureau of International Labor Affairs, United States Department of Labor, February 14, 1994.

2. John H. Hovis, President, United Electrical, Radio and Machine Workers of America (UE), Submission and Request for Review Before the United States National Administrative Office, In re: General Electric Company, February 10, 1994. See also: Allen R. Myerson, "Big Labor's Strategic Raid in Mexico," *New York Times*, September 12, 1994.

3. Dan La Botz, *Mask of Democracy: Labor Suppression in Mexico Today* (Boston: South End Press, 1992).

4. I dealt with some of the same material presented in this chapter somewhat differently in my articles: "Making Links Across the Border," *Labor Notes*, August 1994, 7-10, and "Tackling the Maquiladora Zone," in *CrossRoads*, November 1994, 18-20.

5. Author's interview with Phoebe McKinney, Juárez, Mexico in May, 1994.

6. Author's interview with Dave Johnson, Juárez, Mexico in May, 1994.

7. Author's interview with Báldemar Velázquez, Juárez, Mexico in May, 1994.

8. Author's interview with Mexican organizer who prefers to remain anonymous, Juárez, Mexico in May, 1994.

9. Author's interview with Mary Tong, Juárez, Mexico in May, 1994.

10. Author's interview with Susan Mika, by telephone, July 1994.

11. Asra Q. Nomani, "Unions Angry After Administration Rejects Complaints About Mexico Plants," *Wall Street Journal*, October 14, 1994.

9. MEXICAN WOMEN

1. Author's interview with María Atilano Uriarte, Mexico City, August 1994.

2. Andrés Oppenheimer, "The Harsh Life of Chiapas Women," *Miami Herald*, March 28, 1994, 9A in *Mexico NewsPak.*.

3. José Steinsleger, "The Zapatista Women's Revolution," *InterPress Service*, Peacenet, March 6, 1994 in *Mexico NewsPak*.

4. Private communication from Lynn Stephen, March 1995. Also, Sara Lovera, "Three Tzeltal Women Subpoenaed in Rape Case," *La Jornada* (Mexico City), September 11, 1994, 11, from *Mexico NewsPak*.

5. Anna Macías, *Against All Odds: The Feminist Movement in Mexico to 1940* (Westport, CT: Greenwood Press, 1982) Chapters 2 through 4.

6. Macías, *Against All Odds*, Chapter 6, quotation from 144.

7. The account of contemporary feminism comes largely from Ana Lau Jaiven, *La nueva ola del feminismo en México* (Mexico: Grupo Editorial Planeta). See also the chapter "México: Feminismo y Movimiento Popular en México," in Coordinación de Grupos Organizadores de las Jornadas Feministas (a collective author), *Jornadas Feministas, México, D.F. Noviembre de 1986, "Feminismo y Sectores Populares en América Latina"* México, D.F.: Jornadas Feministas, 1987; and Elaine Burns, "Women and Feminism" in Tom Barry, ed., *Mexico: A Country Guide* (Albuquerque: Inter-Hemispheric Education Resource Center, 1992).

8. Author's interview with Rosario Ibarra, Los Angeles, June 1994. See: Anthony De Palma, "Among the Ruins of the Left, a Pillar Stands," *New York Times,* October 5, 1994.

9. See, for example, an account of feminist organizing among domestic workers: Mary Goldsmith, "Politics and Programs of Domestic Workers' Organizations in Mexico" in Elsa M. Chaney and Mary García Castro, *Muchachas No More: Household Workers in Latin America and the Caribbean* (Philadelphia: Temple University Press, 1989) 221-244.

10. Vivienne Bennett, "Gender, Class and Water: Women and the Politics of Water Service in Monterrey, Mexico," *Latin American Perspectives* (Women in Latin America) Spring, 1995, 22(2) 76-99.

11. Juanita Darling, "Activism Rooted in Mexico's Culture," *Los Angeles Times*, 29 June, 1993, 3H, from *Mexico NewsPak*.

12. For a view of women organizers among the urban poor see: Kathleen Logan, "Women's Participation in Urban Protest," in Joe Foweraker & Ann L. Craig, *Popular Movements and Political Change in Mexico* (Boulder: Lynne Rienner Publishers, 1990) 150-159. For an account of the Urban Popular Movement up to the mid-1980s see: Juan Manuel Ramírez Saiz, *El Movimiento Urbano Popular en México* (México, D.F.: Siglo Veintiuno Editores, 1986) and Juan Manuel Ramírez Saiz, "Urban Struggles and their Political Consequences," also in Foweraker and Craig, *Popular Movements*, 234-246.

13. Dan La Botz, *Crisis of Mexican Labor* (New York: Praeger, 1988) 167-176. For another point of view see: Teresa Carrillo, "Women and Independent Unionism in the Garment Industry," in Joe Foweraker & Ann L. Craig, *Popular Movements and Political Change in Mexico* (Boulder: Lynne Rienner Publishers, 1990) 213-233.

14. Hugo García Michel, *Mas Allá de Laguna Verde* (Mexico: Editorial Posada, 1988), Part 2, Chapter 2, "Algunos datos sobre la historia del movimiento antinuclear Mexicano," 229-257.

15. Carlos Monsiváis, *Entrada libre: Crónicas de la sociedad que se organiza* (Mexico: Ediciones Era, 1992) 284.

16. Ruben Torres Jiménez, "Women, Victims of Violence at Home," *Interpress Service* (Peacenet), 24 October 1993 in *Mexico NewsPak*.

17. Author's interview with María Atilano Uriarte, Mexico City, August 1994.

18. Author's interview with Patricia Bracho, Mexico City, August 1994.

10. THE NATIONAL DEMOCRATIC CONVENTION

1. All of those quoted in this chapter were interviewed by the author at the Convención Nacional Democrática, San Cristóbal de las Casas and Aguascalientes (near Guadalupe Tepeyac), Chiapas, August, 1994.

2. Francisco J. Santamaría, *Diccionario de Mejicanismos*, s.v. "barzón."

3. These figures come from "Resolutivos aprobados por la Convención Nacional Democrática," in the section "Perfil de La Jornada," *La Jornada*, 20 August 1994. They differ from the lower figures found in the original convention reports distributed to the press in San Cristóbal de la Casas.

11. THE FIGHT FOR ELECTION REFORM

1. Discussions of the Mexican election reforms in this chapter are based on: Instituto Federal Electoral, *Código Federal de instituciones y procedimientos electorales* (Mexico: IFE, 1994). For a laudatory summary of the reforms in

English see: Theodore C. Sorensen, "The Prospects for a Free, Fair and Honest Election in Mexico: A Report to El Consejo Coodinador Empresarial (The Business Coordinating Council)" (New York: Paul, Weiss, Rifkind, Wharton & Garrison [attorneys], August 15, 1994). For a critical summary see: Washington Office on Latin America and Academia Mexicana de Derechos Humanos, "The 1994 Mexican Election: A Question of Credibility," August 15, 1994."

2. Author's interview with Luz Rosales, Chiapas and Mexico City, August 1994.

3. In addition to Movimiento Ciudadano por la Democracia were: Convergencia de Organismos Civiles por la Democracia, Consejo para la Democracia, Fundación Arturo Rosenblueth, Academia Mexicana de Derechos Humanos (AMDH), Instituto Superior de Cultura Democrática and Acuerdo Nacional por la Democracia (ACUDE).

4. Author's interview with Luz Rosales, Chiapas and Mexico City, August 1994.

5. "Observadores Electorales: Informe Especial," El Financiero, May 8, 1994.

6. Annual reports and other documents of the National Endowment for Democracy. See also, Jim Cason and David Brooks, "Recibiría Alianza Cívica-Observación 94 hasta 140 mil dólares de apoyo," La Jornada, June 5, 1994.

7. WOLA and AMDH, "The 1994 Mexican Elections," 34.

8. "Observadores Electorales: Informe Especial," El Financiero, May 8, 1994.

9. Marta Anaya, "ONU: 15 mil Observadores de las ONG's en Todo México," Excelsior, May 14, 1994; David Aponte, "400 ONG aceptan la asesoria de la ONU," La Jornada, May 15, 1994; Mónica Martín, "Posiblemente el Próximo Martes se Firme el Acuerdo de Colaboración Electoral Entre la ONU y las ONGs," Excelsior, May 18, 1994; David Aponte, "ONG, cruciales en comicios: expertos," La Jornada, June 1, 1994.

10. María Elena Media, "Observadores: ruta a la legalidad," Reforma, July 2, 1994.

11. Mireya Cuellar, "Aprueba la ONU entregar l.5 mil a Alianza Cívica," La Jornada, July 16, 1995. The article is accompanied by a table with a detailed breakdown of the budget.

12. Marta Anaya, "Acreditados ya, más de 50 mil Observadores Electorales: provienen de Diversas ONGs del País," Excelsior, July 4, 1994. There were 950 foreign visitors, 700 from the U.S., 50 from Canada, and the rest mostly from Latin America and Europe.

13. Georgina Salierna V., "Para Elba Esther Gordillo la elección es legal y transparente," La Jornada, August 25, 1994, 16. See also, "¿Qué es y cómo funciona la observación electoral del magisterio?" Perfil de La Jornada section, La Jornada, August 20, 1994.

14. Federal Electoral Institute, Regimen financiero de los partidos políticos (Mexico: IFE, 1994) in WOLA-AMDH, "The 1994 Mexican Elections," 40, 44.

15. WOLA and AMDH, "The 1994 Mexican Election," 3.

16. Mexican Academy of Human Rights in collaboration with Civic Alliance/Observation 94, "The Media and the 1994 Federal Elections in Mexico: A Content Analysis of Television News Coverage of the Political Parties and Presidential Candidate" (Mexico: Mexican Academy of Human Rights, May 19, 1994), 2-5 and two pie charts on unnumbered pages. See also, Tim Golden, "Mexican TV Picks Its Political Shots," *New York Times*, July 23, 1994.

17. WOLA and AMDH, "The 1994 Mexican Election," 3.

18. José Barberan, "Balance de la discusión del padrón," Perfil de La Jornada section in *La Jornada*, August 12, 1994; and IFE, "Informe del IFE sobre los homonimias en el DF," in Perfil de la Jornada section in *La Jornada*, August 14, 1994.

19. Jorge G. Castañeda, *Utopia Unarmed: The Latin American Left After the Cold War* (New York: Knopf, 1993) Chapter 8, "La Guerre Est Finie: The Latin American Left and the Fall of Socialism," 227-266, and Chapter 14, "A Grand Bargain for the Millenium," 427-76.

20. "Latin Revolutionaries Learn to Love the System," *Business Week*, October 18, 1993, 13.

21. Nidia Marín, "'Pacto de Concordia', Propone el Grupo San Angel," *Excelsior*, June 25, 1994, 4.

22. Méndez Asensio and Robles Gil, *El Jefe Diego* and Luis Alberto García Orosa, *La Verdad sobre Diego: Biografía NO autorizada* (Mexico: Edamex, 1994).

23. Gonzalo Martre, *El Debate: Los 90 Minutos de democracia que transformaron a México* (Mexico: Grupo Editorial Planeta, 1994) 29.

24. Ibid., 36-37.

25. *Ibid.*, 134-37.

12. THE ELECTION OF ZEDILLO

1. Interview with international observer, Italian actress Giovanna Cavasola, Mexico City, August 1994. Interview with Luciano Pascoe and Andres Pascoe, Mexico City, August 1994; the Pascoes, two young PRD supporters also videotaped an interview with such a woman. Virtually identical stories were reported in the press as well.

2. I interviewed 17 Mexican, European, Latin American, Canadian, and U.S. international visitors. In addition, I attended the meetings of international observers organized by Alianza Cívica immediately after the election, and heard the discussion among dozens of Canadian, European, and Latin American observers.

3. Author's interview with Steve Baileys, Mexico, August 1994. Also: Steve Baileys, "Report on Mexican National Elections of August 1994," a 20-page typescript.

4. Alianza Cívica/Observación 94, "Report on the Stratified Sample," August 23, 1994, typescript. Also, "Elecciones Mexicanas del 21 de agosto de 1994, grupo de visitantes Europeos y Latinoamericanos, observaciones sobre el proceso electoral en las casillas, informe," typescript.

5. Tim Wise, "Press statement from the second international working group of U.S. visitors invited by Civic Alliance," typescript, August 24, 1994. See also, Katharine Kilbourn, Grassroots International, "U.S. Delegation Finds Widespread Fraud in Oaxaca, Mexico," typescript, August 24, 1994.

6. Global Exchange, "Global Exchange International Visitors Report," typescript, August 23, 1994.

7. Gonzalo Martre, *El Debate: Los 90 minutos de democracia que transformaron a México* (Mexico: Planeta, 1994), 9.

8. Silvia Gómez Tagle, *La Fragil democracia mexicana: Partidos políticos y elecciones* (Mexico: GV Editores, Mujeres en Lucha for la Democracia, A.C., Medio Día, 1993) 17.

EPILOGUE

1. For a good discussion of the technical economic aspects of the crisis see: James M. Cypher, "NAFTA Shock: Mexico's Free Market Meltdown," *Dollars and Sense*, March/April 1995, 22-25 and 39.

2. Ken Silverstein and Alexander Coburn, "Major U.S. Bank Urges Zapatista Wipe-Out: 'A litmus test for Mexico's stability'," *Counterpunch*, 2(3), February 1, 1995.

3. Tim Golden, "Mexico's New Offensive: Erasing Rebel's Mystique," *New York Times*, February 11, 1995, 1.

4. Todd Robberson, "Mexico Home Front Sees No End to Crisis," *Washington Post*, May 1, 1995, p. 14A, in *Mexico NewsPak*. And: "Los trabajadores recuperaron el Zócalo en una jornada masiva de inconformidad," *La Jornada*, 2 mayo 1995, On-line edition.

BIBLIOGRAPHY

BOOKS, PAMPLETS, AND DISSERTATIONS

Alberto Aguirre et al., *El Asesinato del Cardenal, ¿Un error?* Mexico: Planeta, n.d. [1994?].

Manuel Aguilar Mora. *El Bonapartismo mexicano*. Mexico: Juan Pablos Editor, 1982. 2 vols.

Amnesty International, *Human Rights in Rural Areas: Exchange of Documents with the Mexican Government on Human Rights Violations in Oaxaca and Chiapas*. London: Amnesty International, 1986.

Andrew Arato. *From Neo-Marxism to Democratic Theory: Essays on the Critical Theory of Soviet-Type Societies*. Armonk, NY: M.E. Sharpe, 1993.

José Arias and Luis Barquera, eds. *¿Laguna Verde? ¡No Gracias!* Mexico: Claves Latinoamericanas, 1988.

Tom Barry. *Mexico: A Country Guide*. Albuquerque: The Inter-Hemispheric Education Resource Center, 1992.

Thomas Benjamin. *A Rich Land, A Poor People: Politics and Society in Modern Chiapas*. Albuquerque: University of New Mexico Press, 1989.

Guillermo Bonfil Batalla. *México profundo: Una civilización negada*. Mexico: Grijalbo, 1990.

Miguel Angel Calderón. *El impacto de la crisis de 1929 en México*. Mexico: SEP, 1982.

Roderic A. Camp. *Entrepreneurs and Politics in Twentieth Century Mexico*. New York: Oxford University Press, 1989.

Barry Carr. *Marxism & Communism in Twentieth-Century Mexico*. Lincoln: University of Nebraska, 1992.

Jorge G. Castañeda. *Utopia Unarmed: The Latin American Left After the Cold War*. New York: Alfred A Knopf, 1993.

José Luis Cecena. *México en la orbita imperial*. Mexico: El Caballito, 1991.

Miguel Angel Centeno. *Democracy within Reason: Technocratic Revolution in Mexico*. University Park, PA: Pennsylvania State University Press, 1994.

James D. Cockroft. *Mexico: Class Formation, Capital Accumulation and the State*. New York: Monthly Review, 1983.

John L. Cohen and Andrew Arato. *Civil Society and Political Theory*. Cambridge, MA: MIT Press, 1992.

George A. Collier. *Basta! Land and the Zapatista Rebellion in Chiapas*. Oakland, CA: The Institute for Food and Development Policy, 1994.

Coordinación de Grupos Organizadores de las Jornadas Feministas [a collective author]. *Jornadas Feministas, México, D.F. Noviembre de 1986, "Feminismo y sectores populares en América Latina."* Mexico, D.F.: Jornadas Feministas, 1987.

Arnaldo Córdova. *La política de masas del cardenismo*. Mexico: Ediciones Era, 1974.

Wayne Cornelius, Ann L. Craig and Jonathan Fox, eds. *Transforming State-Society Relations in Mexico: The National Solidarity Program*. San Diego: Center for U.S.-Mexican Studies, UCSD, 1994.

Guillermo de la Peña. *A Legacy of Promises*. Austin: University of Texas, 1981.

Denise Dresser. *Neopopulist Solutions to Neoliberal Problems: Mexico's National Solidarity Program*. San Diego: Center for U.S.-Mexican Studies, 1991.

Ejército Zapatista de Liberación Nacional (EZLN). *Comunicados y correspondencia: Del 1o de enero al 21 de abril de 1994*. N.p.: Unión Nacional de Trabajadores, miembro de la CONAC-LN, n.d.

—————————. *La palabra de los armados de verdad y fuego*. Mexico: Editorial Fuenteovejuna, 1994.

—————————. *Voice of Fire: Communiques and Interviews from the Zapatista Army of National Liberation*, eds. Ben Clarke and Clifton Ross, (Berkeley: New Earth, 1994).

Equipo Pueblo [a collective author]. *Crónica del Nuevo México*. Mexico City: Equipo Pueblo, 1989.

Arturo Escobar and Sonia E. Escobar. *The Making of Social Movements in Latin America: Identity, Strategy, and Democracy*. Boulder: Westview Press, 1992.

BIBLIOGRAPHY

Nancy M. Farriss. *Maya Society Under Colonial Rule: The Collective Enterprise of Survival.* Princeton, N.J.: Princeton Unversity Press, 1984.

Joe Foweraker. *Popular Mobilization in Mexico: The Teachers' Movement 1977-87.* New York: Cambridge University Press, 1993.

Joe Foweraker and Ann L. Craig, eds. *Popular Movements and Political Change in Mexico.* Boulder: Lynne Rienner Publishers, 1990.

Jonathan Fox. *The Challenge of Rural Democratisation: Perspectives from Latin America and the Philippines.* Portland, OR: Frank Cass, 1990.

Antonio García de León. *Resistencia y Utopía: Memorial de agravios y crónicas de revueltas y profecías acaecidas en la provincia de Chiapas durante los últimos quinientos años de su historia.* Mexico: Ediciones Era, 1993.

Hugo García Michel. *Más allá de Laguna Verde.* Mexico: Editorial Posada, 1988.

Luis Alberto García Orosa. *La Verdad sobre Diego: Biografía NO autorizada.* Mexico: Edamex, 1994.

Carlos B. Gil, ed. *Hope and Frustration: Interviews with Leaders of Mexico's Political Opposition.* Wilmington, DE: Scholarly Resources, 1992.

Adolfo Gilly. *El cardenismo, una utopía mexicana.* Mexico: Cal y Arena, 1994.

——————————, ed. *Cartas a Cuauhtémoc Cárdenas.* Mexico: Ediciones Era, 1989.

——————————. *México, la larga travesía.. * Mexico: Editorial Nueva Imagen, 1985.

——————————. *Nuestra caída en la modernidad.* Mexico: Joan Boldo i Climent, Editores, 1988.

——————————. *Por todos los caminos: Escritos sobre América Latina, 1956-1982.* Mexico: Editorial Nueva Imagen, 1983.

——————————. *La Revolución interrumpida.* Mexico: El Caballito, 1971.

Silvia Gómez Tagle. *La Frágil democracia mexicana: partidos políticos y elecciones.* Mexico: GV Editores, Mujeres en Lucha por la Democracia, A.C., and Mediodía, 1993.

——————————. *De la alquimia al fraude en las elecciones mexicanas.* Mexico: GV Editores, Mujeres en Lucha for la Democracia, A.C., and Mediodía, 1994.

Jürgen Habermas. *The Structural Transformation of the Public Sphere: An Inquiry into a Category of Bourgeois Society*. Cambridge, MA.: MIT Press, 1994.

Nora Hamilton. *The Limit of State Autonomy: Post-Revolutionary Mexico*. Princeton, NJ: Princeton University, 1982.

Neil Harvey. *Rebellion in Chiapas: Rural Reforms, Campesino Radicalism, and the Limits to Salinismo*. San Diego: Center for U.S.-Mexican Studies, UCSD, 1994.

Francisco Hernández Juárez and Maria Xelhuantzi López. *El sindicalismo en la reforma del Estado*. México: Fondo de la Cultura Económica, 1993.

Eduardo Huchim. *México 1994: La Rebelión y el magnicidio*. Mexico: Nueva Imagen, 1994.

Ana Lau Jaiven. *La nueva ola del feminismo en México*. Mexico: Grupo Editorial Planeta.

John Keane, ed., *Civil Society and the State*. New York: Verso, 1988.

—————————. *Democracy and Civil Society*. New York: Verso, 1988.

Won-Ho Kim. "The Mexican Regime's Political Strategy in Implementing Economic Reform in Comparative Perspective: A Case Study of the Privatization of the Telephone Industry." Ph.D. Diss, University of Texas at Austin, December 1992.

Alan Knight. *The Mexican Revolution*. Lincoln: University of Nebraska Press, 1986. 2 vols.

Dan La Botz. *Chiapas and Beyond: Mexico's Crisis and the Fight for Democracy*. Detroit: Solidarity, May, 1994.

—————————. *The Chiapas Rebellion: A Political Analysis*. Detroit: Solidarity, January, 1994.

—————————. *Crisis of Mexican Labor*. New York: Praeger, 1988.

—————————. *Edward L. Doheny: Petroleum, Power and Politics in the United States and Mexico*. New York: Praeger, 1991.

—————————. *Mask of Democracy: Labor Suppression in Mexico Today*. Boston: South End Press, 1992.

Jorge Laso de la Vega, ed. *La corriente democrática: Hablan los protagonistas*. Mexico: Editorial Posada, 1987.

BIBLIOGRAPHY

Juan Felipe Leal. *La burguesía y el estado mexicano*. Mexico: El Caballito, 1972.

——————. *México: Estado, burocracia y sindicatos*. Mexico: El Caballito, 1980.

Penny Leroux. *Cry of the People: The Struggle for Human Rights in Latin America—The Catholic Church in Conflict with U.S. Policy*. New York: Penguin, 1982.

Jan Jozef Lipski. *KOR: A History of the Workers' Defense Committee in Poland, 1976-1981*, translated by Olga Amsterdamska and Gene M. Moore. Berkeley: University of California Press, 1985.

Anna Macías. *Against All Odds: The Feminist Movement in Mexico to 1940*. Westport, Conn.: Greenwood Press, 1982.

Gonzalo Martre. *El Debate: Los 90 minutos de democracia que transformaron a México*. Mexico: Grupo Editorial Planeta, 1994.

Karl Marx. *Capital*. New York: International Publishers, 1967.

Rigoberta Menchú. *I, Rigoberta Menchú: An Indian Women in Guatemala*. New York: Verso, 1991.

Luis Méndez Asensio and Pedro Reygadas Robles Gil. *El Jefe Diego*. Mexico: Ediciones Temas de Hoy, 1994.

Luis Méndez Asensio and Antonio Cano Gimeno. *La guerra contra el tiempo: Viaje a la selva alzada*. Mexico: Editorial Temas de Hoy, 1994.

Mexican Academy of Human Rights in collaboration with Civic Alliance/Observation 94. "The Media and the 1994 Federal Elections in Mexico: A Content Analysis of Television News Coverage of the Political Parties and Presidential Candidate." Mexico: Mexican Academy of Human Rights, May 19, 1994.

René Millan. *Los Empresarios ante el estado y la sociedad*. Mexico: Siglo Veintiuno, 1988.

Robert P. Millon. *Zapata: The Ideology of a Peasant Revolutionary*. New York: International Publishers, 1972.

Carlos Monsiváis. *Entrada libre: Crónicas de la sociedad que se organiza*. Mexico: Ediciones Era, 1987.

Barrington Moore. *Social Origins of Dictatorship and Democracy: Lord and Peasant in the Making of the Modern World*. Boston: Beacon, 1966.

DEMOCRACY IN MEXICO

Ward M. Morton. *Woman Suffrage in Mexico*. Gainesville: University of Florida Press, 1962.

Abraham Nuncio. *El Grupo Monterrey*. Mexico: Editorial Nueva Imagen, 1982.

Juan Manuel Ramírez Saiz. *El movimiento urbano popular en Mexico*. Mexico, D.F.: Siglo Veintiuno Editores, 1986.

Pedro Reygadas, Ivan Gomezcesar, Esther Kravzov, *La guerra de año nuevo: Crónicas de Chiapas y Mexico 1994*. Mexico, D.F.: Editorial Praxis, 1994.

Alan Riding. *Distant Neighbors: A Portrait of the Mexicans*.
New York: Vintage, 1986.

Diego Rivera and Bertram D. Wolfe. *Portrait of Mexico*. New York: Covici-Friede, 1937.

Rodolfo Rojas Zea, ed. *Tres huelgas de telefonistas*. Mexico, D.F.: Editorial Uno, S.A., 1980.

John Ross. *Rebellion from the Roots: Indian Uprising in Chiapas*. Monroe, Maine: Common Courage Press, 1995.

Philip L. Russell. *The Chiapas Rebellion*. Austin: Mexico Resource Center, 1995.

—————————. *Mexico Under Salinas*. Austin: Mexico Resource Center, 1994.

Ramón Eduardo Ruíz. *The Great Rebellion: Mexico, 1905-1924*. New York: W.W. Norton, 1980.

Carlos Salinas de Gortari. *Producción y Participación Política en el campo*. Mexico: Universidad Nacional Autónoma de México, 1980.

Harley Shaiken. *Mexico in the Global Economy: High Technology and Work Organization in Export Industries*. San Diego: Center for U.S.-Mexican Studies, 1990.

Jesus Silva Herzog. *Breve historia de la revolución mexicana*. Mexico: Fondo de la Cultura Económica, 1973.

Theodore C. Sorensen. "The Prospects for a Free, Fair and Honest Election in Mexico: A Report to El Consejo Coodinador Empresarial (The Business Coordinating Council)." New York: Paul, Weiss, Rifkind, Wharton & Garrison [attorneys], August 15, 1994.

BIBLIOGRAPHY

Shirlene Ann Soto. *The Mexican Woman: A Study of Her Participation in the Revolution, 1910-1940*. Palo Alto, California: R&E Research Associates, 1979.

Susan Street. *Maestros en movimiento: Transformaciones en la burocracia estatal (1978-1982)*. Mexico: CIESAS, 1992.

Luis Suárez. *Lucio Cabañas: El guerrillero sin esperanza*, Mexico: Grijalbo, 1984.

Paco Ignacio Taibo II. *Cárdenas de cerca: Una entrevista biográfica*. Mexico: Grupo Editorial Planeta, 1994.

John Tutino. *From Insurrection to Revolution in Mexico* Princeton, NJ: University of Princeton, 1986.

Arturo Warman. *"We Come to Object": The Peasants of Morelos and the National State*. Baltimore, MD: Johns Hopkins University Press, 1980.

Washington Office on Latin America and Academia Mexicana de Derechos Humanos. "The 1994 Mexican Election: A Question of Credibility," August 15, 1994."

Mark Wasserman. *Persistent Oligarchs: Elites and Politics in Chihuahua, Mexico: 1910-1940*. Durham, NC: Duke, 1993.

Robert Wasserstrom. *Class and Society in Central Chiapas*. Berkeley: University of California Press, 1983.

Eric Wolf. *Peasant Wars of the Twentieth Century*. New York: Harper, 1969.

John Womack. *Zapata and the Mexican Revolution*. New York: Vintage, 1968.

ARTICLES

Vivienne Bennett, "Gender, Class, and Water: Women and the Politics of Water Service in Monterrey, Mexico," *Latin American Perspectives* 85 (Spring 1995) 76-99.

Frank Cancian and Peter Brown, "Who is Rebelling in Chiapas?" *Cultural Survival Quarterly* (Spring 1994) 22-25.

Enrique Cárdenas, "The Great Depression and Industrialisation: The Case of Mexico," in: Rosemary Thorp, *Latin America in the 1930s: The Role of the Periphery in World Crisis*. New York: St. Martin's Press, 1984, Chapter 9, 222-241.

George Collier, "Peasant Politics and the Mexican State: Indigenous Compliance in Highland Chiapas," *Mexican Studies/Estudios Mexicanos* (Winter 1987) 3 (1), 71-98.

—————————. "The Rebellion in Chiapas and the Legacy of Energy Development," *Mexican Studies/Estudios Mexicanos* (Summer 1994) 10 (2) 371-382.

—————————. "Roots of the Rebellion in Chiapas," *Cultural Survival Quarterly* (Spring 1994) 14-18.

James M. Cypher, "NAFTA Shock: Mexico's Free Market Meltdown," *Dollars and Sense*, March/April, 1995, 22-25 and 39.

Duncan Earle, "Zapatismo and Nationalism," *Cultural Survival Quarterly* (Spring 1994) 26-30.

Jonathan Fox, "The Challenge of Democracy: Rebellion as Catalyst," *Akwe:kon: A Journal of Indigenous Issues* (Summer 1994) XI (2) 13-19.

Mary Goldsmith, "Politics and Programs of Domestic Workers' Organizations in Mexico" in: Elsa M. Chaney and Mary García Castro, *Muchachas No More: Household Workers in Latin America and the Caribbean*. Philadelphia: Temple University Press, 1989.

Gary H. Gossen, "Comments on the Zapatista Movement," *Cultural Survival Quarterly* (Spring 1994) 19-21.

Stephen H. Haber, "Assessing the Obstacles to Industrialisation: The Mexican Economy, 1830-1940," *Journal of Latin American Studies* (February 1992).

Neil Harvey, "Playing with Fire: The Implications of Ejido Reform," *Akwe:kon: A Journal of Indigenous Issues* (Summer 1994) XI (2) 20-27.

Dan La Botz, "Making Links Across the Border," *Labor Notes*, August 1994, 7-10.

—————————. "Manufacturing Poverty: The Maquiladorization of Mexico," *Multinational Monitor*, January/February, 1991.

—————————. "Tackling the Maquiladora Zone," *CrossRoads*, November 1994, 18-20.

Carlos Morera Camacho, "Los grandes cambios en los grupos financieros en 1988-1992," *Coyuntura* (PRD's official magazine), September 1993.

James D. Nations, "The Ecology of the Zapatista Revolt," *Cultural Survival Quarterly* (Spring 1994) 31.

Lynn Stephen, "The Chiapas Rebellion," *Radical America*, 25 (2) 7-17.

Dimitris Stevis and Stephen P. Mumme, "Nuclear Power, Technological Autonomy, and the State in Mexico," *Latin American Research Review*, 26 (3) 1991.

John Summa, "Mexico's New Super-Billionaires," *Multinational Monitor*, November 1994.

Jaime Tamayo, "Social Democracy and Populism in Mexico," in: *Social Democracy in Latin America: Prospects for Change*. Boulder: Westview Press, 1993.

Judith Teichman, "Dismantling the Mexican State and the Role of the Private Sector," in: Ricardo Grinspun and Maxwell A. Cameron, *The Political Economy of North American Free Trade*. New York: St. Martin's Press, 1993.

Carlos M. Vilas, "The Hour of Civil Society," *NACLA*, September/October 1993, 38-42.

Evon Z. Vogt, "Possible Sacred Aspects of the Chiapas Rebellion," *Cultural Survival Quarterly* (Spring 1994).

Robert Wasserstrom, "Spaniards and Indians in Colonial Chiapas, 1528-1790," in: Murdo J. MacLeod and Robert Wasserstrom, eds., *Spaniards and Indians in Southeastern Mesoamerica: Essays on the History of Ethnic Relations,* Lincoln: University of Nebraska, 1983, 92-126.

LEGAL DOCUMENTS

John H. Hovis, President, United Electrical, Radio and Machine Workers of America (UE), Submission and Request for Review Before the United States National Administrative Office, In re: General Electric Company, February 10, 1994.

Judith Scott, General Counsel and Earl V. Brown, Jr., Associate General Counsel, International Brotherhood of Teamsters, Complaint Before the United States National Administrative Office Bureau of International Labor Affairs, United States Department of Labor, February 14, 1994.

NEWSPAPERS AND WEEKLY MAGAZINES

La Jornada	*El Financiero*
Mexico NewsPak	*Proceso*
New York Times	*San Diego Union*

PHOTO DESCRIPTIONS
AND CREDIT

All photographs are by Dennis Dunleavy

INDEX

INDEX

and Carlos Salinas de Gortari, 10-11
and civil society, 196-98, 202-3, 205-8
and Cuauhtémoc Cárdenas, 208, 210-12, 227
and Diego Fernández de Cevallos, 19, 208-12, 227
and Ernest Zedillo, 208, 210-12, 227
and fraud, 130-31, 133, 193-94, 200-202, 213-14, 216-20, 222-27
and funding, 199-200
and Global Exchange, 226-27
and international observation, 194-97, 215-17, 220-22, 225-27
and Jorge Castañeda, 203-8
measures, 198-202
and media, 199, 200, 208, 210-12
and National Action Party (PAN), 208-12
and San Angel Group, 205-8
and women, 86, 160-61
See also Elections
Elections
and Carlos Salinas de Gortari, 91, 99, 104-5
and Cuauhtémoc Cárdenas, 83-85, 90-94, 121-22, 129-37, 208, 210-12, 227
and Institutional Revolutionary Party (PRI), 8, 9, 10-11, 13, 14-15, 17-19, 129-37, 193-95, 198-202, 208-12
and 1988, 83-85, 90-94, 99, 104-5, 121-22
and 1989-1993, 129-37
and Party of the Democratic Revolution (PRD), 129-37
and social democracy, 129-37
and Zapatista Army of National Liberation (EZLN), 8, 9, 13, 14-15, 17-19
See also Election reform
Elections, 1994. *See* Election reform
Emiliano Zapata Peasant Organization (OCEZ), 37
Energy. *See* Environment
Environment
and anti-nuclear movement, 75-80, 88, 165
and border industries (maquiladoras), 139, 142, 153
and Committee for the Ecological Defense of Michoacán (CODEMICH), 77
and electricity, 21, 29
and Lacandón rainforest, 30
and mining, 46, 112
and oil industry, 29, 55, 60, 110-11
EZLN. *See* Zapatista Army of National Liberation

F

FALN. *See* Armed Forces of National Liberation
Farm Labor Organizing Committee (FLOC), 148-49. *See also* Agriculture
FAT. *See* Authentic Labor Front
FDN. *See* National Democratic Front
Federal Agrarian Reform Law, 36-37. *See also* Agriculture

Federation of Unions of Firms of Public Goods and Services (FESEBES), 116
Feminism, 40, 111
and gay/lesbian movement, 162-63
rise of, 158-67
and Rosario Castellanos Group, 157-59, 167-70, 173-74
and Women in Solidarity Action (MAS), 161-62
and Women in Struggle for Democracy (WSD), 159-61, 170-74
and Women's Revolutionary Law, 40, 158-59
See also Women; Workers
Fernández de Cevallos, Diego, 19, 208-12, 227
FESEBES. *See* Federation of Unions of Firms of Public Goods and Services
FLOC. *See* Farm Labor Organizing Committee

G

Galván, Rafaél, 68, 162
García Arias, Ramón, 184, 185
García Michel, Hugo, 77, 79-80
Garment Workers Union, 164-65
Garza Sada, Eugenio, 59
General Electric, 139, 141-42, 145-48, 154
General Motors, 139, 150
General Union of Workers and Peasants (UGOCM), 62
Gilhool, Bridget, 217-18
Gilly, Adolfo, 54, 84-85, 95-97
Global Exchange, 226-27
González Garrido, Patrocinio, 8
González Luna, Efraín, 58
Gramsci, Antonio, 71
Guervara, Genaro, 78-79
Gutiérrez, Efraín, 27
Guzmán Cabrera, Sebastián, 111

H

Haciendas, 25-26, 44-45. *See also* Agriculture
Harp Helu, Alfredo, 14, 19
Hernández Galicia, Joaquín, 110-11
Hernández Juárez, Francisco, 113-16
Hernández Morales, Juan, 177-78
Homosexuality, 162-63
Honeywell Corporation, 139-42
House of the World Worker, 49-50. *See also* Workers
Huerto, Victoriano, 48-49
Human rights, 6, 8, 15-16, 133, 134
and Liberation of Theology, 35-36
See also Civil society; National Democratic Convention (CND)

I

Ibarra de Piedra, Rosario, 163, 173-74

INDEX

INDEX

Ruíz, Samuel, 4, 11, 12, 34, 37
Ruíz Massieu, José Francisco, 229-30
Russell, Philip, 221-22

S

Salgado, Esteban, 179-80
Salinas de Gortari, Carlos
and Chiapas rebellion, 2-3, 5-9
and Committee for Popular Defense (CDP), 108-9
economic program of, 103, 110-19, 230
and elections, 10-11, 91, 99, 104-5
and labor unions, 110-19
and National Solidarity Program (PRONASOL), 105-10
political rise of, 103-5
and technocrats, 101-3
San Angel Group, 205-8
SEP. *See* Minister of Education
SITUAM. *See* University Workers Union
Social democracy
and Mexican Socialist Party (PMS), 93, 123-24
and National Democratic Front (FDN), 121-22, 197-98
and 1989-1993 elections, 129-37
and Party of the Democratic Revolution (PRD), 122-26
and Porfirio Muñoz Ledo, 126-29
and Salvador Nava Martínez, 131-137
and women, 135-36
See also Civil society; National Democratic Convention (CND)
Socialism, 95-97, 123-25, 160, 174. *See also* Social democracy
Socialist Workers Party (PST), 63, 93
SPP. *See* Ministry of Programming and Budget
State Council of Indigenous and Peasant Organizations (CEOIC), 12
Stephen, Lynn, 159
STI. *See* Union of Indigenous Workers
STIMAHCS. *See* Metal Workers Union
Stock market. *See* Economics
STPRM. *See* Petroleum Workers Union
Strikes, 1, 111
coffee workers, 26
mining, 46, 112
railroad, 121, 129
Spicer autoparts, 128
university, 13
See also Labor unions; Political action
STRM. *See* Telephone Workers Union
Student movements. *See* Universities
SUTIN. *See* Nuclear Workers Union

T

Talamantes, Aguilar, 123
Tanner, Liz, 217

TD. *See* Democratic Tendency
Technocratic counter-revolution. *See* Salinas de Gortari, Carlos
Telephone Workers Union (STRM), 112-16
TELMEX. *See* Mexican Telephone Company
Theology of Liberation, 34-36, 40
Tlatelolco massacre (1968), 18, 31, 62-63
Tong, Mary, 152-53
Trotskyists Revolutionary Workers Party (PRT), 34, 63, 93, 163

U

UAM. *See* Metropolitan Autonomous University
UE. *See* Ejido Unions; United Electrical Workers
UGOCM. *See* General Union of Workers and Peasants
UNAM. *See* National Autonomous University of Mexico
Utopia Unarmed (Castañeda), 126, 203-4
Union of Indigenous Workers (STI), 27
Union of Unions (UU), 38
Unions. *See* Labor unions
United Electrical Workers (UE), 68, 145-48
United States
and border industries (maquiladoras), 116-17, 139, 140, 141, 142, 143, 144-49, 151-55
and capitalism, 46, 56, 233-234
and Cuba, 32
and Mexican economy, 45-46, 52-53, 56, 60-61, 195-96, 230-31, 233-34, 237
and Mexican election reform, 194-97
and Mexican nuclear energy, 76
and National Endowment for Democracy (NED), 195-96
and North American Free Trade Agreement (NAFTA), 3, 24, 25, 110, 117, 119, 143, 154
Universities
and Metropolitan Autonomous University (UAM), 13
and National Autonomous University of Mexico (UNAM), 72-75
and strikes, 13
and student movement, 72-75, 165
and teacher unions, 34, 38
and University Student Council (CEU), 74-75
and University Workers Union (SITUAM), 13
University Student Council (CEU), 74-75
University Workers Union (SITUAM), 13
Urban Front of Mexico City of the Zapatista National Liberation Army, 7
Urbina, Erasto, 27
UU. *See* Union of Unions

V

Velázquez, Báldemar, 148-49
Villa, Francisco "Pancho," 47, 49-50

ABOUT DAN LA BOTZ

Dan La Botz is a the author of several books on U.S. and Mexican labor and politics. His book *Mask of Democracy: Labor Suppression in Mexico Today* (South End Press, 1992) was frequently cited in the debate over workers' rights and the North American Free Trade Agreement (NAFTA). He is also the author of *Rank and File Rebellion: Teamsters for a Democratic Union* and the widely used labor organizing manual, *The Troublemaker's Handbook: How to Organize Where You Work and Win.*

La Botz is a candidate for a Ph.D in U.S. History at the University of Cincinnati, working on a dissertation titled, "Slackers: American War Resisters in Mexico, 1917-1925." In 1995 La Botz received a Fulbright fellowship for research in Mexico, and now lives in Mexico City.

ABOUT SOUTH END PRESS

South End Press is a nonprofit, collectively-run book publisher with over 175 titles in print. Since our founding in 1977, we have tried to meet the needs of readers who are exploring, or are already committed to, the politics of radical social change.

Our goal is to publish books that encourage critical thinking and constructive action on the key political, cultural, social, economic, and ecological issues shaping life in the United States and in the world. In this way, we hope to give expression to a wide diversity of democratic social movements and to provide an alternative to the products of corporate publishing.

Through the Institute for Social and Cultural Change, South End Press works with other political media projects—*Z Magazine;* Speak Out!, a speakers bureau; the Publishers Support Project; and the New Liberation News Service—to expand access to information and critical analysis. If you would like a free catalog of South End Press books, please write to us at South End Press, 116 Saint Botolph Street, Boston, MA 02115. Also consider becoming a South End Press member: your $40 annual donation entitles you to two free books and a 40% discount on our entire list.

Related Titles from South End Press

Mask of Democracy: Labor Suppression in Mexico Today
     by Dan La Botz
Zapata's Revenge: Free Trade and the Farm Crisis in Mexico
     by Tom Barry
Haiti: Dangerous Crossroads
     edited by NACLA
Global Village or Global Pillage: Economic Reconstruction from the Bottom Up
     by Jeremy Brecher and Tim Costello
50 Years is Enough: The Case Against the World Bank and the IMF
     by Kevin Danaher
Roots of Rebellion: Lan d and Hunger in Central America
     by Tom Barry